LLEWELLYN'S 2019

Sabbats
ALMANAC

Samhain 2018
to
Mabon 2019

D0424897

Llewellyn's Sabbats Almanac:
Samhain 2018 to Mabon 2019

Cover art © Carolyn Vibbert
Cover design by Ellen Lawson
Editing by Aaron Lawrence
Interior Art: © Carolyn Vibbert, excluding illustrations on pages 38, 76, 108 145, 185, 220, 257, 290, which are © Wen Hsu

You can order annuals and books from *New Worlds*, Llewellyn's catalog. To request a free copy call toll free: 1-877-NEW WRLD, or order online by visiting our website at http://subscriptions.llewellyn.com.

ISBN: 978-0-7387-4611-1

Llewellyn Worldwide Ltd.
2143 Wooddale Drive
Woodbury, MN 55125-2989
www.llewellyn.com

Printed in the United States of America

2018

JANUARY
S	M	T	W	T	F	S
	1	2	3	4	5	6
7	8	9	10	11	12	13
14	15	16	17	18	19	20
21	22	23	24	25	26	27
28	29	30	31			

FEBRUARY
S	M	T	W	T	F	S
				1	2	3
4	5	6	7	8	9	10
11	12	13	14	15	16	17
18	19	20	21	22	23	24
25	26	27	28			

MARCH
S	M	T	W	T	F	S
				1	2	3
4	5	6	7	8	9	10
11	12	13	14	15	16	17
18	19	20	21	22	23	24
25	26	27	28	29	30	31

APRIL
S	M	T	W	T	F	S
1	2	3	4	5	6	7
8	9	10	11	12	13	14
15	16	17	18	19	20	21
22	23	24	25	26	27	28
29	30					

MAY
S	M	T	W	T	F	S
		1	2	3	4	5
6	7	8	9	10	11	12
13	14	15	16	17	18	19
20	21	22	23	24	25	26
27	28	29	30	31		

JUNE
S	M	T	W	T	F	S
					1	2
3	4	5	6	7	8	9
10	11	12	13	14	15	16
17	18	19	20	21	22	23
24	25	26	27	28	29	30

JULY
S	M	T	W	T	F	S
1	2	3	4	5	6	7
8	9	10	11	12	13	14
15	16	17	18	19	20	21
22	23	24	25	26	27	28
29	30	31				

AUGUST
S	M	T	W	T	F	S
			1	2	3	4
5	6	7	8	9	10	11
12	13	14	15	16	17	18
19	20	21	22	23	24	25
26	27	28	29	30	31	

SEPTEMBER
S	M	T	W	T	F	S
						1
2	3	4	5	6	7	8
9	10	11	12	13	14	15
16	17	18	19	20	21	22
23	24	25	26	27	28	29
30						

OCTOBER
S	M	T	W	T	F	S
	1	2	3	4	5	6
7	8	9	10	11	12	13
14	15	16	17	18	19	20
21	22	23	24	25	26	27
28	29	30	31			

NOVEMBER
S	M	T	W	T	F	S
				1	2	3
4	5	6	7	8	9	10
11	12	13	14	15	16	17
18	19	20	21	22	23	24
25	26	27	28	29	30	

DECEMBER
S	M	T	W	T	F	S
						1
2	3	4	5	6	7	8
9	10	11	12	13	14	15
16	17	18	19	20	21	22
23	24	25	26	27	28	29
30	31					

2019

JANUARY
S	M	T	W	T	F	S
		1	2	3	4	5
6	7	8	9	10	11	12
13	14	15	16	17	18	19
20	21	22	23	24	25	26
27	28	29	30	31		

FEBRUARY
S	M	T	W	T	F	S
					1	2
3	4	5	6	7	8	9
10	11	12	13	14	15	16
17	18	19	20	21	22	23
24	25	26	27	28		

MARCH
S	M	T	W	T	F	S
					1	2
3	4	5	6	7	8	9
10	11	12	13	14	15	16
17	18	19	20	21	22	23
24	25	26	27	28	29	30
31						

APRIL
S	M	T	W	T	F	S
	1	2	3	4	5	6
7	8	9	10	11	12	13
14	15	16	17	18	19	20
21	22	23	24	25	26	27
28	29	30				

MAY
S	M	T	W	T	F	S
			1	2	3	4
5	6	7	8	9	10	11
12	13	14	15	16	17	18
19	20	21	22	23	24	25
26	27	28	29	30	31	

JUNE
S	M	T	W	T	F	S
						1
2	3	4	5	6	7	8
9	10	11	12	13	14	15
16	17	18	19	20	21	22
23	24	25	26	27	28	29
30						

JULY
S	M	T	W	T	F	S
	1	2	3	4	5	6
7	8	9	10	11	12	13
14	15	16	17	18	19	20
21	22	23	24	25	26	27
28	29	30	31			

AUGUST
S	M	T	W	T	F	S
				1	2	3
4	5	6	7	8	9	10
11	12	13	14	15	16	17
18	19	20	21	22	23	24
25	26	27	28	29	30	31

SEPTEMBER
S	M	T	W	T	F	S
1	2	3	4	5	6	7
8	9	10	11	12	13	14
15	16	17	18	19	20	21
22	23	24	25	26	27	28
29	30					

OCTOBER
S	M	T	W	T	F	S
		1	2	3	4	5
6	7	8	9	10	11	12
13	14	15	16	17	18	19
20	21	22	23	24	25	26
27	28	29	30	31		

NOVEMBER
S	M	T	W	T	F	S
					1	2
3	4	5	6	7	8	9
10	11	12	13	14	15	16
17	18	19	20	21	22	23
24	25	26	27	28	29	30

DECEMBER
S	M	T	W	T	F	S
1	2	3	4	5	6	7
8	9	10	11	12	13	14
15	16	17	18	19	20	21
22	23	24	25	26	27	28
29	30	31				

Contents

Ostara

Beltane

Litha

Lammas

Contents

Mabon

Introduction

NEARLY EVERYONE HAS A favorite sabbat. There are numerous ways to observe any tradition. This edition of the *Sabbats Almanac* provides a wealth of lore, celebrations, creative projects, and recipes to enhance your holiday.

For this edition, a mix of writers—Melanie Marquis, Peg Aloi, JD Hortwort, Susan Pesznecker, Michael Furie, Dallas Jennifer Cobb, Deborah Castellano, Suzanne Ress, and more—share their ideas and wisdom. These include a variety of paths as well as the authors' personal approaches to each sabbat. Each chapter closes with an extended ritual, which may be adapted for both solitary practitioners and covens.

In addition to these insights and rituals, specialists in astrology, history, cooking, crafts, and family impart their expertise throughout.

Charlie Rainbow Wolf gives an overview of planetary influences most relevant for each sabbat season and provides details and a short ritual for selected events, including New and Full Moons, retrograde motion, planetary positions, and more.

Linda Raedisch explores the realm of old-world Pagans, with a focus on traditional gravestone symbols we often associate with Samhain, as well as some unique sabbat festivals tied to the Nordic culture.

Blake Octavian Blair conjures up a feast for each festival that includes an appetizer, entrée, dessert, and beverage.

Natalie Zaman offers instructions on DIY crafts that will leave your home full of color and personality for each and every sabbat.

Mickie Mueller provides directions for portable magic rituals and rites for celebrating your favorite sabbat on the go.

About the Authors

Blake Octavian Blair is an eclectic Pagan, ordained minister, shamanic practitioner, writer, Usui Reiki Master-Teacher, tarot reader, and musical artist. Blake blends various mystical traditions from both the East and West along with a reverence for the natural world into his own brand of modern Paganism and magick. Blake holds a degree in English and Religion from the University of Florida. He is an avid reader, knitter, crafter, and practicing pescatarian. He loves communing with nature and exploring its beauty whether it is within the city or hiking in the woods. Blake lives in the New England region of the USA with his beloved husband. Visit him on the web at www.blakeoctavianblair.com or write him at blake@blake-octavianblair.com.

Deborah Castellano writes for many of Llewellyn's annuals and writes a blog on PaganSquare about unsolicited opinions on glamour, the muse, and the occult. *Glamour Magic: The Witchcraft Revolution for Getting What You Want* (Llewellyn Publications). Her shop, the Mermaid and the Crow, specializes in handmade goods. She resides in New Jersey with her husband, Jow, and two cats. She has a terrible reality television habit she can't shake and likes St. Germain liqueur, record players, and typewriters. Visit her at www.deborahmcastellano.com.

Dallas Jennifer Cobb practices gratitude magic, giving thanks for personal happiness, health, and prosperity; meaningful, flexible, and rewarding work; and a deliciously joyful life. She is accomplishing her deepest desires. She lives in paradise with her daughter in a waterfront village in rural Ontario, where she regularly swims and runs, chanting: "Thank you, thank you, thank you." Contact her at jennifer.cobb@live.com or visit www.magicalliving.ca.

Michael Furie (Northern California) is the author of *Spellcasting for Beginners*, *Supermarket Magic*, and *Spellcasting: Beyond the Basics* published by Llewellyn Worldwide. Furie has been a practicing Witch for over twenty years. An American Witch, he practices in the Irish tradition and is a priest of the Cailleach. You can find him online at www.michaelfurie.com.

JD Hortwort resides in North Carolina. She is an avid student of herbology and gardening. JD has written a weekly garden column for over twenty years. She is a professional and award-winning writer, journalist, and magazine editor and a frequent contributor to the Llewellyn annuals. JD has been active in the local Pagan community since 2002, and she is a founding member of the House of Akasha in Greensboro, N.C.

Kristoffer Hughes is the founder and Chief of the Anglesey Druid Order in North Wales, UK. He is an award-winning author and a frequent speaker and workshop leader throughout the United Kingdom and the United States. He works professionally for Her Majesty's Coroner. He has studied with the Order of Bards, Ovates and Druids, and is its 13th Mount Haemus Scholar. He is a native Welsh speaker, born to a Welsh family in the mountains of Snowdonia. He resides on the Isle of Anglesey.

Melanie Marquis is a lifelong practitioner of magick, the founder of United Witches global coven, and a local coordinator for the Pagan Pride Project in Denver, Colorado, where she currently resides. Melanie is the author of numerous articles and several books, including *The Witch's Bag of Tricks*, *A Witch's World of Magick*, *Beltane*, and *Lughnasadh*, and she's written for many national and international Pagan publications. She is the co-author of *Witchy Mama* and the co-creator of the Modern Spellcaster's Tarot. An avid crafter, cook, folk artist, and tarot reader, she offers a line of customized magickal housewares as well as private tarot consultations by appointment. Connect with her online at www.melaniemarquis.com or facebook .com/melaniemarquisauthor.

Mickie Mueller is an author, artist, and illustrator who explores the realms of magic with both visual mediums and the written word. Her mixed media artwork is created magically; she combines colored pencil techniques with paint that is infused with magical herbs that correspond to the subject, bringing the power of spirit into her magical artwork. Mickie's black and white illustrations have been published in various books since 2007, and she has illustrated tarot and oracle decks including Voice of the Trees oracle, which she also wrote, and Mystical Cats Tarot. She has also written for several of the Llewellyn annuals and the book *The Witch's Mirror*. She is a Reiki Master/Teacher, ordained Priestess, and loyal minion to two cats and a dog.

Susan Pesznecker is a writer, English teacher, nurse, practicing herbalist, and hearth Pagan living in Oregon. Sue holds an MS in professional writing and loves to read, watch the stars, camp, and garden. Sue has authored *Yule: Rituals, Recipes, & Lore for the Winter Solstice* (Llewellyn 2015), *The Magickal Retreat* (Llewellyn 2012), *Crafting Magick with Pen and Ink* (Llewellyn, 2009), and contributes to the Llewellyn Annuals.

Linda Raedisch is a card-carrying Muggle with an abiding interest in witches, ghosts, goblins, and Galaxy Class Starships. This is her seventh year contributing to the *Sabbats Almanac*. Linda is also a soapmaker, housecleaner, amateur ethnobotanist, and rabid autodidact whose first professional writing assignment was to ghostwrite a children's book about Halloween. Since then, she has written *Night of the Witches: Folklore, Traditions and Recipes for Celebrating Walpurgis Night* and *The Old Magic of Christmas: Yuletide Traditions for the Darkest Days of the Year* (Llewellyn Publications), and the fantasy novella *The Princess in the Mound: A Visitor's Guide to Alvenholm Castle* (2017).

Suzanne Ress has been practicing Wicca for about twelve years as the leader of a small coven, but she has been aware of having a special connection to nature and animal spirits since she was a young child. She has been writing creatively most of her life—short stories, novels, and nonfiction articles for a variety of publications—and finds it to be an important outlet for her considerable creative powers. Other outlets she regularly makes use of are metalsmithing, mosaic works, painting, and all kinds of dance. She is also a professional aromatic herb grower and beekeeper. Although she is an American of Welsh ancestry by birth, she has lived in northern Italy for nearly twenty years. She recently discovered that the small mountain in the pre-alpine hills that she inhabits with her family and animals was once the site of an ancient Insubrian Celtic sacred place. Not surprisingly, the top of the mountain has remained a fulcrum of sacredness throughout the millennia, and this grounding in blessedness makes Suzanne's everyday life especially magical.

Natalie Zaman is a regular contributor to various Llewellyn annuals. She is the author of *Color and Conjure: Rituals and Magic Spells to Color* (Llewellyn, 2017), *Magical Destinations of the Northeast* (October 2016), and writes the recurring feature "Wandering Witch" for *Witches & Pagans* magazine. Her work has also appeared in *FATE*, *SageWoman*, and *newWitch* magazines. When she's not on the road, she's chasing free-range hens in her self-sufficient and Pagan-friendly back garden. Find Natalie online at http://natalie-zaman.blogspot.com.

Samhain

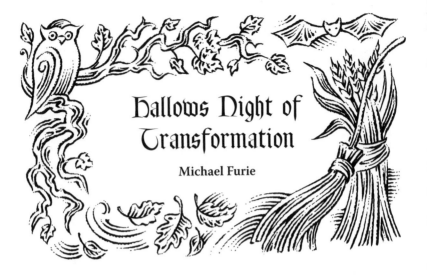

Hallows Night of Transformation

Michael Furie

SAMHAIN IS SUCH A unique time—both an ending and a new beginning. While it is magically linked to its opposing holiday, Beltane, this holiday has an energy that is set above and apart from all the other sabbats. On this night, or more accurately during this time, the culmination of the power and promise of the entire years' worth of growth and decline comes together as a magical "grand finale" of sorts; laying the groundwork for a new year. If properly constructed, our rituals and even our mundane celebrations can become templates of magical intention for the future; we have the power to harness some of the energy present now in order to help manifest our goals all the way through the next year's cycle.

The sabbat known as Samhain can vary greatly depending on the tradition one practices, but for me, it is celebrated as a three-day festival from October 30st to November 1st. On the first day, all the wonderful preparations can be made: altars set up, decorations arranged, the feast menu finalized (and some of the food cooked), outfits chosen, ritual outline double-checked, etc. The second day is, of course, "the big day": when the main ritual for Samhain is conducted. For many of us, it is a double duty type of day, with the modern Halloween celebrations having the focus for most of the daytime and early evening hours and the Samhain observance commencing at night. On the third day, all of the offerings are buried with honor and thanks. In addition to the reverent activities, the third day is also the practical time for cleanup of dishes, costumes, and decorations. I usually prefer to keep most of the interior decorations up for a few weeks after the Sabbat in order to help preserve the energy.

Personally, I've always found it strange that so many people seem to be in a rush to take down decorations as soon as the holiday is over, especially when the holiday is a sabbat. I think that in our modern culture where our eyes are always trained to be focused on the next thing coming over the horizon, the appreciation of the here and now has fallen out of favor. The sabbats are celebrated as both a peak of power and an initiator into a new cycle, so the idea that once Samhain is "over" we should immediately turn our focus away from its meaning makes no sense to me. This holiday is (among other things) a beginning: a portal into the dark half of the year, and the power of this change continues throughout the month of November and realistically all the way until Yule further modifies the energy. All too often are the relatively modern Thanksgiving and Christmas holidays rushed forward, leaving Halloween and its "spookiness" in the dust. Speaking from a witchy perspective, the autumn equinox is the time to give thanks for what we have and the time of Samhain is where we acknowledge and honor what we've lost and also to make our magical blueprints for the future. If we plan carefully, we can harness and align with the inherent power present at this time, channeling our vision into the greater energy flow so that our intention becomes part of the natural unfolding of events, which is one of the secrets of manifestation; working with the natural energetic tides is more effective than working against them.

Since Samhain is considered the "Witches' New Year," it not only represents the traditional themes of honoring departed loved ones and the Ancestors but also the hope and promise of starting over.

Magically speaking, if you design the entire Samhain celebration around a magical goal, a vision of how you would like things to be throughout the coming year, you can project a clear and powerful intention. In essence, this means that if you are seeking prosperity in the coming year, the decorations, costumes, and ritual accessories should steer away from the spooky, grim, or grotesque and instead be focused on joyful and elegant. In this case, royal costumes with lots of golden or silver-colored accessories or an outfit adorned with play money could be worn to help empower the intention. Instead of horror-themed decorations, happy jack-o'-lanterns or ones carved with magical symbols, glittering shiny candles and favorite foods and treats; anything that carries a prosperous and joyful feeling to you can be added to the festivities.

Other intentions can follow a similar pattern. If your desire is to increase psychic ability in the coming year, playing up the magical and Otherworldly, divinatory aspects of the holiday can be a great way of projecting this wish. Dress in your witchy finest or in a "fortune-teller" type of costume, lay out all of your favorite tools for divination, like tarot decks, scrying mirrors, crystal balls, etc., and make the decorations etheric and slightly spooky. Owl, bat, and ghost decorations work well for this magical goal; anything that gives the feel of Otherworldly messenger, magical power, or second-sight. If love is the strongest intention, dressing up as a deity known for love, such as Venus or Eros, can be an excellent costume choice not only to represent your desire but also to help draw in the deities to aid in your magic (if you choose to do so). If your desire is to enhance your magical ability in the coming year or if you want to achieve greater confidence and inner strength, the witch archetype can be fully embraced. Black hooded cloaks, bubbling cauldrons, large mystical-looking jewelry, a handy broomstick, or a magic wand can all become a part of the festivities. Magically-themed jack-o'-lanterns carved with pentagrams, elemental symbols, or special sigils can be created and charged with intent.

The possibilities for decorations and costumes are almost endless, but there is one major exception; horror or "evil" themes should be avoided. The reason for this is pretty straightforward, in that it is usually a bad idea to encourage chaos, violence, or horror into our lives especially at a time of such magical potential. This is the time to cultivate our highest potential, especially since the effects can last for an entire year or realistically, much longer. Skulls, bats, ghosts, and other such decorations are not considered horrific or evil and so can all be included in the holiday. Movie killers, devils, demons, and monsters, on the other hand, are not the best choices when trying to connect to the magic of this day. Living in such a tumultuous world already, none of us need to conjure up any more frightening images or energies, especially in our own lives. By carefully planning the energy and intention that we wish to project out into the world, we can avoid any misdirected magic or negative backlash.

Keeping a nice failsafe condition such as "with harm to none" in the back of your mind while working any magic on Samhain is also a wise idea to help minimize any unforeseen problems or mishaps. Magical manifestations need never result from harm. Please note that I'm not advocating ignoring our "shadow sides" or any dark aspects of the holiday. I am merely saying that when trying to create a magical effect, it is better to stick with the accessories and intentions that will encourage the best possible results. As an example, a red "devil" costume wouldn't be the best choice for a magical intention of greater power. Even though it could be argued that the horned, red man with cloven hooves, a pitchfork, and a tail is most likely a vilified version of the horned god grafted onto Lucifer, and therefore could be used without any "evil" connotation, it is still a symbolic emblem of evil in the popular mind and would potentially pose a problem to the complete fulfillment of the magic. Spiritual power would be better expressed as a witch, wizard, or deity costume and mundane power would better be expressed as royalty or as a corporate CEO. There are myriad ways to express any magical goal and we can just keep searching and planning until we find one that feels right.

One of the most wonderful mundane aspects of Samhain to me is the fact that most of our witch tools can be openly displayed in our homes at this time even if you are not necessarily a public witch. Cauldrons, brooms, wands, crystals, candles, skulls, etc., are all perfect Halloween decorations and fly right under most people's radar. Usually people will just think you're really into Halloween. In this way, we are given the advantage of setting our magical intentions early in the day and allow them to "simmer" while we go out and fulfill our regular obligations, like taking kids trick-or-treating or handing out candy ourselves. Normally wearing special ritual garb out in the everyday world is frowned upon (with some exceptions of course), but on Samhain we're encouraged to break the rules and disrupt our normal patterns, so turning a costume into a magical garment is a perfect way to enhance the magic. Clothing, jewelry, shoes, and other accessories usually carry a power and ability to make us feel a certain way; gym shoes and sweat pants give us a much different vibe than formal wear for example, and this inherent quality can be greatly enhanced through magic. You can choose just the right costume and accessories and bring them together, blessing them to become vessels to fulfill your magical goal. To do so, place the outfit on your altar, hold your hands over it, and visualize the end result of your intention. Infuse as much emotion into this visualization as you can, visualizing the way you want to feel when your goal is achieved and then mentally willing this power to flow down through your arms and hands into the costume. Fix in your mind that this energy will stay in the outfit until you choose to release it in ritual and also that this energy will remain intact, unaffected by any others. This way it can be worn out into the world without the worry of its power being diminished.

In my personal practice, I choose not to compartmentalize my magical life and my "regular" life, the two walk hand in hand. I think it is empowering to carry my magic into the everyday world, not in an overbearing way but in a subtle yet effective manner. Some witches and Pagans prefer to avoid the Halloween aspects of this day, feeling that it takes away from the true meaning of Samhain to participate in the candy-coated frolic of trick-or-treating or parties. In my opinion, I feel that the power lies in nature and in the individual Witch and that we can draw upon this power and connection no matter where we are or how we choose to celebrate. It is our choice whether or not to bring our magic with us into the everyday world.

The power of Samhain is that of limitless potential. Being a cross-quarter day, it is at its heart, a crossroads where the past and the future converge into the now. This quality is what makes it such an effective time for initiating change; the key is to unleash and project what you desire in the coming year as a clear concept and end result. When we place our vision of the future and what we desire into currents of energy that are already present, we not only help achieve our own goals but also help to turn the wheel from one seasonal cycle to another. By becoming active participants in the inherent rhythms of the earth, we are performing one of the most sacred and significant magical acts that a witch can do; a merging with the powers of nature. May your Samhain celebrations bring you joy, fulfillment, and wonderful magical success! Blessed Be.

Cosmic Sway

Charlie Rainbow Wolf

SAMHAIN OPENS WITH THE opportunity to finally break free of some of that recent karmic opposition involving the north nodes. Pluto and Saturn have disentangled themselves, and the Sun's recent opposition to Uranus—which is still going backward—is probably one of the most influential aspects for Samhain. Expect the unexpected, because it's likely to happen!

This has the potential to be a bit of a stressful period because of the way the changes manifest. It's vital to concentrate on going with the flow and remain flexible in your plans—especially if you have Samhain rituals or ceremonies. Accept changes as they occur, even if they're not what you wanted to happen. They may open the doors to something even better, although you can't see it at the time.

This transit also incubates nervous energy. The good news is the spontaneity that this aspect brings might just be the kick you need to try something different or to start thinking outside the box. Do something a bit different in order to scratch that restless itch, or you might find yourself getting a bit clumsy or careless.

Remember that this aspect is influencing everyone, so people may be more unpredictable than usual. They could need their own personal freedom or want to try things their own way. Uranus and Taurus are both fixed here, so there's not going to be a lot of compromise, and that's only going to add tension and frustration to this aspect.

Venus moves into a critical degree over the two-day Samhain celebration. This brings restraint and frustration to relationships. Fortunately Venus is a swift-moving planet and will be out of this position within a day. In the meantime, take any disappointments in stride. Venus in Sagittarius is generally a positive aspect, and once it leaves the critical degree, you should be in for some interesting socializing.

Samhain opens with the Moon in Sagittarius and closes with the Moon in Capricorn. While on its travels, the Moon makes a conjunct with Jupiter in its ruling sign of Sagittarius. This is a very positive aspect indeed! It's a wonderful Moon for socializing, and it takes some of the sting out of the Sun's opposition with Uranus. Of course, like all lunar transits, it's a fleeting thing. Make the most of it—once the Moon moves into Capricorn, events are going to take a turn for the more serious, and the more practical.

Mercury changes stations on the thirty-first, and Mercury retrograde is always challenging. Its saving grace is that it happens frequently enough that we've gotten used to its shenanigans. This time it's retrograde in Scorpio, and that might make things a bit intense. Like any retrograde, it's a period for the *re* words—review, reflect, reconsider—particularly when it comes to communication and travel plans. Don't take anything for granted. Repeat things so that you know you understand them, and ask others to do likewise so that you're sure you've been heard. Have a backup plan, just in case!

This sabbat also sees Mars making a hard aspect to Neptune and Saturn. The aspect with Neptune lowers the energy, and while this may be a good thing with that solar angle to Uranus, it also opens the doors for suspicion, guilt, and lethargy. Relationships with others seem hard going and confusing. It's not a good time for any long-term commitments. This energy will dissipate in about a week, so try to defer anything important until then.

I find the Saturn aspect intriguing, for it was very similar back around Beltane—the opposite festival on the wheel. Look back at what was happening then; with Saturn being the Lord of Karma, anything left undone may arise again, on both a personal and a global scale. There's certainly a week or so of stress around this transit.

Saturn sextile Neptune is pretty big news, for the influence of this aspect will be around for several days. The energy of Neptune is creative and dreamy, while the energy of Saturn is practical and hard working. The two combined mean that there's a good chance to make dreams a reality, to take plans and make them manifest.

This aspect should see complex issues disentangling and a sense of reliability seeping in when it comes to intentions taking form. Things that were uncertain—and possibly daunting or challenging—become less intimidating. It's easier to take things at face value, because the faces are now becoming clearer. Stability is on the increase, and headway is made through issues that were once standing in the way of progress.

There is a chance that this aspect might bring to light any weaknesses or flaws when it comes to getting projects off the ground, but it should be easy to turn this into an asset. After all, if you know the foundation is wobbly, you can fix it at the beginning, making it a sturdier structure. Remember, Saturn is the disciplinarian; if you ignore this initial failing, it will more than likely return to haunt you with an even bigger problem.

Samhain Ceremony: A Dumb Supper

In the Mabon ritual we honor the dead as those who had left their earthly bodies behind. In this Samhain ceremony, we're honoring the dead once again, but this time it is as the spirits of all those who have gone before. Samhain is opposite Beltane on the Wheel of the Year, and some traditions saw these dates as the pivotal forces and more important than the solstices and equinoxes.

This ceremony invites the dead to come and mingle with you. Many different paths had a "silent supper" or a "dumb meal" (dumb meaning *silent*, in this instance, not foolish) at this time of year, where they picnicked on the graves of their departed and feasted with them, or set a table at their own dinner table. This is something you can do alone or with a group; the requirements are the same.

There's not a lot of ritual prep to do for this one. You simply carry out your Samhain activities as usual, but when it comes to the food, it's more of a formal sit-down meal than a socialize-and -mingle occasion. Prepare a place for the dead, and serve the food and drink as you would if there was a person sitting there. If you like, you can choose an ancestor and place their photo at the place setting.

What makes this meal different is that no one is to look or to talk to the dead during the course of the repast. No one is to speak to anyone else. This is done reverently, in silence. Spend your time communing with the spirit that has graced you with their presence. Listen to what they bring to you, and pay attention to the influence it has on you.

At the end of the meal, silently clear away the untouched food and drink from the position where the spirit was sitting. Take them outside and leave them for the fairies and nature spirits to consume as they will. Only then can the conversation resume. If you're doing this as a group activity, it may be helpful to discuss your thoughts and feelings. If you're doing it by yourself, you might want to journal the experience.

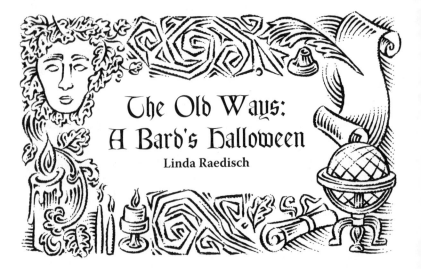

The Old Ways:
A Barb's Halloween
Linda Raedisch

WE'VE ALL HEARD OF "Double, double, toil and trouble," but as "Hallowmass" approached, Shakespeare's contemporaries would have been just as likely to suffer from the earworm, "Mingle, mingle, mingle, in the pingle,/Join the cantrip with the jingle." You, dear reader, may already be aware that a cantrip is a witch's incantation. (A pingle, in case you are wondering, is a little lidded pot used for cooking a child's porridge.) The above is a line from the Galloway Song, one of a number of Jacobean greatest hits having to do with witches.

If any of the action in Macbeth is meant to take place on All Hallows' Eve, Shakespeare does not mention it. October 31 was regarded as a night of prophecy, so it would have been entirely appropriate for Macbeth to have his first run-in with the Three Witches on that date. History tells us that King Duncan was killed in August (in battle, not in his bed), but when has Shakespeare ever allowed history to get in the way of creativity? (History also tells us that Macbeth enjoyed a long and more-or-less successful reign before he met his doom at Lumphanan.) The fact that Shakespeare did not invoke the occasion of Halloween to lend eeriness to the scene tells us that, in his day, Halloween was a fairly low-profile holiday.

We know that Shakespeare was acquainted with the feast at the end of October, but his single reference to it, "to speak puling, like a beggar at Hallowmass," in *Two Gentlemen of Verona* has no spooky ring to it at all. In both Elizabethan and Jacobean England, Halloween was indeed an understated affair. "Souling" was technically no longer allowed under the newfangled Church of England, but children roamed the streets nevertheless in hopes of receiving "soul cakes," in gratitude for which they were supposed to pray for the souls trapped in Purgatory. In the countryside, Catholic holdouts quietly fed bonfires in memory of the dead, but in Shakespeare's imagination, ghosts were more likely to walk abroad on Christmas Eve.

In Scotland, it was a different story. There, Halloween bonfires remained *de rigeur*, ostensibly to "burn the witches," as the accompanying chants made clear. In Macbeth's own Moray, blazing fir candles were thrown into the flames to keep fairies away too. The smoke imparted blessings while the soot could be used to blacken the face, a convenient disguise for the youths who ran amuck, pinching cabbages out of the neighbors' gardens and flinging them at the cottage doors. Hence Scotland's other name for Halloween, Cabbage Night.

The flames of the bonfire were fed with bracken, peat bricks, barrels of pine tar, old furniture, and even bits of houses, which may explain why there is now nothing left of the two witches' houses that Sir James Sinclair clearly marked on his map of Dunsinane in 1772. Sinclair's map also included a "Witches' Stone", but I believe any witch in Dunsinane would have been lucky to survive so long. The last witch to be tried and executed in Scotland, indeed in the British Isles, was Janet Horne in 1727. Had witches still been living at Dunsinane fifty years later, I'm sure they didn't appreciate Sir James drawing a path to their doorsteps.

The houses, as Sinclair has rendered them, are quite ordinary-looking. With peaked roofs and doors in their gable ends, they radiate all the spookiness of Monopoly hotels. Back in the 1600s, playwright Ben Jonson displayed a little more imagination. His witch, Maudlin, in *The Sad Shepherd*, dwells "within a gloomie dimble...Down in a pitt, ore-growne with brakes and briars," a "dimble" being a narrow valley and a "brake" a thicket. And earlier, in *The Faerie Queen*, Elizabethan poet Edmund Spenser described the typical witch's abode as "a little cottage built of sticks and reedes/In homely wise, and wald with sods around." Like Jonson, he situates the cottage in "a gloomy hollow."

But what were the witches who lived in these quaint little cottages supposed to be up to at Halloween? Surely, they were not whining for soul cakes with the children in the streets? Fortunately for us, but very unfortunately for the accused men and women, we have several accounts of supposed witchy doings in the Scotland of the time. On "Allhollow Even" 1590, accused witch Agnes Sampson partied with two hundred other witches in a churchyard in North Berwick in the Lothians, the party guests arriving at the venue in sieves. There they drank wine and danced to the music of a "Jew's trump," led by the devil's secretary, John Fian. In Craigleuch, near Aberdeen, we hear of a coven of witches dancing round a stone on Halloween 1597. Dances, especially ring dances, often come up in accounts of the so-called Witches' Sabbath. The witches were said to dance withershins, counterclockwise, thereby reversing the fertility of the land.

Did these sixteenth-century gatherings of witches ever really take place? Probably not, but the defendants, in their desperation, told their torturers what they thought they wanted to hear. When Macbeth's Three Witches "Round about the cauldron go" in Act 4 Scene I , they're enacting a Jacobean stereotype, one which has persisted into the twenty-first century, thanks to the play's popularity.

The magical cooking vessel of Celtic mythology survives on the one hand as the Holy Grail and on the other as the witch's cauldron. In both cases, it is a source of life and a sign of covenant. By the 1500s, the ingredients of the witch's brew had become the subject of wild fantasy and disgusted fascination. But whether it contained "eye of newt and toe of frog" as in Macbeth or "May dew and fumart's tears" as in the Galloway Song, the most important aspect of the witch's brew was the idea that it should be cooked and consumed together with other witches in the presence of their leader, each witch dipping in with a little horn spoon which she kept on her belt just for that purpose. In this way, the witches affirmed their identity as a coven and sustained their individual magic powers until the next gathering.

All in all, the Christian observance of All Souls' and All Saints' Day was not all that different from the Samhain-tide gathering of the ancient druids, when all members of the community, living and dead, came together to reaffirm their bond. The Witches' Sabbath, as it existed in the Elizabethan and Jacobean imagination, was basically the same ritual turned on its head.

It is amusing to note that the practice of trolling the streets for soul cakes was once as frowned upon by the Church of England as its robust offspring, trick-or-treating, is in many American communities today. So whether you are all decked out in Druids' robes and headed for the sacred groves or are simply dressed as a Jacobean witch at Hallowmass, rest assured that it's all part of the same life-affirming ritual.

Resources

Aitchison, Nick. *Macbeth: Man and Myth.* Gloucestershire, England: Sutton Publishing Limited, 2000.

Briggs, K. M. *Pale Hecate's Team: An Examination of the Beliefs on Witchcraft and Magic among Shakespeare's Contemporaries and His Immediate Successors.* New York: The Humanities Press, 1962.

Hutton, Ronald. *The Stations of the Sun: A History of the Ritual Year in Britain.* New York: Oxford University Press, 1996.

McNeill, F. Marian. *Scottish Folklore and Folk-belief.* The Silver Bough, Volume One. Glasgow: William Maclellan, 1957.

Feasts and Treats

Blake Octavian Blair

SAMHAIN, THE THIRD OF the harvest festivals, is upon us! This harvest brings us yet another rotation of tasty seasonal ingredients available for our feasting pleasure. It also brings thoughts of the beloved dead to mind. This Samhain menu will give a nod to both of those elements. With pumpkins on our porches, it's only fitting in my mind that we put them on our feast tables, both in the form of decor as well as in the meals on our plates. In this menu you'll find one of the favorite savory pumpkin dishes, as well as my own adaptation of pesto, featuring seasonal greens and some modern updates to kick up the flavor. To finish it all off is a recipe for a sweet treat, left to us by one of my departed ancestors. Create a delightfully witchy feast table decor by throwing in a few skeleton-themed items among the pumpkins to hearken to the ancestral currents in the air.

Pumpkin Slow Cooker Oatmeal

It has been said breakfast is the most important meal of the day, so why not start your Samhain out in style with delicious homemade pumpkin oatmeal! This one is a cinch, just make it while wearing your pajamas the night before in your slow cooker and let it slowly cook itself into a seasonal pumpkin deliciousness to greet you in the morning! It's so easy and so tasty that it's sure to become one of your holiday traditions!

Prep time: Less than 10 minutes
Cook time: Overnight
Serves: 5–6

1 cup steel-cut oats
4½ cups liquid, including; water, milk, and cream
1 cup canned pumpkin
¼ cup raisins
2 tsp cinnamon
¼ tsp ground clove
¼ tsp ground nutmeg

Combine all ingredients into a 3 quart slow cooker. Set to "warm" and cook overnight.

The cooking process will release a fair amount of natural sugars. Therefore, I do not specify to add any additional sugar to this dish. However, you can place a sugar bowl on the table when serving so your diners can add it to their tastes as needed.

Note: the "warm" setting is more than sufficient for cooking the oatmeal overnight, and this reduces the severity of burning at the bottom of the crock (as opposed to cooking it at a higher setting). There will be some no matter what but this minimizes it to the thinnest of layers. The crock is easily cleaned after by soaking in hot water.

Kale Pesto Pasta

This dish makes both a wonderful entrée as well as a delightful hearty side dish. Kale is actually in season in October, the Samhain season in the Northern Hemisphere, so for many of us it is the perfect opportunity to use a fresh seasonal ingredient in our sabbat feast. This kale pesto isn't likely to resemble a pesto recipe of your ancestors, with inclusion of sriracha and soy sauce as rather exotic ingredients for a pesto. However, as odd as it sounds, I've found through my culinary adventures that this combination gives the dish a delightful kick and body that isn't overpowering yet full of dimension.

Prep time: 5 minutes
Cook time: 25 minutes
Serves: 6

¼ cup shelled pumpkin seeds (or to taste)
Salt
5–7 large leaves of kale
1 lb spaghetti pasta
¾ cup olive oil
2 tbsp sriracha
2 tbsp soy sauce

Add the pumpkin seeds to a cold dry skillet and turn on to medium heat, stirring frequently until aromatic and a slight golden brown color and glistening appearance are achieved. Remove from heat and set aside.

Add a few pinches of salt to a large pot of water and bring to a boil. Add kale to pot and cook for 3 minutes. Place kale in ice water for one minute. Drain kale.

Add spaghetti to same pot and water kale was cooked in and cook until al dente. (Approximately 9–12 minutes.) Drain in a colander.

While the pasta is cooking, you can proceed to simultaneously prepare the pesto sauce as follows.

In a blender or food processor, combine the kale leaves, olive oil, sriracha, soy sauce, and half the pumpkin seeds. Blend until saucy, or desired consistency is achieved. You should be able to finish making the pesto sauce in the time it takes for the pasta to finish cooking. Note: you may want to adjust the ratios of oil and kale leaves to achieve the consistency you desire. Some prefer an oilier pesto, some like a thicker pesto. Similarly, you can adjust the amount of sriracha for your desired heat level. As written, I find the pesto not to be very spicy, yet it has a nice mild spice that brings out the other flavors.

Add the drained pasta and the pesto sauce back into the large empty cooking pot from the pasta and toss until all the pasta appears evenly coated with the pesto sauce.

Serve into bowls and sprinkle the top of each with some of the remaining pumpkin seeds.

Stuffed Baked Pumpkins

What is Samhain without a dish to honor this squash that serves as star ambassador of the season? This savory dish is the perfect entrée for your Samhain feast! Plus, it looks awesome and festive on the table and your family and guests will have a priceless expression when you set an entire pumpkin down in front of them.

Prep time: 15 minutes
Cook time: 2 hours (mostly inactive)
Serves: 4

4 sugar/pie pumpkins (approx. 1 lb each)
Kosher salt (to taste)
Cracked black pepper (to taste)
¼ onion, diced
1 tbsp butter
2 cloves minced garlic
12 ounces vegetarian sausage crumbles
4 ounces fresh baby spinach
1 cup cooked wild rice
2 cups stuffing mix
1 cup shredded fontina, gruyere, or cheddar cheese

Preheat oven to 350 degrees F. Begin preparing the pumpkins by removing the tops, seed, and loose fibers (pumpkin guts!). You can set aside and save the seeds for future roasting, they make a great snack. Season the interior of the pumpkins with a sprinkling of salt and cracked black pepper.

Next dice the onions and then place into a skillet on medium low heat, sweat the onions in butter until they are aromatic and translucent in appearance, approximately 5–7 minutes. Then add the garlic and sweat for an additional minute.

Next add the vegetarian sausage crumbles to the skillet until heated through and the crumbles are slightly browned, approximately 7–10 minutes.

Then add the spinach to the skillet and stir for 1–2 minutes until it becomes wilted, and then season with salt and black pepper.

In a large mixing bowl, add the sausage mixture, cooked rice, stuffing mix, and cheese. Mix until all ingredients are evenly distributed. Tightly pack the stuffing into each of the pumpkins and replace the tops. Place packed pumpkins into a glass baking dish and into the 350 degree oven for 1 hour. After an hour, remove the pumpkin tops and bake an additional 20–30 minutes or until the flesh of the pumpkins is tender. When done, replace tops and serve.

Grandma's Scottish Shortbread

I'm sure we all have foods we associate with loved ones who have since passed away. This, dear reader, is one such recipe for my husband and I. His grandma was famous among her circles for her homemade Scottish shortbread. Grandma was in fact a proud Scotswoman, born and raised. She was a small woman with a formidable yet lovable personality. We too, came to love our shortbread, not purely for the happy memories associated with grandma, but also because it was so delicious. In fact, I'm willing to bet you can't eat just one piece. It's important to buy the best butter you absolutely can for this recipe. The entire recipe only has three ingredients, the fewer the number of ingredients the more important their quality tends to become. This is why I specify to use imported Irish butter. Trust me, Grandma would insist. This shortbread works wonderfully for cakes and ale ceremonies in ritual, as a delicious snack, or a satisfying desert. Tip from Grandma: it goes great with a cup of tea as well.

12 ounces all-purpose flour
4 ounces castor sugar
8 ounces imported Irish butter (softened)

Preheat an oven to 325 degrees F. Sift together the flour and sugar into a large mixing bowl. Next, incorporate the butter into the mixture using your fingertips until an even consistency is achieved. You want the consistency of a crumbly, mealy dough.

Next, divide the dough in half and then shape each half into a round (approx. ¼ to ½ inches in thickness) on a cookie sheet.

Place cookie sheet with rounds into the oven for 20–30 minutes, until the rounds have a golden appearance. When finished baking, sprinkle the rounds with additional caster sugar while warm, and cut into wedges when cooled.

Crafty Crafts

Natalie Zaman

CONFESSION: I'M A CRAFT-SUPPLY hoarder, particularly when it comes to glitter. Powders, discs, mirrors, sequins, silver, gold, every color of the rainbow—I probably have it. This was a truth I had to face when we decided to move and the inevitable purge began. There's nothing like a good clear-out to reveal just how much stuff you've accumulated, especially after being in the same house for two decades. It didn't, however, negate my desire to create. I want to keep making stuff, but not add to the pile. What's a witch to do? I found a very satisfying (not to mention sparkling) answer in consumable crafts.

Even before my massive and still ongoing dump-o-rama I'd embraced the idea of consumables, especially with gift giving. The downside: a consumable gift isn't a permanent reminder of kindness. The upside: consumable gifts give over and over and over again. Consumable gifts and crafts are interactive. From start to finish they give pleasure, in their making, giving, and using—after which, your recipient is free of any obligations to keep, display, or otherwise curate a thing. And—important, this—you're free to make more.

All of this year's Crafty Crafts are consumable in some way, shape, or form. Burn them, mix them, melt them, scrub them, deck yourself out in them, use them up until they're gone. They're tailored to specific sabbats and were designed with magic and ritual in mind (hence the presence of efficacious and symbolic herbs, stones, essential oils and the ever-important intention). With a few adjustments, any of them can be made for a variety of occasions—or they can just be made, no esoteric agenda necessary.

Some things to note before we crack open the glitter cannisters:

I tend to work with plants that I can wild harvest or grow in my garden, so I use lots of rosemary, lavender, lemon balm, honeysuckle and blackberry leaves and berries when I make things. If a project calls for the use of plants, it's likely that one or more of these will appear in the list of items to procure. All of them are suggestions and can be swapped out for other herbs and flowers.

About aesthetics ... while I would dearly love my finished products to be Pinterest-perfect, most of the time they look homemade rather than handmade. Still, I love the creative process and the idea that I've created something useful—which brings me to another reason to love consumable crafts: I'm not afraid to destroy them because of their beauty.

Chances are you'll probably find many of the other necessary supplies for these projects in your pantry or, if you're like me, your craft stash. Most are inexpensive and can be easily acquired at your local market, craft, or thrift shop. I like using things up (many a project has evolved around the phrase, "what can I do with the rest of this...") and using free things—save glitter. On THAT I will splurge.

And speaking of glitter...the aforementioned substance somehow finds its way into almost everything I make. It's a personal taste, so feel free to omit it if it's not your thing. Before you do however, consider this: besides being fabulously blingy, the shiny stuff is, literally magical. Glitter attracts light and also reflects it—which means it draws positivity to your work, and then reflects it outward. Shine on!

Sparkling Monogram Memory Lights

The addition of initials to anything—a handkerchief, a doormat, a cake—conveys instant pride in one's identity. Monograms are personal sigils and date back to the ancient world where coins were marked with the initials of rulers to claim what was theirs—that whole "render unto Caesar" thing. Craft some candles with your ancestors' initials as an elegant means of honoring them at Samhain (or any time!).

Time Lavished: Making a monogram memory light will take up about an hour of your time, maybe two, depending on how much you want to devote to cutting out beeswax letters (or in my case, re-cutting them).

Coinage Required: The supplies to make 4–6 monogram memory lights will set you back about $30–$40. You can save some money and do some upcycling at the same time by repurposing crayons as well as leftover wax from candles that didn't burn down all the way. Remember to save any wax scraps when you cut your monograms. These can be melted down to make other candles or added to the wax you're using for this project.

Supplies

Old tea cups. (You can also use mugs or small bowls—chips add character!) By using a cup with a history, you're keeping the past alive. *What is remembered, lives*—that is, after all, the purpose of this craft. Bonus points for using a cup that belonged to an ancestor. (Unless, of course, it's fragile. In that case—keep out of reach of crafty hands!)

Wooden candle wicks and tabs to hold them in place. You can use traditional candle wicking, but I find it fussy, plus, you can write messages on wooden wicks.

Heat-proof receptacle to melt candle wax. (Never melt wax in a microwave or over direct heat—it's a fire hazard!)

Candle wax. You can buy candle wax, but since its Samhain and the new year, it's a good time to clear up and clean out. Repurpose wax from candles that didn't burn all the way, as well as broken crayons. (Peel any paper off your crayons before melting them.) Smudge any upcycled material you're using with sage, lavender, or your favorite cleansing herbs before you melt it to clear it of any past workings or connotations that may be attached to it. You can also place the wax in a salt water bath before you melt it.

Cypress or myrrh essential oil. Both of these oils are good for spirit connection work, however, if you associate a specific scent with your ancestor(s), use those or any others that hold personal meaning for you.

Glitter. Black is seasonal and protective while white, silver and purple are colors for working with the spirit realm. Again, use your intuition as well as traditional knowledge to determine what colors to use (for this, or any Craft!).

Beeswax sheets. Most beeswax sheets come in standard square (8" × 8") or rectangular (8" × 17") sizes. You'll be cutting the initials from this material, so any size will work, and any left-over remnants can be melted down to make other candles later. If you have a choice of colors, black, as stated above, is seasonal and protective, but you can use any color. In fact, the whole point of a monogram is personalization. Think of your ancestors' favorite colors.

Small scissors and/or a craft knife.

A store-bought pillar candle. Don't have tea cups or lots of time? No problem—there's a quick way to make a monogram memory light—read on!

Crystal chips. Quartz will magnify your intention while stones like lepidolite, celestite, petrified wood, selenite, and amethyst are good for spirit communication.

Begin by turning your cup upside down and placing it on top of a sheet of beeswax. Trace the outline of the cup opening, then cut it out. Using a stencil or your own mad skills, carefully cut your ancestor's initial(s) from the beeswax disc you just made. You don't have to make the letters circular in shape (or the shape of the cup

opening), but this will ensure that your monogram will fit. (You'll be placing it on top of the candle.)

Next, clean and dry your cup. Before inserting the wick into the tab, write your ancestor's name on it, and if space allows, a simple message. Center the wick tab in the bottom of the cup, then secure it in place with a few drops of melted wax. Once you've poured your candle and the wax has hardened, you may need to trim the wick depending on the size of the cup.

Melt the wax, then take it off the heat and let it cool and thicken slightly before mixing in the essential oils. The wax should still be liquid when you do this. Adding essential oil to too-hot wax lessens the potency of its scent.

Pour the wax into the cup, leaving a little space at the top—you'll need some room for your monogram. As the wax starts to set, sprinkle glitter on the top of the candle.

Let the wax harden and set completely (mine took about an hour) before adding your monogram, which will sit on top of the candle. First, trim the wick if needed; you should see about an inch of it above the wax. Center the monogram around the wick. Depending on the letter, you may need to make a slice or slit in the wax with your scissors or craft knife to accommodate the wick. Don't worry if you cut the letter; simply place it on top of the candle in pieces. Trim any excess so that it fits in your cup, and gently press it into place. Press a few crystal chips into the cells of the beeswax. Place them randomly or in a pattern, outline the letters, or fill them in completely. These are just suggestions—do what feels and looks right to you.

In a hurry? You can skip the candle making process and purchase a pillar candle. Cut your letters from the beeswax sheet (the size of the letters will depend on the size of your candle). Use a hair dryer or heat gun to soften one side of the candle and the back side of the monogram. Gently press the monogram into the candle. If the letter fails to stick, use a bit of craft glue to hold it in place.

Dress the candle with the oils and gently spread glitter on the sides and top of the candle. Press the crystal chips into the cells of the beeswax. Place the stones around the edge of the letters to outline them, or incorporate them into the letters randomly or in a pattern. Again, do what looks and feels right to you.

Monogram candles can be used for many other special occasions—weddings, birthdays or any time that you want to acknowledge the uniqueness of a certain special someone—including yourself. Go forth shining!

Portable Magic

Mickie Mueller

SAMHAIN HAS BECOME A really busy time of the year for many of us. Since the spiritual celebration of Samhain dovetails with the secular celebration of Halloween, it can create special challenges. As we dash around stocking up on candy, carving pumpkins, and of course all of our other usual commitments, it can be a challenge to remember Spirit during this pivotal time of the year. It can be especially perplexing when the actual sabbat falls on a weekday, as Samhain does this year. Many of us have work or school early the next morning. We often plan our group or solitary celebrations on the closest weekend when we have more time. I love to do some bits and bobs of magic on the actual sabbat too. Over the years I've come up with simple ways to take my magic on the go. The Wheel of the Year stops for no witch, and on Samhain that is doubly true! As we welcome in the Celtic New Year, let's think about ways to keep our magic close at hand. In all the hubbub of daily life we can still find ways to remain mindful of the real reason for the sabbats, and Samhain is the perfect place to begin a new tradition of sabbat magic on the go.

Skulls or Stones: Jewelry to Honor the Dead

I always see lots of jewelry in the fall that most people would wear only for Halloween but you and I might wear all year long! Jewelry is a wonderful way to bring magic with you wherever you go. Skull or skeleton jewelry can be fun and kitschy or dark and serious, but for a witch they can be a perfect talisman to focus on remembrance, a reminder that life is both beautiful yet impermanent. If you prefer there are also some stones that can specifically help you tap into the energy of this festival of spirit. A few of these include carnelian, jet, moonstone, jasper, bloodstone, obsidian, and onyx or fossil stones. Once you've found the perfect piece of jewelry to wear on Samhain, enchant it before you wear it that day.

Cleanse the jewelry by waving it through incense smoke and visualizing any negative energies dissipating. Next simply hold your jewelry in your hands over your heart to charge it with joyful memories of loved ones and thoughts of appreciation of the gifts your ancestors gave you. Wear your special piece on Samhain and let it be a reminder that life is precious and that the spirits guide you lovingly from the other side.

Death and Rebirth Tarot Card Spell

You'll need your favorite Death card from one of your tarot decks, a slip of cardstock paper about the same size as the tarot card, and a 3" × 5" rigid plastic sleeve to protect your card. You can find a pack of these wherever baseball cards or gaming cards are sold, or on online. I love these for tarot card spells and meditations to keep my cards safe.

The Death card carries energies for clearing away the old to make way for the new, so on the slip of paper thoughtfully write at least three things you want to banish from your life and what you want to replace them with. As examples, "Banish my anger, replace it with understanding. Banish stress, and replace it with peace and balance." Stack the list on the back of the tarot card and slide both into the sleeve so that you carry it with you all day on Samhain.

When it's protected in the sleeve, you can toss it in your purse, pocket, and easily bring it along throughout the day. As you go about your everyday business, other things will come up that you would like to banish from your life, add them one by one to your list and place it back next to the card in the sleeve. In the evening, set the whole thing on your altar or a shelf next to a candle and leave it there all Samhain night until the next morning. You can replace the Death card back into your deck, the list can be burned in a fireproof bowl or cauldron to send it into the realm of spirit.

Wear Colors of the Day

When you get dressed on Samhain morning, consider the clothes you wear and the significance of the colors corresponding with the magic of the sabbat. Wearing Samhain colors can help you embody the energies of the magic in the air all day.

Black is the most obvious color to wear on Samhain; this is a color that's great for neutralizing outside energies, so it's a color for psychic protection. It's also a stabilizing color and associated with divination, which might come in handy in your wardrobe when the veil between the worlds is thin.

Gray is a ghostly color, and yes, it's associated with the realm of spirits. You can also wear gray to enhance balance, visions, and dreams.

Orange in all its shades is a color of the harvest. If you don't look great in bright orange, try a more golden shade or deep pumpkin or just an accessory. This is a color that breaks down barriers representing the thinning veil between the worlds. Orange can also bring happiness and strength, which we need to build up to see us through the winter months.

Purple is a color that has recently become associated with the secular celebration of Halloween, but witches have known that purple is a color to wear for spiritual protection and psychic powers for ages. You can also wear purple on Samhain to help heal emotions and usher in spiritual blessings for the witches new year. Purple has often been a symbol of occult power.

Sabbat on the Go Tips:

If you work in an office or someplace where you can have flowers, put a vase of marigolds or rosemary (or both) on your desk as a message to the spirits of loved ones who've crossed over to let them know that you're thinking of them on Samhain.

Bring a snack of pomegranate seeds and/or pumpkin seeds along on your daily travels. Both are connected to the underworld and also represent fertility and love; pumpkin seeds are full of abundance magic. Focus on these properties while you enjoy these Samhain treats.

Wear any of these oils today: frankincense, patchouli, rosemary oil, or a drop of each. All these oils are perfect for Samhain due to their ability to purify, protect, and impart their high spiritual vibrations assuring only positive experiences with roaming spirits as well as good luck for the coming year.

Carry a charm bag for good luck. Use some or all of the following: pumpkin seeds, crushed eggshell, a coin, crescent moon charm, small piece of broom straw, jasper, carnelian, star anise, allspice, cinnamon, cloves. Keep in mind that in a charm bag, a little of each goes a long way. Place all your items in the middle of a six inch square piece of fabric, gather it up in a bundle, and tie it with twine or ribbon.

Samhain Wishcraft Ritual

Michael Furie

THIS RITUAL WILL HELP harness the energy present on Samhain and channel it toward fulfilling your desire and laying the groundwork for a joyous new year filled with promise.

Items Needed

Costume that corresponds to the magical wish

"Halloween" themed decorations that relate to the wish

4 direction candles (or four lit jack-o'-lanterns, one for each direction)

Sage incense (cone, stick, or raw)

3 black candles

2 white candles

1 silver or gray candle

1 orange candle

Wish written on a piece of paper

1 small freestanding mirror

Cauldron (or heat-proof bowl)

Censer (and self-lighting charcoal if using raw incense)

Chalice of water

Athame

Determine the four cardinal directions of north, east, south, and west in your working area, and place either a sturdy candle or a jack-o'-lantern at each of the four points. Generally speaking, each direction is linked to one of the four elements and most often north is connected to earth, east is connected to air, south is connected to fire, and west is connected to water. If using the direction point candles, elemental colors can be chosen (green for earth, white for air, red for fire, and blue for water). If jack-o'-lanterns are used to mark the points, they can be carved with magical symbols or animal faces that you feel align with their direction and element. For the earth, a pumpkin, a tree, pentagram, or upside-down triangle with a horizontal line through the middle can be carved. For air, a bird, clouds, or a right -side up triangle with a horizontal line through the middle can be made. For fire, flames, a dragon, or a right-side up triangle can be created. For water, a fish, cauldron, or upside-down triangle can be carved. Once the jack-o'-lanterns or candles have been decided upon, place them at their directional points and decide how large you wish to make the circle boundary. If you choose to mark the circle's circumference, cords, ribbons, crystals, nuts, or flowers, etc. can be used as boundary markers.

After the circle has been prepared, it's time to focus on the altar. Arrange an altar by placing one of the black candles at the left rear corner and then moving right, the silver or gray candle followed by the censer in the middle, then another black candle and finally, a white candle resting in the rear right corner. These candles shall serve as the goddess and god candles with the two on the left representing the goddess in both her dark and light sides and the two on the right symbolizing the god in his dark and light aspects as well. Setting the cauldron in the center, place the third black candle and the chalice filled with water to its immediate left. Put the orange candle and the athame to the right of the cauldron and the other white candle in front of it (nearest to you), this will be the "work candle." Place the mirror in the middle, behind the cauldron and in front of the censer. Light the incense and the black and orange candles on either side of the cauldron (which represent the dark time of the year and the bounty of the harvest, respectively).

Through smoke and flame, I begin this rite, to honor the power of Samhain night. Goddess and God, Ancestors all, I ask for your blessings, please hear my call.

Once all of the preparations have been made, cast the circle. Starting in the north and moving clockwise, hold the athame out and send energy through it to form the circle with words such as,

I cast this circle to create a sacred space and to protect those within from any forces that would bring harm. This circle is made. So mote it be.

Once you have completed the circle, stand at the north point and call to the earth element saying,

Power of earth, come this night, bring your power to this rite.

Move to the east and call to the element of air saying,

Power of air, come this night, bring your power to this rite.

Go to the south and call,

Power of fire, come this night, bring your power to this rite.

At the western point, call to the element of water saying,

Power of water, come this night, and bring your power to this rite.

Finally, move to the center and placing both hands on the altar, mentally connect to the spiritual essence and declare,

Power of spirit, enter this circle, bless the altar and all in attendance.

Light the white work candle with the intention that its flame shall help carry your magic out to manifestation. Light the black goddess candle saying,

I kindle this flame in honor of the dark goddess, she who reigns in the time of decline.

Light the silver or gray candle saying,

I kindle this flame in honor of the light goddess, she who reigns in the time of growth.

Light the black god candle, saying,

I kindle this fire in honor of the dark god, he who reigns through the time of decline.

Light the white god candle saying,

I kindle this fire in honor of the light god, he who reigns in the time of growth.

Declare your intent by saying,

On this sacred Samhain night, I seek to create a new path forward, out of the shadows and into the light, my wish be granted, success assured.

Pick up the paper with your wish written on it and read it aloud then look at yourself in the mirror. Look deep into your own eyes and feel your power, that inner fire, the accumulation of all of your ancestors' energy and knowledge that paved the way for you and fuels your magic. Now, focus on your costume and intention, immersing yourself in the feeling of having your wish already granted. Visualize the complete achievement of your goal: the end result. Pouring all of your built up thought and emotion into the paper with your wish written on it, mentally "see" your intention-infused energy streaming from your hands into the paper. When you feel that it has reached its peak, ignite the paper in the flame of the white work candle and drop it in the cauldron to burn saying,

Unleashing a clear desire to claim, creating new form, future revise; with Samhain fire to achieve my aim, (state intention) be

gained, I catalyze, with harm to none, the power set free, to work the magic, so mote it be.

Conclude the rite with thanks to your ancestors and deities by holding up the chalice in salute to them, taking a sip of the water and then pouring the rest into the cauldron to ensure that the paper is completely extinguished. Finally, release the quarters by going to the west, south, east, and north points and saying,

Thank you to the element of (state respective element), may you go in power.

Using the athame, "cut" the circle by walking it in a counter-clockwise direction visualizing the energy being absorbed back into the knife. Extinguish the candles in reverse order of lighting them: the white and black god candles, then the silver and black goddess candles, then the work candle and finally, the orange and black candles. Remove the costume and carefully fold it (if possible) and place it on or near the altar until the next day.

On the next day, give the contents of the cauldron to the earth by preferably burying water and ashes in the ground but if that is not possible, pouring them into a flowerpot will do. Afterward, clean up the altar and ritual area, carefully putting things back and reverently disposing of any perishable remnants (pumpkins, etc.) and put the costume away in a special place to remind you of the magic. Leave as many of the decorations up as you can for at least a week after Samhain to reinforce your intent.

Notes

Notes

Yule

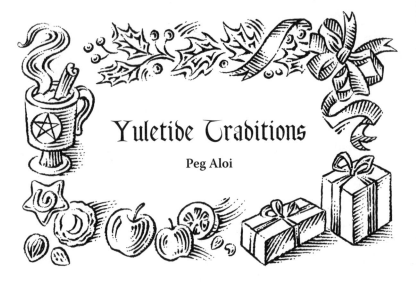

Yuletide Traditions

Peg Aloi

DESPITE BEING RAISED CATHOLIC, my family were not terribly insistent churchgoers, and Christmas often felt like a very secular, if not Pagan, affair. We traipsed through snowy woods to chop down our Christmas tree. We strung popcorn and cranberries onto string to decorate the tree, then after the tree came down, we hung them outside for the birds. We cut out sugar cookies in the shapes of reindeer, stars, holly leaves, and candles, and decorated them with frosting, colored sugars, sprinkles, and tiny silver balls. We'd sing carols while my mom played on her Hammond organ. We dug traditional treats out of our stockings: shelled nuts, oranges, chocolates. If we went to midnight mass, where I mostly remembered beautiful singing from the choir, that I joined with happily, my siblings and I were allowed to walk the ten or so blocks home, a magical time of night often with snow glittering like sugar in the streets. The colored lights on peoples' doors and shutters and the candles in their windows all looked so festive and inviting; we'd pass people getting into their cars after holiday dinners or themselves returning home from mass, maybe to open a gift or share some hot chocolate. Laughter rang like bells, calls of "Merry Christmas!" wafted across streets, people waved to strangers. The neighborhood was a community united in common celebration of family bonding and pleasing rituals of food and drink, games and fun. If it was snowing, we helped clear each other's cars and sidewalks, while the kids had snowball fights and built snowmen. As we walked toward our house, the smell of woodsmoke wafting from chimneys around the neighborhood completed this sensual tapestry of hospitality and holiday comfort.

The Magic of Yule

There'd be a fire in our own fireplace in the living room, where stockings were hung, red felt embroidered with angels and our names in block letters, made by my grandmother in the 1960s. There were plates of cookies and bowls of nuts, maybe a Dean Martin Christmas album playing on the stereo. The excitement was palpable, even years after believing in Santa Claus was no longer important. A magical feeling defined Christmas Eve in those days; and in years since, when I've been in cities far from where I grew up, it still felt that way, although I found myself much more aware of what a quiet and lonely night it could be, too, with all the shops and restaurants closed. How lonely to be without family or friends on this night, I have often thought, and yet I have been alone on December 24th a number of times. Invariably, I think about Yuletides past, good and bad, like some Dickensian ritual of remembering, coming away with a cautionary reminder to live in the moment and to be ready for change when, inevitably, it arrives. Accepting, if not embracing, change is a lesson many Pagans and witches struggle with, and nature is a powerful teacher in this regard. Seasonal sabbats based in changes of the landscape help us to observe the changes within us—the ebb and flow of energy and emotion, creativity and reflection.

Memories of the Yuletide season have always been significant for me, and it's always both surprising and comforting to me each year when I encounter them: the magical sight of colorful outdoor lights decorating houses (especially when driving in the countryside at night); the jubilant scent of evergreen trees and boughs indoors; the sudden warmth of a fireplace or wood stove as one comes in from the brisk cold; the taste of traditional treats made by myself or others (I happily make decorated sugar cookies each year from my mother's excellent recipe); old-fashioned carols played over loudspeakers in store or on the radio. Despite the insistence that Christmas is overly commercialized (and indeed, it is), I still manage to feel a certain magic when this time of year comes around. And I realize the sights and sounds that resonate most are more closely related to a Pagan concept of winter solstice as opposed to the Christian celebration of Christ's birth.

The Lean Months of Winter

Many of us know that old Pagan festivals were usurped by Christian holidays as a way to lend credibility and authority to the Church in modern European history. The uneducated rural folk observed this time of the coming darkness by celebrating the return of the light, as days started to grow longer after the solstice. In the days of feudalism, the poor worked the farms of landowners for their own subsistence, and had to make sure they put by enough food for the winter. That honoring of light in the darkness was a symbolic embrace of hope, a sign to stay strong and resilient during the coming months of harsh weather. Just as autumnal harvest festivals celebrated the abundance of farms and fields, they also observe hunting (the blood moon, for example) as a way to give thanks for their food sources. We tend to take it for granted these days that food is easily procured at the holidays, but our ancestors were not so lucky, and the Yuletide feasts they enjoyed (often prepared by landowners for their serfs and servants) marked a time just before the lean months of winter. "Eat, drink, and be merry" meant take advantage of abundance while you have it.

Since becoming a practicing witch as a young adult, my celebration of Yuletide has, strangely enough, retained many of the sensory delights I remember from the Christmases of my youth, and it's been comforting to realize that my upbringing was actually fairly Pagan all along. My dad was an avid outdoorsman. I still decorate the mounted deer's head, named Percy, that I inherited when he passed away; he once hung it on our porch with lights and ribbons and I (a sensitive teenager) was mortified. No, I proudly hang holly boughs and lights from this old piece of taxidermy, in his honor and also to honor the deer's life. My father was not one to collect hunting trophies: he mainly hunted for food, so this rare piece, from a deer he hunted when he was fairly young, is one I still treasure. The image of the stag, associated with the Horned God, is one I've always honored at this time of year. Images of deer, animal representatives of the woodland horned gods, consorts to our forest goddesses who embody the deep soul and mystery of nature, are for me deeply entwined with Yuletide, and of course I include reindeer, elk and other animals in this magical menagerie. I see deer by the side of the road in late autumn, eating at twilight to fatten themselves for winter. I know some will be hunted, but others will survive and increase their herds. The decline in natural predators in many areas has meant deer overpopulation; in years when wild apple and acorn yields are low and winter is harsh, this can mean starvation. At such times, I go to their local hangouts near me (wooded edges to parks and wooded areas on campus land) to leave them apples, carrots and grain.

My mom was a gardener, cook, and baker, and she had many artistic talents as a musician, painter, and writer. I never thought I'd be a professional gardener or baker, but that is part of how I support myself now and it allows me to remember and honor my mother's memory, to appreciate the skills and appreciation she taught me, every time I create an outdoor holiday display for a client, or bake extra Christmas cookies or gingerbread for the busy holiday season. Holiday celebrations are often interwoven with memories of family and youth, and the pagan pleasures of Yuletide in my childhood remain part of my observance of the winter solstice. These memories are sensual in nature; indeed, the olfactory centers of the brain are closely linked to our memory function, and so the delightful smells of holiday treats can immediately transport us to memories from years, even decades, earlier. Candy canes, hot chocolate, sugar cookies, spicy gingerbread, eggnog, roast turkey and ham, fruitcake, and in the Italian feasts of my family gatherings, anise-flavored pizzelles, savory antipasto, roast chicken, spicy marinara sauce over meatballs and braciola, and many fish dishes prepared for Christmas Eve.

Whatever our ethnic or cultural backgrounds, the favorite holiday foods consumed in winter, when food fortifies us for cold weather and dark nights, seem to nourish us in a special way. I've always been deeply grateful for having such a rich family history in this regard; as an adult, I've attended some holiday meals where store-bought desserts, take-out side dishes, and tasteless entrees were served, and I felt real pity for people who did not choose to make something special. As a Pagan, some of the best food I've ever eaten has been at Pagan potlucks, where those preparing and sharing the food understood the simple truth that food has a deeply spiritual significance and can also be very magical. Just as our rituals and magical workings can be very simple or elaborate, yet still effective, the foods we prepare for sharing during holidays are all about the intention and love we imbue them with.

Yuletide Rituals

I've attended Yuletide rituals that were incredibly varied and all very magical in their own way. One was an all night candlelight vigil to honor the longest night, with people gathered in the home of friends who lived in the country for a quiet night with hot drinks and snacks, leaving their candle lit on an altar if they needed a bit of shut-eye, and then at dawn we bundled up to do some "wassailing" of fruit trees in the orchard. When I lived in Boston, I walked snowy city streets with an amateur "churchless church choir" led by a director who understood that adults who no longer engage in school or church-based choral groups still derive great pleasure from singing traditional carols. We stood in the public library in an acoustically sensitive stairway and gentle hummed "Silent Night" in four part harmony—one of the most powerful holiday musical memories I've been part of. I've created ritual altars for my coven for this festival full of votive holders of candles, of all shapes, sizes, and colors, festive to look at but also resembling the memorials we erect to the dead—for what season brings home the melancholy feelings of grief and loss more than winter?

Our rituals to observe the winter solstice may also be seen as a way to usher in the new year, and this includes themes of forgiveness, renewal, creativity, and hope. Some contemporary Pagan traditions honor the festival of Samhain as the beginning of the new year, but my own coven celebrates the new year at winter solstice. This makes more sense to me; not only is this the traditional start of the new year as it is marked in most of our secular calendars, but the rebirth of the sun and beginning of the longer, lighter days feels like a fitting way to welcome in a new year.

Some Pagans also refer to Yule as Midwinter in the same way we refer to Midsummer. Some people are confused by this, because, they ask, why would the beginning of the season be referred to as the middle? But these words are based on an older understanding of the word, referring to the true beginning of the season (at least in this hemisphere), when the landscape and weather really look and feel like a reflection of the season. In those days, Samhain was more of a "true" start to the autumnal season than the autumn equinox, for example.

The notion that Pagans and witches choose to view winter as a time for looking inward for reflection, reading, study, crafts and "inner work" that has to do with dreams, journaling, and personal transformation is also a frequent theme discussed by many of my pagan compatriots over the years. Practices do seem to be doing many things differently these days compared to when I first entered the community, with many people who are new to Wicca and Paganism finding their information via social media instead of books.

There is far less reading of books, much more watching of videos. Even reading for pleasure has been replaced for many people with binge-watching their favorite TV shows and discussing them on social media. I think these changes may also be reflected in how contemporary practitioners see winter in a magical context—how can we best spend our time in this fallow season, when our thoughts and reflections can turn us inward for self-examination? The ritual we do to mark Yuletide can help us begin our winter work.

The coven I work with (the Order of Ganymede in Boston, established 1968: I joined in 1990) observes our Yuletide ritual as a rite of renewal, but also of letting go. This ritual has a fascinating component: we suspend a holly bough from the ceiling, hanging over a cauldron containing boughs of evergreen with candles nestled into them. Near the end of the rite, people walk under the bough, alone or in twos, as a rite of forgiveness and absolution for the new year, reciting a traditional poem by Scottish poet Charles MacKay. It begins like this:

Ye who have scorned each other,
Or injured friend or brother,
  In this fast-fading year;
Ye who, by word or deed,
Have made a kind heart bleed,
  Come gather here!

Let sinned against and sinning
Forget their strife's beginning,
  And join in friendship now.
Be links no longer broken,
Be sweet forgiveness spoken
  Under the Holly-Bough.

The poem is only four stanzas, and we repeat it as long as necessary, until every coven member has passed under the holly bough, taking our time to embody this spirit of forgiveness and renewal. I have always found this rite to be very healing and beautiful. Below is a ritual for Yule that is based upon this principle of letting go. You may make any changes you like, incorporating MacKay's poem or other traditional carols, like "The Fairest Maid," which has a sort of Celtic faery imagery:

Now sing we of the fairest maid,
With gold upon her toe,
And open up the eastern door,
To let the old year go.
For we have brought fresh holly,
All from the grove so near,
To wish you and your company
A joyful healthy year.

Cosmic Sway

Charlie Rainbow Wolf

THE SKIES ARE FAIRLY quiet as we ease into Yule and the holiday season. The biggest news is the annular solar eclipse on the 26th. This is a full eclipse, but not counted as a total eclipse because the Moon's distance from the Sun doesn't quite cover it, and will leave the notable "ring of fire" around the Moon still visible during the transit. The path of the eclipse will be most profound over Indonesia.

Solar eclipses are harbingers of change, and what better portent to have at the end of one calendar year and the beginning of another? Just as the old year is ending and the new year is beginning, the eclipse brings both an ending and a beginning. It may not be life-changing for you, but it will have a knock on effect. Perhaps someone close to you, or something on a more widespread scale, will affect you in some way because of the eclipse.

Sometimes it takes hindsight to see what the eclipse initiated. This eclipse will have some ongoing influences—right through to the next annular solar eclipse at midsummer, 2020. In Capricorn, you should expect the energies of this eclipse to be practical, unassuming, and perhaps a bit uncompromising. It's a good time to sow the seeds of determination and plan for what you want to accomplish in the New Year.

Eclipse patterns occur on (roughly) a nineteen-year cycle, so if you want to see how this eclipse might affect you, look back on where your life was taking you nineteen years ago! Of course, other planets will be in different positions, and that has to be taken into consideration. However, the Sun represents your personality, your authentic self, so this reflection isn't a bad measure of what is influencing you, and a reflection on what you might want to change this time around.

This eclipse also makes a conjunction with Jupiter, meaning that the changes the eclipse instigates will take on an expansive and somewhat philosophical slant. New ideas are plentiful, but you'll have to remain diligent to see whether they hold water or not. This is also an aspect that could highlight foreign affairs—either personal exchanges or political events. Because eclipses have a tendency to make things seem larger than life, it's usually best to wait until the dust settles before making any important decisions.

Jupiter is playing nicely with Uranus as Yule opens, too. This is usually a good influence, one that brings favorable results. The atmosphere is optimistic and uplifting, and pleasant surprises are possible. What better way to celebrate the festive season than with these two guys playing "Father Christmas" in the skies?!

Expectations may not be met, but that's okay. It's easy to get ruffled, but it's also easy to recover. The disappointments are usually minor, with other opportunities coming along that make up for what might have been missed. It's a period for taking calculated risks, for being hopeful about their outcome, and for pursuing a bit of what you fancy rather than spending too much time listening to others. This transit brings a broader vision and open-mindedness, and that's usually a good thing!

Another interesting planetary feature is the ongoing dance between Mars and Pluto. They're quite chummy at the moment, after being at loggerheads several times this year. This is an aspect of perseverance, of taking the initiative, of making necessary changes that will lead you to your goals. You've heard the old saying, "Either I will find a way or I will make one"? That sums up this aspect in a nutshell. It's likely to be hard work, but it has the potential for sowing seeds that will reap great rewards in the long term.

There's really not a whole lot else going on as Yule opens. Venus is on its way through Aquarius, Mercury is direct and behaving itself in Sagittarius, and Mars is quite at home in Scorpio; all the inner planets seem fairly content. Apart from the stellium in Capricorn at the time of the eclipse, the skies are fairly quiet, which should lead to some favorable frequencies for seasonal celebrations!

Yule Celebration: Welcoming the Light

Yule is the date when the Oak King takes back his crown from the Holly King, and the daylight starts to lengthen. It's opposite Litha on the wheel of the year, so it's only fitting that the celebration be one that echoes Litha's themes. Welcoming back the light during Yule (which lasts into January) seems even more apt because of the solar eclipse on the 26th. You'll need the following items:

Holly leaves (fresh, not plastic; if you can't obtain fresh ones, use paper cut outs)

Scraps of wool fabric, about 4" in diameter. If this isn't possible, use an old t-shirt or bed sheet. Any natural fiber will do.

Small scraps of paper

A pen

Wool yarn. This must be wool and not man-made.

A Yule log or candle.

As soon as the sun sets, or as soon after that as possible, light your Yule log or candle. If you wish to welcome any spirits, or cast a circle, now is the time to do so. It's best if you can do this after you've bathed and before you've had anything to eat, but as this is a sunset ceremony, that may not be possible, and that's okay. Remember, it's always your intent that is the most important, not what you actually do.

Next, write what you'd like to banish in the new year. Maybe there's a habit you want to break, or a personality trait you're working on improving. It doesn't have to be anything elaborate, just a word or even a symbol will do. Put this and the holly leaf or its representation onto the scrap of fabric . This symbolizes the Holly King being taken down by the Oak King. Tie the pouch shut with the wool yarn.

Once everyone has made their bundles, continue with your usual Yule food and activities. What you do with your ties next is entirely up to you. It's very fitting to hang them on an oak tree, and if you have one on your property, by all means do so. If no oak trees are available, tying them onto your Yule tree is also appropriate. Leave them there until the 6th night, and then when you take down the tree, remove the ties and bury or burn them. If you've done this as a community activity, the ties might be used collectively, or each participant could take their tie home with them. Remember to remain reverent, and to respect the death of the Holly King as he fell in battle once again so that the light might return.

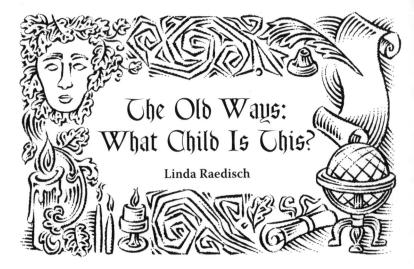

The Old Ways: What Child Is This?

Linda Raedisch

THE FIRST COLONISTS TO venture into southern New Jersey's Pine Barrens were probably looking for farmland. They burnt off the bracken, cut down a few of the oaks, white cedars, pitch and short-leaf pines, gave it a go and quickly gave up. Some of them, like the native Lenape before them, left to seek greener pastures while the rest turned to hunting, woodworking, ironworking, charcoal burning, and the intensive gathering of all those wonderful Christmas presents the forest offers up each year: cranberries for the table and the Christmas tree; bayberries for making soap and candles; mistletoe, pine cones, holly and laurel for decking the walls and the windows, and long ropes of ground cedar for winding round the pewter plate on the fireplace mantle.

The wilderness that is the Pines is also a good place to hide. If we are to believe all of the stories told over the last few hundred years, you would think you couldn't walk so much as a mile along one of the sandy tracks without running into a witch, ghost or monster. One of my favorites is Peggy Clevenger, a woman of Hessian extraction who kept an inn in Red Oak Grove and could turn herself into a lizard or hare. But there is another even more famous witch who has no given name. I suppose she must once have had one, but it was long ago eclipsed by the long shadow her youngest son has cast over the Pines. Today she is remembered only in relation to him, as Mother Leeds, or occasionally Mrs. Shourds, mother of the Jersey Devil.

She is not without antecedents. Like Norse mythology's Angerboda, whose name means "she who offers sorrow," and who gave birth to the wolf that will one day devour the sun, Mother Leeds gave birth to a monster whose fame only seems to grow with each passing year. And like the fearsome mother of Grendel, the monstrous villain of Beowulf, she inhabits a world of dense thickets and sandy bogs. In some versions of the story, she is a full-fledged witch, but the more prevalent view seems to be that she was an ordinary woman who simply had too many children. When she realized she was pregnant with her thirteenth, she snapped and declared that it could come out a devil for all she cared.

Leeds was probably not her surname; she was named for Leeds Point, New Jersey, which was named for Leeds Castle in Kent, back in the old country. Her infamous thirteenth child is also known as the "Leeds Devil." If there was ever a Father Leeds (or Mr. Shourds) he has long ago disappeared from the story.

Few agree on exactly when Mother Leeds and her brood were supposed to have lived. A highly creative piece of journalism that appeared in the *Atlantic Monthly* in 1859 assigns the Jersey Devil a birth date of 1735. The article goes on to identify the Devil with Caliban, the unfortunate man-monster from Shakespeare's *The Tempest*. A tempest was supposed to have raged the night of our Devil's birth, the newborn chimera flying out the window and into the storm, according to the article, instead of up and out the chimney as most other versions have it.

With a date of 1735 in hand, I am going to suppose that Mother Leeds would have celebrated Christmas, if she celebrated it at all, on our January 6. The American colonists adopted the Gregorian calendar in 1752, but I imagine someone like Mother Leeds, after a long life of hardships, would not have taken kindly to change and would have continued to keep Christmas according to the old Julian calendar. There are so many questions I would like to ask her: Was she born here in the Pines or did she come over from the British Isles? Was she a practicing witch like Peggy Clevenger or simply a neighborhood outcast? Did she utter her famous curse because she was worn out with caring for twelve children or because she was tired of giving birth to them only to have to watch them die as so often happened in those days? And what exactly did happen on that dark and stormy night when she gave birth to her thirteenth?

Since bayberry candles were precious, the birthing room would have been lit only by rushlights. Hopefully, Mother Leeds was not all alone but had a midwife or her older daughters to attend her. What did they see that night?

Descriptions of the Jersey Devil vary. Usually, it's a pair of black bat wings that carry him up the chimney in the moments after his birth. Subsequent sightings have mentioned horse's hooves and a horse's face, sometimes a dragon's face or a face that is a cross between a horse's and a dragon's. Whatever the truth of the matter, it must have been severely deformed. I am guessing that Mother Leeds was never allowed to see her baby, that the midwife folded it in a towel and whisked it from the room. Nowadays, such a child, if born alive, would have been rushed to the NICU, diagnosed, and hopefully gone on to live a fulfilling life. But that night, the horrified midwife would have had nowhere to turn but the fireplace. If there ever was a Mother Leeds, and if she ever did give birth to a thirteenth child, I imagine his tiny body was turned to ashes long ago. Perhaps one of her other children saw the midwife drop the sad bundle in the fire. Perhaps he or she ran outside in order not to witness such a horror, and, looking up, saw some winged creature flapping its way over the rooftop and away. "No, the baby didn't die," that child might have told anyone willing to listen, "He flew up the chimney and away."

It has been suggested, quite plausibly, that the Jersey Devil is nothing more than a Great Blue Heron, a long-beaked wading bird that stands four feet tall and haunts the wetlands throughout New

Jersey. Some believe he is a folk memory of the gargoyles that adorn the Gothic cathedrals of the Old World. An exorcism performed in 1752 was supposed to have banished the Jersey Devil for 100 years, but many of the tales have him popping up again every seven years. Seven was already a mystical number in the minds of the Anglo-Saxon colonists, but in the Pine Barrens it has a curious significance. Natural forest fires are common throughout the area, and in the mysterious dwarf forests deep within the Pines, they occur roughly every seven years. Could the dragon-like Jersey Devil be the embodiment of these fires which, though dangerous if you're caught in the middle of one, help preserve the forest itself?

The Jersey Devil has long outlived his nameless mother. He still puts in an appearance now and then, most infamously in a week-long rampage in 1909, and most recently...well, he can always be counted on to terrorize troops of Girl Scouts camping in the Jersey woods, even as far north as Morris County's Great Swamp.

I like to think that if the thirteenth child somehow did escape up that chimney, that he never forgot his mother and that he might still have come to visit her once a year on Old Christmas Eve. How happy Mother Leeds would have been to see him! She would have put the pewter plate away, out of the candlelight, so he wouldn't be startled by his reflection, and then she would have cut him a large piece of cranberry cake and told him how handsome he was.

Resources

Cohen, David Stephen. *The Folklore and Folklife of New Jersey*. New Brunswick, New Jersey: Rutgers University Press, 1983.

McCloy, James F. and Ray Miller, Jr., *The Jersey Devil*. Moorestown, New Jersey: Middle Atlantic Press, 2005.

McPhee, John. *The Pine Barrens*. New York: Farrar, Straus and Giroux, 1968.

Feasts and Treats

Blake Octavian Blair

THE YULETIDE SEASON HAS many rich food traditions and memories for many of us. We associate Yuletide meals with hearty menus served gathered around the feast table with loved ones, whether the festivities are elaborate or simple. While we gather to celebrate the return of the Sun, we are reminded of the other blessings that are sources of metaphorical light and warmth even in the dark times of our lives. The light will return! The selection of Yuletide recipes presented here offers some versions of old favorites, while offering a less traditional but satisfying lighter alternative to the traditional Yuletide entrees of many. There is even a delightful drink included so we may toast the rising sun! Prepare your feast table with winter and solar inspired decor such as gold candles, paper snowflakes, and pine cones.

Garlic Rosemary Baked Salmon

Prep time: 10 minutes
Cook time: 6—15 minutes
Serves: 2

Cooking spray
2 salmon fillets

3 tbsp olive oil
3 sprigs chopped fresh rosemary
3—6 cloves garlic, chopped finely
Salt (to taste)
Cracked black pepper (to taste)
1 lemon (sliced into wedges)

Preheat oven to 450 degrees F. Coat a metal baking sheet with non-stick spray or wipe with olive oil. Place the salmon fillets onto the baking sheet and brush with olive oil.

Once fillets are coated with olive oil, rub the chopped garlic onto them as evenly as possible. Next, sprinkle the fillets evenly with the chopped rosemary. Then sprinkle with a few pinches of salt and cracked black pepper to taste.

Place baking sheet with fillets into the preheated oven. Cook six minutes for each half inch of the fillets. Approximately 6—15 minutes for most fillets depending on thickness. Keep a close eye so as to not overcook, as the fish can cook extremely fast. The salmon is done when tender and flaky. Serve with fresh lemon wedge.

Everybody's Favorite Brussels Sprouts

Some vegetables have a more beloved reputation than others. Brussels sprouts can be a challenge to get people to eat. However, the following preparation has turned many a person from abhorring the little leafy green balls to requesting them as one of their favorite holiday side dishes. This is why they are titled "Everybody's Favorite Brussels Sprouts." Any recipe that has that much success I want others to share the joy in. So here I present to you my favorite way to dish up and serve this unfairly maligned vegetable.

1 lb brussels sprouts
2 tbsp butter
4 cloves garlic, crushed
Salt (to taste)
Cracked black pepper
1—2 cups vegetable broth

To begin, prepare the Brussels sprouts by cutting off the bottom stem portion and remove any loosely attached leaves. Cut each sprout in half from top to bottom. The sprouts will likely need to be cooked in two batches.

Heat 1tbsp butter in a large cast iron skillet on medium heat until butter coats bottom of skillet. Add half of the Brussels sprouts to the skillet cut (flat) side down in a single layer. All cut sides must be touching buttered surface. Sprinkle with salt and cracked black pepper. Dob tops of sprouts with half of the crushed garlic.

Cook for 4 to 5 minutes undisturbed. Carefully, add between ½ and 1 cup vegetable broth to cover bottom of skillet. Now, cover the skillet for an additional 4 to 5 minutes. Transfer the sprouts to a medium covered bowl or casserole dish.

Carefully, wipe the pan clean with a paper towel and repeat the entire process to cook the second half of the Brussels sprouts. When second batch is finished, keep in covered dish until ready to serve.

Baked Sweet Potato Casserole

This is one of my all-time favorites! When I think of Yuletide dinner, I think of baked sweet potato casserole and all its marshmallowy goodness. Many of us have certain dishes we always had for certain occasions growing up and incorporate into our traditions—this is one of mine. Plus, any excuse to have a sweet side dish, right? I've noted below I serve generous portions. Depending on how much you serve and make, this makes a wonderful "leftover" to look forward to.

Prep time: 20 minutes
Cook time: 55 minutes
Serves: 4—6 (generous sized portions)

2 (29 ounce) large cans of sweet potatoes or yams
½ stick butter (4 tbsp)
½ cup brown sugar

Cinnamon (to taste)
Raisins (to taste)
Marshmallow cream (to taste)

Heat yams in a large pot in the liquid from the can. When yams are hot, drain and place in a large mixing bowl.

Using an electric mixer, mash the yams while adding the butter, brown sugar, and cinnamon. When well combined, and of desired texture (think mashed potatoes), add desired amount of raisins and continue to mix just long enough to incorporate and evenly distribute the raisins throughout the mixture.

When well mashed and combined, place in a casserole dish and bake in a preheated 375 degrees F oven for approximately 30—40 minutes. Then, remove and add marshmallow cream with a greased rubber spatula to the surface and then heat under broiler until the fluff begins to get a brown toasted color.

Note: Many people's version of this dish uses plain whole marshmallows sprinkled on the top. The reason I do not is that I like to make this dish vegetarian friendly and most commercial marshmallows contain gelatin as an ingredient. Marshmallow cream, sometimes referred to as "fluff," does not contain gelatin generally, and has the same finished effect. Sometimes around the holidays in specialty and health food groceries you can find whole marshmallows that are vegetarian.

Solstice Sunrise Mimosas

One tradition my husband and I created together for ourselves is that of solstice sunrise mimosas. We always get up before sunrise on the day of the winter solstice, make mimosas, and watch the sun rise. It's a rather indulgent solar inspired celebration. Mimosas are indeed a perfect fit though, in their radiant orange glory, don't you think? The suggested garnish also provides a visual homage to a glowing orange rising sun. Plus, when it's pre-dawn, you couldn't pick a simpler drink to make.

Prep time: 5 minutes
Serves: 4—6

1 bottle of your favorite champagne
½ gallon of orange juice (no pulp preferred)
1 orange, cut into slices.

Take your orange and cut into circular slices. Add a slit from one edge to the center of each slice.

Now, to each glass, add equal parts champagne and orange juice. However, you can vary the ratio depending on your taste and desired strength. Garnish each glass by sliding the slit orange slice over the rim of the glass.

It is also possible to make a nonalcoholic version of the mimosa as well. Simply substitute either ginger ale or sparkling white grape juice instead of the champagne. Garnish as mentioned earlier then serve, toast the return of the sun, and enjoy!

Crafty Crafts

Natalie Zaman

I HAVE A THING for oldish British TV shows, especially when they involve cooking. A favorite is *River Cottage*, and I have a special fondness for the first Christmas special, probably because the host, Hugh Fearnley Whittingstall, goes out to a forest with the local hedge witch to find Yule logs.

The Well-Dressed Yule Log

I like the idea of finding a Yule log in the woods, but it's something I've never done. There were years where our Yule log was one of those manufactured logs (made from sawdust, nutshells, wax, and other things and compressed into a log shape), or just a candle in a log-shaped holder when we had no fire place or fire pit. For a few years I managed to store the trunk of the previous year's Yule tree and cut that up to use as a Yule Log. As the trunk yielded several logs, I got an idea for a unique holiday gift: Garbed in herbs, oils, words, cords, and, of course, glitter, it seems almost a pity to put a match to a well-dressed Yule log, but that's the point—it's meant to go up in smoke! And, of course, you can make a well-dressed log for any occasion that calls for a bonfire.

Time Lavished: The actual dressing of the Yule log will take only an hour of your time. Having all of your materials laid out before hand, a large space in which to work, and an extra pair of hands or a support to hold the log steady if it tends to roll or rock when placed on a flat surface will save time as well as frustration. Crafting the log can also be a ritual. If you choose to do this, allow time for the creation of sacred space and any other preparations your tradition dictates.

Coinage Required: $20—$30 will buy you everything you need to dress several logs. But remember—logs can certainly be found, and herbs grown and wild harvested.

Supplies

One log of wood. Found, part of a cord, or a man-made (of recycled materials) log—anything you can (legally and safely) get your hands on.

An uplifting essential oil. I love lemon balm and lemon verbena, but orange blossom and ylang-ylang work well too.

Paint, paint markers, or sharpies

A large bundle of rosemary (for remembrance and gratitude) lavender and sage (for cleansing)

Jute, cotton, hemp, or wool cord. Everything will be burned, so natural is better.

Scissors

Masking tape

Craft glue

Glitter

Small tumbled crystals, crystal points or crystal chips—I used tigers eye (for success), rose quartz (for love) and quartz crystal (for clarity).

Beeswax candle or sealing wax

The suggested stones and herbs can be replaced with others that resonate with you. Always work with materials with which you are comfortable.

Brush any dust and debris from your log.

Write the outgoing year on one end of the log and the incoming year on the other with the markers. On the body of the log, write out some statements of gratitude for the old year, and hopes and wishes for the new year. Brush the log with your sunny essential oil, and roll it in the glitter.

If you're working with a man-made log, the initial prep work is a bit different, but make no mistake, this type of log is just as good as a natural log. First, remove the packaging and rewrap the log with masking tape and plain brown paper, butcher paper, or a double or triple layer of blank newspaper (newspaper is a bit thin and can tear easily.). Avoid wrapping your paper too tightly as it acts as kindling for these logs; you want the log to have a bit of breathing room. Write the outgoing and incoming years on the new wrapper as well as any intentions and statements of gratitude. Brush the paper with a thin layer of glue and sprinkle it liberally with glitter—there's no such thing as too much—before blessing it with a few drops of oil.

Cut five 24-inch lengths of cord. (Each one should be long enough to tie around the log and knot it.) Lay them out one underneath the other, spacing them evenly. The length of the space from the top cord to the bottom one should match the length of the log. Center the log on top of the cords; they'll be the initial means of securing the herbs and flowers to the log before you bind them with a longer length of cord.

Divide your bunch of lavender in half. Place one half on the log so that the tips of the flowers line up with the edge of the log, then do the same on the other end. You should have two bundles of flowers on top of the log, flowers facing outward and the cut stems facing each other.

Place the rosemary in the center of the log, on top of the lavender. The rosemary should cover the parts of the lavender stems that have no flowers.

Place the sage in the center of the log on top of the rosemary. Carefully adjust the layers so that the entire log is covered and that there are no blank spaces.

One at a time, tie up each cord to secure the herbs and flowers to the log.

Next, cut a longer length of cord (about 5 feet long). Lay it out on your workspace, then place the log on top of it. Line up the cord with one end of the log.

Carefully pull the cords up so that you have even lengths on both sides, crisscross them over the herbs and flowers, then wrap them around the back of the log. Work slowly and methodically, crisscrossing the cords over and under the log until you get to the other end. If you didn't cut a cord long enough to do this, simply knot it off, cut another length of cord and pick up where you left off. You can bind the log once, or several times. When you're finished, the log will look like a giant smudge stick.

As a finishing touch, stud the log with the crystals. Staring at one end of the log, drop several drips of sealing or beeswax directly onto the herbs until you have a blob the size of a dime. Press the crystals into the wax while it is still warm and liquid. I set my stones in a row down the log, but you can do it in other patterns, or randomly.

Both the making and the burning of the well-dressed Yule Log can be a ritual. Dress the log with intention: Say, sing, or think about things that happened in the waning year for which you are grateful, and the things for which you are hopeful in the coming year. If your log is a gift, personalize it by visualizing the recipient and all of the good things you wish for her as the old year turns to the new.

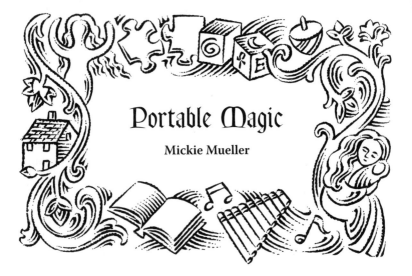

Portable Magic

Mickie Mueller

YULE IS A MAGICAL time, and since the winter solstice falls on a Friday this year, many people will be excited to celebrate this winter sabbat on the weekend. The days have grown so short now that I personally feel rushed when it starts getting dark so early. To me I feel like the day is done long before it really is. I love bringing magic on the go with me at Yule for many reasons. My kids are grown, some with little ones of their own, but years ago we started having them all spend the night with us for Yule. Since the rest of the extended family celebrates Christmas, Yule became very special for us. My husband and I work from home, but it's still our busiest time of the year, so simple celebrations and magic that can come along with me while I get orders packed and to the post office and prepare for our family celebration is a must. I started coming up with ways to keep this sabbat in focus back when I worked commercial retail and food service jobs and seldom had the option to ask for the day off that time of year, so I brought my magic with me.

Rebirth of the Sun Crystal Talisman

If you have a small citrine, sunstone, or a clear or rutilated quartz crystal, you can fill it with the energy of the sun on the solstice morning and carry that energy of rebirth with you all day. First rinse it in cool water before sundown on the eve of the solstice; as you do, visualize it becoming clear and pure, vibrating with its own energy. Pay attention to where the sun is visible when it sets, a window or porch at your home and set the stone there so that it will capture the last of the light as the sun sets. Once the sun has gone down, move your stone to sit in a location where it will receive the sun's rays as it rises in the morning, triumphant from the longest night of the year. Leave it there overnight. Grab the stone from its sunny spot as you leave the house in the morning and carry it in your pocket as a reminder of the power of light to overcome darkness. If you have to leave the house before the sun comes up, still bring it along, pop outside at your first opportunity once the sun is up to let it capture the fresh new light. As you go throughout your day, touch the stone whenever you think of it and think about the days growing longer again from this point on.

Holly, Ivy, and Mistletoe

Holly, ivy, and mistletoe are three plants of the season that each hold special powers and can easily be incorporated into your magic on the go this Yule. Holly's used in magic for courage, wisdom, and overcoming challenges. Holly represents the Holly King, and since it's green all year, it's a symbol of immortality. Ivy is the feminine half of the duo from the old English Yuletide folk song "The Holly and the Ivy." If Ivy was brought into the household before the holly on the Solstice, the woman of the house would rule the year. Ivy brings luck, protection, healing, and grants powers of tenacity. Mistletoe goes way back as a winter solstice plant, used on the Roman celebration of Saturnalia and harvested by the Druids with golden sickles. It's a plant of fertility, luck, protection, and, of course, passion.

Working magic on the go with these plants is easy. You can carry a sprig of one or all of them in a simple charm bag made from fabric tied with ribbon to impart their energies throughout the day. You can also wear jewelry with representations of the plant. They can be high end, handmade, or inexpensive fun costume pieces. Hold them in your hand and call in the spirit of the plant to bless the jewelry piece with its energy, and let that magic fill your day with their blessings.

Chai Tea Holiday Blessings Spell

Chai is not only one of my favorite hot beverages, it's also full of traditional Yuletide spices and herbs. Ginger, cardamom, cinnamon, fennel, and clove—what's not to love?! It promotes a feeling of peace and has many health benefits too; I personally love using chai for magic. Place a chai teabag in a plastic ziplock bag and carry it with you on Yule as you work, shop, or run errands. Every time you experience something happy that puts joy in your heart, you hear a kind word, see a good deed or anything special, let that feeling fill your lungs, open the plastic bag, and blow that feeling into it, filling your chai teabag with good vibes. Brew that tea and enjoy it when you're home, or wait until the next morning after the sun rises from the longest night, and let it fill you with happiness and good will.

Wear Colors of the Day

Wearing something festive can really help you to hold the winter solstice in the forefront of your mind, whether a simple t-shirt or a classic ugly sweater. Think about the colors and what kind of magical energies they hold as you choose your wardrobe for Yule.

Green boughs were brought into homes on the winter solstice during ancient times as a symbol of immortality. Wear green on Yule to represent life and surviving and thriving through the winter. It can also be a color for healing, finances, and luck.

Red can give you strength and is a color of fire relating back to the sun on this solar celebration. Red is a color to wear for passion, joy, and renewal on Yule.

White is a nice color to wear for Yule, representing snow and ice as we recognize and embrace the spirits of nature. White is also a color of new beginnings and rebirth as we think about the return and newly growing power of the sun.

Gold is an obvious solar reference and perfect to celebrate the energy of the sun conquering darkness. Wearing gold in your wardrobe even if it's just gold threads woven through another color can boost energies of abundance and wealth. As the sun grows in power, may also your prosperity.

Sabbat on the Go Tips

Make a safe travel charm bag for your car to combine with your safe driving habits while on the road this winter. Include any or all of these: mint, rosemary, juniper, holly berries, ivy leaf, moonstone, black tourmaline, a small sun charm. Wrap it up in a piece of gold colored fabric, tie it closed with red twine or ribbon, and tuck it inside your glove compartment.

Peppermint brings wealth, so carry peppermint candy along with you and eat a little piece every time you spend or donate money on the solstice as you visualize the universe replenishing your finances.

Wear frankincense oil alone or combined with myrrh for Yule blessings and to keep you feeling peaceful and de-stressed in the face of holiday shopping.

Ritual for Yuletide

Peg Aloi

DECORATE THE AREA WITH evergreen boughs and holly. If you can, tie a branch of holly so that is hangs from the ceiling; you can use a simple tack to do this. You could also place the holly in a vase and put it on a high shelf. Place a cauldron in the center of the circle, and a seven day candle inside. Each directional altar should contain some candles in votive holders, but don't light them until you're ready to begin. You can use votive holders or candles in the colors of the four elements, or all white candles to signify the beginning of the new year. White cloths on the altars will also reflect light and enhance the look of the greenery. Place statuary or other decorations on the altar as you wish but keep your design simple to allow you to focus your energy. Before beginning the rite, you can enter into a ritual state of mind while decorating and preparing your ritual area. Perhaps put on some instrumental traditional Yuletide music that you enjoy. Wear robes appropriate to the season: white for winter, or silver or gold, or red or green to symbolize fire and evergreen, two important images in this rite. Have some frankincense and myrrh resins, if available, on the Eastern altar in an incense burner on a charcoal block, and start this charcoal burning before you begin the rite. Cakes and wine, or other simple food and drink, should be on the north altar.

Before beginning, light one candle on each altar. Cast your circle as you normally do. If you don't belong to any specific tradition, you may trace a circle with a knife, wand, sword or branch of evergreen, visualizing a circle of light and protection around the space. Some witches call upon particular gods or goddesses for their circle casting; you can do that now if you wish. This rite will call upon the Lady of the Woods and the Horned God as her Consort. If you prefer to use specific names for these deities that is fine.

When the circle is cast, go to the cauldron in the center and light the candle, saying:

The center is the place of beginning. May my/our inner flames be rekindled with the rebirth of the sun.

Go to the eastern altar and invoke the Horned God in his eastern element. (If you have frankincense and myrrh resin, now is the time to add some resin to the burning charcoal) You may finish lighting the other candles on the altar before or while you do this:

God of light and of dawn, of newness and hope, of inspiration and endeavor, be with us now and kindle in us the fire of creativity and new beginnings.

Move to the southern altar, and invoke the Horned God in his southern element. Light the candles, saying:

Horned One, consort of the Great Mother, God of forest creatures and wild nature, god who sets the head alight with flames, god of desire and the will, be with us now and kindle in us the fire of imagination and passion.

Move to the western altar, and invoke the Lady in her western element. Light the candles, saying:

Lady of the oceans and of the stars, whose tears wash us clean with rain, wise goddess who governs all mysteries of the world, be with us now and kindle in us the fire of curiosity and compassion.

Move to the northern altar, and invoke the Lady in her northern element. Light the candles, saying:

Lady of the Woods, of the dark places within and without, goddess who gives us birth and grants us death, bringer of all joys and sorrows, giver of wisdom, be with us now and kindle in us the fire of courage and awareness.

Now move to the center of the circle, standing beneath the holly bough (or holding it above your head or another participant's head), and look upon the candlelight all around, and in the cauldron. (You can adjust this part of the rite for the number of people present) Turn in place under the holly bough, and say:

By the candle flames burning bright, I release the strife and sadness of the year before. By the green life of the holly bough, I enter the year ahead with joy. By the starlight in the winter sky, I look forward with hope. By the warmth of the solstice sun reborn, I move forward with compassion.

Repeat this three times, or as many times as needed. You may choose to recite this slowly while moving around the circle to raise energy, holding hands with others. You may choose to play some instrumental music at this time to enhance the energy raising, or not.

To ground the energy and end the rite, it is traditional to have cakes and wine (or bread and juice or whatever you prefer). Your group may have a specific way you always do this. One general blessing that comes in handy:

Bless this spiritual food and drink unto our bodies, bestowing upon us health and strength and love and joy and peace. So mote it be.

You can now open the circle or close the right according to your practice. It is enough to put the candles out and bless each quarter and thank the God and Goddess for attending. Some choose to leave some food and drink for the fey folk overnight. Bring some of the greenery into other areas of your home to remind you of the rite and inspire you during the winter.

Notes

Imbolc

Imbolc

JD Hortwort

AT IMBOLG, WE MARK the first cross-quarter of the year. Winter is half over; spring is coming closer. It's not one of the more fanciful Pagan observations—especially if you compare it to the excitement of Yule or Samhain.

That might be because, as best we know, *Imbolg* (originally *i mBolg* in Old Irish) is an agrarian festival in the truest sense. A translation of the word comes down to "in the belly" or "in milk." Another word for this seasonal observation is *Oimelc*, possibly meaning "ewe's milk." Try to explain the significance of that to someone not accustomed to the intricacies of animal husbandry!

To be fair, students of Pagan lore still debate the significance of Imbolg to ancient worshippers. Some have suggested this was not so much a day of celebration but a season of purification, perhaps lasting a week or more.

The evidence sways on the scale. On the one hand, Imbolg is not mentioned on the Coligny calendar, unlike the cross-quarter observations of Beltaine and Lughnasahda. The Coligny calendar was discovered near Lyon, France, in 1897 as an etched bronze plaque measuring roughly two feet high and four feet across. The calendar is written in Gaulish in Roman letters and is believed be from the first century CE. It is the best hard historical evidence so far of how Celtic people marked the passage of days.

On the other hand, the Neolithic Mound of Hostages at Tara in Ireland was set up to mark the rising sun on Imbolg and Samhain. This is a passage tomb believed to have been built sometime around 3000–2500 BCE. The Celts didn't build it, but they did utilize it. The point is, you don't arbitrarily construct an artificial mountain nine feet tall and forty-nine feet in diameter, investing many hours of manual labor. If the ancients oriented the entrance to the tomb to capture the sun on this day, they must have considered the day important.

Plus, there is ample evidence that the time around the end of January and the beginning of February in ancient times was marked by cleansing and anticipation. Ancient people could clearly see their flocks beginning to produce milk again and they could see the evidence of new growth in the fields. It's safe to assume they welcomed these new signs of vitality as though their lives depended on it—because they did.

Still, as one of the leaders of a Pagan group in my area, I can say it's not easy to get people excited about sheep giving birth or nursing their young. And, despite the fact that this cross-quarter festival is a celebration of the end of winter, the chilly days of February often give lie to that promise. It's cold outside, even in the Mid-Atlantic states. In the north tier of the U.S., winter hangs on desperately with gray days, persistent snow or ice, and howling winds.

Skeptical Pagans can hardly be blamed for raising an eyebrow at the pronouncement that, "Spring is just a few weeks away!" "Oh, yeah?" is the response. "Tell us again around Ostara."

Fortunately, if modern Pagans don't always grasp the idea of sheep coitus, they usually have a good understanding of the nature of seeds. For the group with which I practice, that has become the reason for this very Pagan season.

Imbolg is a stirring, a quickening just before something wonderful comes forth. We celebrate it in Bridget, daughter of the Dagda. Her mother might have been the Morrigan, or she might have been

Boann. That really depends on the region doing the celebrating, way back in pre-Roman days.

Bridget may have been a triple goddess. She certainly had enough names including Bride, Brighid, Brigit, Briggidda, Brigantu, and Brid. Many Pagans believe she was Pan-Celtic even in the early days—known and accepted by Celts across Europe, Britain, and Ireland.

She is thought to be the goddess of the hearth and of the forge. She is patron goddess of poets and story tellers—those who lived by the light of the divine spark of inspired performance. Bridget is a fertility goddess and a healer. She takes over from the Old Crone of Winter, the Cailleach, as ruler of the lighter half of the year.

The Crone stomps around the winter landscape, striking and freezing the ground with her staff. Only on Imbolg will she occasionally delight in a sunny day. But her motive is sinister. She allows the sun only so that she can gather more wood for the home fire and prolong the cold outside.

Bridget is the divine spark. She walks back into our lives with a single candle light. It's just a flickering ember, but that tiny flame is a perfect metaphor for what is going on in nature. We don't walk in on spring like we walk into a room of Yule decorations. Spring doesn't show up overnight. The first signs of spring aren't brilliant like the bright eggs we dye for Ostara.

They are the delicate first blades of grass that tentatively poke up from under the fallen leaves. As the sun warms the ground, down below seeds begin to break their hulls; sap begins to rise in the trees; the smallest flower buds begin to swell.

This idea of the first stirrings is behind modern observations of Groundhog's Day. In some cultures, people watched for badgers or bears as indicators for how long winter would last. On the European continent, certain regions watched for the first appearance of the hedgehog.

This takes us back to the agrarian roots of Imbolg. If your food supplies are running low and the wood pile is getting smaller, the reappearance of spring is about much more than cabin fever. It's about survival. Early settlers from Europe believed if the hedgehog saw its shadow winter would go on for another six weeks. If not, spring might come early, before the actual vernal equinox.

Americans didn't have hedgehogs. They had bears and badgers. Both of those can be especially ornery when they first step out of the den. Who would want to be the person standing there waiting on either one?

What we had in abundance was groundhogs. Groundhogs kind of look like hedgehogs and badgers. They can be mean-tempered but are much more manageable than angry bears. So, our German forefathers grafted their expectations onto this American critter and kept on prognosticating the weather with it.

Probably without realizing it, those American ancestors were also marking the very Pagan ritual of Imbolg and Bridget's message to us. Bridget tells us to get ready for the coming warm weather by cleansing and purifying ourselves and our surroundings.

Bridget tells us to take that broom from the hearth and sweep away the debris of winter and last year's growth. In the days leading up to February 2, we encourage our members to do this both physically and metaphysically. We ask that they give their altar a thorough cleaning. We recommended a deep cleaning of their home. We also suggest they indulge in a long cleansing shower or bath ritual with herbs and oils that strip away negative energies and provide a bright, protective aura.

At ritual, members bring ritual tools for cleansing and blessing. At the same time, we cleanse the house's ritual tools. We set up boxes with the candles, incenses, and other items we plan to use for ritual throughout the rest of the year. These will also be blessed during the Imbolg celebration.

In some years, we bring packets of seeds into the ritual. Not all of our members have access to gardening space but most have a sunny window or two. Members pick a seed packet at Imbolg and hold on to it through the ritual. They take it home and place it on their altar. At Ostara, they bring the seed packet back and we all plant the seeds in small pots.

These go back home with the members to be tended and cultivated throughout the season. Hopefully, the members can share the produce from these plantings as the year goes on, whether that is herbs or vegetables or fruit.

The goal of this work is to build anticipation because that is what Imbolg means to us in a modern world. Yule is heavily over-written with the memories of the Christian observations all of us have; so is Ostara. Imbolg is a truly Pagan festival. It's fresh. It's free of baggage—beyond the image of a mean-spirited rodent being hauled out of its burrow at the crack of dawn.

The message of our Imbolg ritual is, it isn't spring yet—but it soon will be! Forget the ceremonies or sorrows of last year because we closed that book at Yule. We are looking, hoping for the future and it can be as grand as our imagination.

Cosmic Sway

Charlie Rainbow Wolf

THE HEAVENS LOOK PRETTY interesting for Imbolc celebrations. Traditionally this is a time of newness and fertility, and this is reflected in the skies. It's a good year to try something a bit different, because the Sun conjunct Mercury in Aquarius blends uniqueness with purpose. It may be hard to plan things; this is kind of a cranky combination, because Aquarius does like things done its own way. Watch that differences of opinions and headstrong personalities don't lead to a clash of words and arguments.

There's some karma around this Sabbat, too. Venus is making a hard aspect to the Moon's north nodes in Cancer. Finding harmony may be hard to achieve, especially as the Moon is so close to Venus in Sagittarius. Emotions have the potential to be strong, but also changeable—even downright unpredictable. Fortunately lunar aspects are fleeting things. Any friction here is likely to be a fleeting thing.

All this plausible petulance is offset by jovial Jupiter making a positive aspect to the seasonal Sun. This helps to put people in a positive frame of mind and brings a sense of optimism to ideas and activities. If you're going to employ the law of attraction, the 8th is the perfect day of the month to do it, according to the skies. This kind of happiness is infectious, and nothing sets the stage for the LoA to work in your favor more than a content countenance.

Uranus in Aries brings some unpredictability, and once again there may be a bit of karma around this because of the aspect to the north nodes. Mars will be catching up with Uranus in time for Valentine's Day! This adds a bit of a wild card to the month, because you'll feel more inclined to take a dare, or step out of your comfort zone, or do something uncharacteristic.

Speaking of Valentine's Day, it's a bit more unsettled this year due to an aspect between Venus and Uranus. This means that relationships have the capacity to be intense while Cupid is around, but they might not be very long-lasting. If you're looking for a fling or something unconventional, you may just find it. Even those in an established relationship may feel like trying something a bit deviant or different. This is an exciting aspect, but how it unfolds will depend on your own mindset and personality, because it easily breeds irresponsibility and undependability.

Uranus turned retrograde this month, too—on the 11th. This is one of the slower moving outer planets, and it spends nearly half the year retrograde, but if it's making an aspect to one of your natal planets or power points, it's worth noting. Overall, the underlying vibe has the potential to be slightly less chaotic than when Uranus is direct.

This month also sees Saturn gaining ground on Pluto, both in Capricorn. Saturn is the natural ruler of Cappy, and feels quite at home here, but Pluto is more of a problem. Both Capricorn and Pluto are strong-willed, but they apply that tenacity in very different ways. Pluto has been in Capricorn since 2008, and it's going to stay here until 2023. You'd think we were used to it by now, and you'd be right—apart from Saturn sneaking into the picture. The actual conjunction won't take place until 2020, but you'll start to feel the pull of the two very different yet both very stubborn energies even now. This is also the aspect of fear, and propaganda is likely to increase throughout the year.

There's a chance to get things back into balance, though. Chiron—the little planetoid that orbits between Saturn and Uranus—is at a critical degree this month. Chiron is referred to as "the Wounded Healer," and it will help to offset some of the harshness of Saturn creeping up on Pluto. Chiron reminds us that anything can be turned into something healing and positive if we're prepared to look it squarely in the eye. The anaretic degree of Chiron is sometimes known as "the degree of fate." It's the end of a cycle, a chance to release ourselves from self-imposed limitations and inhibitions, but it also brings the potential for dwelling on apparent bad luck and lack of opportunities. Old cycles dissolve, but what new cycles will be commenced?

For the astrologers among you, Beltane brings two interesting, and very similar, T-Squares. One involves the north node, Pluto and Mars; the second involves the north node, Pluto, and Uranus. This is yet another aspect that brings with it karma, unpredictability, and perhaps more than a bit of aggravation or animosity. The Uranus T-Square is the strongest. Fortunately, Pluto is far enough out of orbit that it's influence isn't as strong—and maybe not as destructive—as it could have been.

The Mars aspect to Pluto does tend to bring some force with it. Channeled in a positive way, this force is determination and single-mindedness, but it might mean that people overlook the needs or feelings of others while they're aiming to reach their own goals. It's probably not intentional, so don't take it too much to heart, but don't be a doormat, either. When someone shows you who they truly are, believe them, especially during this planetary weather.

Overall, Imbolc is a great time for thinking outside the box. Planning something different keeps you on your toes, but watch your patience and your temper. Your reactions are prone to be more "act first, think later," and that's not always a good thing. However, for cultivating determination, for setting your sights on what you want to accomplish the rest of this year, the heavens are lined up to be an ally.

Imbolc Celebration: Invoking Positive Energy

Imbolc is the time of year to bring new projects and new ideas into the light. To do that, you have to create a space where they can bloom and grow. This ritual is a very simple way of doing just that. It celebrates the return of the light, and it also clears the way for newness.

You will need:

Partly burned candles

Wooden matches

A candle snuffer (optional)

Some small bells (think little "jingle" bells, available at craft stores)

A small cotton or muslin bag

A broom

At sunrise on Imbolc (or when you get up, if you're not an early riser), use the wooden matches to light all your partly burned candles. Place them on windowsills or near windows and doors, taking all the usual safety precautions, of course. Use their flame to invite the energies of the goddess Brigid to come and bless your home. She is the lady of the fire and the keeper of the hearth.

Once your candles are burning, put the bells in your muslin bag and tie it onto your broom. Sweep all the corners of your house clean. If you have a carpet, still sweep the floor anyway, using your broom. Gather up all the dirt and the energies from the room in your broom, and sweep them out of the door. If it's not too cold, open your windows as you do this to really get the energies moving and grooving! This is a wonderful way to gather up any old lingering energies, and get them moving so that new, fresh energies can take their place.

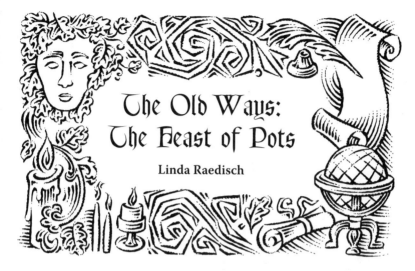

The Old Ways: The Beast of Pots

Linda Raedisch

IF YOU WERE TO show up in Classical Athens on the morning of the fourteenth day of Anthesterion, a lunar month corresponding to our late February/early March, you would find a mess: clay pots lying everywhere on the ground, crusted with dried porridge and buzzing with flies. The three-day spring flower festival of Anthesteria finished up last night and no one is awake yet. Anthesteria is a drinking festival as much as a celebration of flowers, so it will probably take the revelers some time to summon the energy to go outside and clean up.

The first day of the festival, on 11 Anthesterion, was Pithogia, when the *pithoi*, or "jars" of new wine were opened. The second day was Choes, or "cups." This was when the serious drinking started. The third day of the festival, on the unlucky thirteenth day of Anthesterion, was Chytroi, "pots." This was the ancient Greek All Souls' Day. Like our Halloween, Chytroi began at sundown the night before. Chytroi may have been one of the reasons why the Christian All Souls was originally celebrated in springtime, around the time of Beltane.

If you have heard of Chytroi, you are probably either a fan of Classical Greece or you have read Ray Bradbury's classically trippy novel, *The Halloween Tree,* in which some small town American boys look in on many of the ancient world's forgotten festivals of the dead:

> 'Yes.' Moundshroud beamed. 'Their Festival of the Dead: The Feast of Pots. Trick-or-Treat old style. But tricks from the dead if you don't feed them. So treats are laid out in fine banquets on the sill!'[1]

The pots in question were little earthenware pots in which panspermia was cooked and served to the dead—no polished red or blackware for these spirits whose meals were left for them in the garden. The appetizingly named main dish was a porridge made with many if not "all" varieties of seeds and grains and sweetened with honey. Hardly what I would call a "fine banquet," but that's just me. The offerings were left out for all the dead in general and in Athens also for the ghost of a teenage girl named Erigone. Erigone was the daughter of Icarius (not to be confused with the high-flying Icarus or the Icarius who was Odysseus' father-in-law). It was to the mortal Icarius that the god Dionysus bequeathed the gift of wine.

Icarius might have done better to refuse it. When he asked his neighbors round to share a pithoi, they thought he was trying to poison them. So they killed him. When his daughter found his body with the help of the family dog, she was driven mad with grief and hanged herself. But that was not exactly the end of this unfortunate little family, for the gods were kind enough to place them among the stars. Icarius is Arcturus, Erigone is Virgom, and the faithful dog is Canis Major.

A maiden suicide was exactly the kind of restless ghost the Greeks felt they needed to appease. The story of Erigone served to explain why a wine and flower festival should finish up with an offering to the dead. The name Erigone means "born in spring," so one cannot help but wonder if she was once a springtime fertility goddess in her own right. She might just as easily have been a goddess of the harvest, since the ancient Greeks sowed in the fall and

---

1. Bradbury, 2015.

reaped in the spring before the dry heat of summer could sear the crops in the fields.

Actually, the ghosts were believed to start wandering among the living as soon as the first pithoi were breached on the first day of the festival, but they became most active at dusk on the second day. Throughout that night and the day of Chytroi itself, the living took special precautions against these roaming spirits. Front doors were smeared with pine pitch. Pitch was regarded as an especially pure substance, perhaps because its distillation from the wood was such a complicated and time-consuming process. Then again, it may have been that its stickiness could stop a ghost in its tracks.

Another practice was to chew pieces of a shrub called rhamnos, which has been translated as "buckthorn," "blackthorn" and "hawthorn." Buckthorn now answers to the genus name *Rhamnus*, but it should also be noted that the ancient Greeks and Romans liked to bring hawthorn branches indoors to protect the household from demons.

The dead who chose not to roam but kept to their quarters in the underworld were also rewarded on Chytroi with offerings of fruit and lentils. These were not left on the ground but brought to a temple and given into the keeping of Hermes Chthonios. This Hermes was not exactly the same guy as the one in the winged sandals, but his underworld counterpart. Several of the Olympians had such alter-egos who were considered more approachable than full-on chthonics like the Erinyes.

Chytroi was not the only time the Greeks' thoughts turned to the underworld and its denizens. There was the Genesia, the birthday of a deceased person that was celebrated privately by his or her family. In Athens, Genesia observances eventually got sucked into the Nemeseia, a nighttime festival held in honor of the goddess Nemesis on the fifth of the month of Boeodromion, which fell in the midst of our September/October. Nemesis had custody of all those whose lives had been cut short by violence and who required extra placating. (Another of Nemesis' names was Rhamnusia, which I suppose counts as another vote for buckthorn.)

The Athenians and other Classical Greeks seemed to view the spirits of the dead through a haze of fear and superstition, but the earlier Myceneans spent more time trying to commune with the dead than banishing them. In the Odyssey, the hero goes knock-knock-knocking on Hades' door when he wishes to consult the shade of the seer Tiresias. In another episode, he is forced to leave the corpses of his fallen shipmates behind on the plain where they were cut down by the Cicones. Back aboard ship, he utters the "triple cry," calling out the name of each man three times in order to bid him farewell and to encourage his spirit to settle in the cenotaph he will eventually build for him.

But at the close of Chyrtoi, the Athenians were anxious to speed the dead on their way. They informed the ghosts in no uncertain terms that Anthesteria was over and if any of them had slipped from the garden into the house they had better get out. Any spirits still hanging around were made to feel like guests who had stayed too long at a party.

There is one more thing that sets Chytroi apart from some of the more familiar festivals of the dead. On Halloween, trick-or-treaters come home and eat the candy they've collected; on the Mexican Day of the Dead, living family members eat the food whose essence has first been offered to the dead. But none of the offerings left out on Chytroi were consumed by the living. Hence the mess the next morning.

Resources

Garland, Robert. *Ancient Greece: Everyday Life in the Birthplace of Western Civilization*. New York: Harper & Row, 1984.

Lloyd, James. "The Anthesteria." *Ancient History Encyclopedia.* https://www.ancient.eu/The_Anthesteria/. October 1, 2015.

Feasts and Treats

Blake Octavian Blair

THE IMBOLG SEASON ALWAYS conjures cozy thoughts and feelings of nesting at home in a time that is the heart of winter, my favorite season. I enjoy the cold weather and the life rituals that come with it. You see, Imbolg conjures visions of all the creature comforts of home such as cozy knit socks, a good book, some craft projects, and of course comfort food! This menu also aims to honor one of the goddesses most commonly celebrated at this sabbat, Brigid. This goddess oversees not only cows and dairy products such as the eggs, cheese, butter, and cream featured in these dishes, but she is also Goddess of the Forge. The deep orange flame color of cheddar cheese hearkens to the color of a warm hearth fire. Be sure to bedeck your feast table accordingly with a cast iron cauldron as a candle holder for a center piece and maybe even a homemade Brigid's Cross. Enjoy preparing this menu of winter comfort foods!

Baked Macaroni and Cheese

Hot, cheesy, golden baked macaroni and cheese is near the top of my list of comfort foods. Really, when examined, it's a pretty simple entrée but oh so satisfying. It was always a favorite of mine growing up, and when I began college, my aunt gave me her recipe. I adapted it over the years into my own, and now I'm happy to share it with you! For many of us, this sabbat is intimately tied with the honoring of the Goddess Brigid. Among the many things Brigid is associated with, dairy products are one of them, so this dish is a bit of an honoring of Brigid as well. Being that this is a point in the Wheel of the Year that we begin to notice a bit more daylight each day, I rather like that the golden color of this dish pays a bit of homage to that.

Prep time: 10 minutes
Cook time: 1 hour
Serves: Approx. 6

1 lb elbow macaroni
3 tbsp butter
1¾ cups milk
2 cups shredded sharp cheddar cheese
2 tbsp minced onion
1 tbsp mustard
Salt (to taste)
Black pepper (to taste)
Breadcrumbs (to taste)

Add a few pinches of salt to a large pot of water and bring to a boil. Cook pasta for approximately 9–12minutes until al dente. Drain. Transfer pasta into a 10 × 10 casserole dish.

Preheat oven to 350 degrees F.

In a medium saucepan on medium heat, melt butter.

Once butter is melted, add in the milk, and whisk to combine. When mixture is hot, add the cheese, minced onion, and mustard to the pan. Add salt and pepper to desired taste. Combine thoroughly until cheese is melted. Keep the heat on this gentle setting and whisk frequently to assure the milk doesn't scald.

Now pour sauce mixture over pasta in the casserole dish.

Sprinkle the top liberally with breadcrumbs.

Add to preheated oven and bake for approximately 45 minutes. Then, broil until the surface is bubbly and has desired amount of color. Serve and enjoy!

Olive Oil Green Beans

I like to cook with fresh produce whenever possible and these green beans are always a pleasing side dish that are fast to cook up in addition to being quite healthy. Cooking fresh vegetables on the stove top in cast iron gives them a nice finish that boiling frozen vegetables just can't provide. Olive oil is the star secret ingredient here, adding just the right bit of culinary magic to give them a lovely flavor and color while keeping this dish pretty light, thus making them a good compliment to the other heavier dishes in this feast menu. However, you can pair this dish with just about any entrée you could possibly make, and I think it'd go fairly well.

Prep time: 5 minutes
Cook time: 20 minutes
Serves: 4

3 tbsp olive oil
½ tsp minced garlic
1 lb fresh green beans
½ tsp salt (to taste)
Cracked black pepper (to taste)

Add the olive oil to a large skillet (cast iron preferred but not necessary) on medium high heat. Now add the minced garlic and stir around for ten seconds. Now add the green beans to the skillet. Attempt to arrange in an even single layer if possible. Next, sprinkle with salt (to taste, add more than called for if necessary). Now add cracked black pepper (I use a pepper mill but not necessary). Cover. Cook for 5–6 minutes. Stir well, and recover, cook for another 5 or so minutes. Green beans will be tender and have signs of golden color in places when finished. Serve using tongs and enjoy!

Imbolg Custard

My husband's maternal grandma was Scottish and his maternal grandfather, Papa, is English. There are some cultural favorites that have sifted down through the generations and become favorite holiday dishes for us as well. This custard is one of them. Like the macaroni and cheese, it is comprised of rather simple ingredients and has really a rather simplistic preparation. However, it has a satisfying richness that is comforting. Also, custard again pays a bit of homage to the dairy products we often associate with the goddess Brigid this time of year. Thusly, to round out the comfort food theme, we finish off this simple menu with a lovely hearty English desert for your Imbolg feast.

Prep and cook time: Approximately 20–30 minutes (not including cooling)

Serves: 4-6 (Depends highly on portions.)

6 egg yolks
1 cup sugar
2 tsp all purpose flour
1 cup milk
1 cup cream
1 tsp vanilla extract

In a large bowl add the egg yolks, sugar, and all purpose flour. Mix together until well combined and then set aside.

Now, in a double boiler, pour in the milk and cream while whisking constantly. Remove from heat and stop whisking.

Next, begin whisking the egg mixture constantly and slowly, a quarter cup at a time, add the hot milk mixture from the double boiler to the egg mixture. Once you've added half of the milk mixture to the egg mixture, add the contents of the egg mixture bowl back into the warm milk in the double boiler. Whisk double boiler contents until it reaches a thick pudding like consistency.

Then add the vanilla extract and whisk just enough to integrate.

Cool in refrigerator. Serve cold. Note: If done properly, a skin will form on the surface of the custard. This is normal and a sign of a custard done well!

Crafty Crafts

Natalie Zaman

I DON'T SPEND NEARLY enough time in the tub as I should, especially in the winter when the cold seeps into your bones. In February (which I personally consider winter's coldest month here in the Northeast), we celebrate the many talents of Brigid, goddess of fire, blesser of wells, and forger of metals (among other things). Brigid's annual visit is a reminder that Goddess season and warmer weather is on its way.

Brigid's Glittering Milk Bath Melts

This milk bath (milk being a nod to the lady-sheep who are, according to tradition, making milk for their impending lambies) will sooth and relax the body like a hug from Mama Brigid. It will also help to nourish, moisturize, and exfoliate your skin as only milk can.

Time Lavished: You'll fritter away less than an hour mixing up these bath melts, but it's a good idea to let them cure for at least twenty-four hours to fully infuse all the ingredients. Resulting tub time is not counted in this estimate, nor should it be. Stay there for as long as you like.

Coinage Required: $20–$25 will buy you enough ingredients to make about fifteen bath melts with ingredients left over. Given in sets of three, that's five gifts (or a half a month of bath nights for you!).

Supplies

1 cup of cocoa or shea butter. (Different butters will yield different scents. Shea butter has a nuttier, earthier scent, while cocoa butter is warmer and creamier.)

1 cup of base oil (sweet almond or jojoba work nicely)

¾ of a cup of honey (milk and honey was a favorite bathing combination of wonder-woman, Cleopatra!)

Vanilla bean

Knife

Bowl

Spoon

Measuring cups

Sifter

Whisk

Ice cream scoop

3 cups of powdered milk

¼ cup of powdered cinnamon.

Gold and/or copper powdered glitter—I suppose this can be optional, but who doesn't love emerging from a luxurious bath shimmering and glistening? Note: if you have any skin sensitivities, be safe and omit the glitter.

8 × 8 inch squares of cheesecloth

White ribbon

Cinnamon will give the mixture a brown hue. You can use more or less if you like, or you can add cinnamon essential oil for a stronger scent. Use any essential oil with caution. Even though the oil will be diluted with the other ingredients, it's always a good idea to make sure you have no sensitivities or allergic reactions. Visit https://www.aromaweb.com/articles/essential-oil-skin-patch-test .asp to learn how to conduct an essential oil patch test. The cheesecloth and ribbon are optional, but very useful to have on hand just in case things fall apart, literally—read on.

Begin by sifting the powdered milk and cinnamon together so that they're thoroughly combined.

Melt the shea or cocoa butter. You can do this on the stove top or pop it in a microwave safe bowl (preferably glass) for 1½–2 minutes. Split the vanilla bean open and scrape the contents into the butter, then add the oil and honey and blend everything thoroughly with the whisk.

Add the liquid mixture to the dry ingredients a little at a time. Stir it with the spoon first, then work it with your hands. The resulting dough may be a bit crumbly. You'll know that you have the right consistency when you can form a ball of it in your hand and it doesn't fall apart.

Use the ice cream scoop to measure out the bath melts. A regular sized ice cream scoop should hold enough of the mixture to form a two-inch ball.

Dust your palms liberally with more powdered milk (and glitter if you choose to use it) and shape the dough into spheres. Press the dough firmly as you work with it. If you're not confident in the consistency of your mixture, wrap each ball in two squares of cheesecloth, then tie it up with a white ribbon to form a little pouch. Toss the pouch into the bath when you're ready to use it, and the contents will melt out.

Brigid's Milk Bath—
The Less Messier Jar Version (but just as sparkly!)

For a quick, easy, and powdery version of Brigid's milk bath, place a vanilla bean in a mason jar or recycled jar and add:

2 cups powdered milk

1 cup baking soda

1 cup corn starch

10 drops cinnamon oil. (Remember to dilute and test any essential oils before using them for skin sensitivity and allergies!)

¼ cup of white, silver and/or gold powder glitters (Fun and optional—again, if you have any skin sensitivities, omit.)

Cap the jar, shake it up, and pop it in the fridge for a day so the scents will infuse into the dry ingredients. Use at least one cup (or more, if you're feeling particularly decadent) in your bath.

Milk baths aren't just for Imbolc, you know. Switch up the herbs and essential oils to create bath treats for every season: try lavender buds and essential oil for a spring milk bath, rosemary and mint for a refreshing summer bath, and cinnamon, cloves, orange peel, and vanilla bean for a spicy winter warmer.

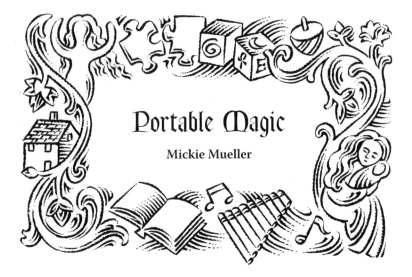

Portable Magic

Mickie Mueller

I've spent many an Imbolc thawing my frozen plumbing, which always made sense since it's a time of the year when we recognize that tenuous moment when spring is teasing us but winter is not quite done with us yet. Everyone else is watching for a weather report from a groundhog, but we witches and Pagans know it's Imbolc, sacred day of the Celtic Goddess Brigid. I like to light a small candle in each room of my house at dusk on Imbolc to purify and bring blessings to my home, but there's lots of other Imbolc magic that I like to carry along with me to keep the powers of healing and renewal close at hand. Imbolc is a time of promise and hope, which makes it very personal for many people who like to do inner work at this time. Because Imbolc is a time of reawakening; personal magic that you actually carry within your energy field can be very effective for spiritual growth, healing, and awakening.

Healing Braid

A bit of healing magic can always benefit us, even if we're not sick. Healing energy can also be beneficial for mind, body, and spiritual maintenance. If it works better for your schedule, you can make this braid in advance of Imbolc and begin wearing it on Imbolc.

If you have never braided, it's really simple. Just search "how to braid string" online and you'll find easy tutorials. Gather one piece of white, yellow, and green embroidery floss about twelve inches long and tie a knot about two inches away from the end. Use a safety pin to pin the knot to the top of a throw pillow, which will hold it in place while you work. As you braid, focus on an image of yourself healed and happy in mind, body, and spirit. Imagine a warm light glowing from within, filling your physical body with energy from the universe and strengthening your aura. Braid it as long as you need it to be for an anklet or bracelet as you prefer. Once it's long enough, knot the end to secure the braid and leave another two inches of unbraided floss past the knot. Tie it to either your wrist or ankle, and every time you notice it as you go about your business on Imbolc, let it remind you of the healing work you've created. Wear it always—once it breaks and comes off, the spell is done and you've absorbed all the healing energy that you summoned up for Imbolc.

Bird Seed Abundance

I love feeding the birds; it's a way to directly connect with nature for me, which is an important part of my spiritual practice. During this time of the year I think of them, knowing that many of their natural resources for food is somewhat tapped out here during the harsh Midwestern winter. When you share a bit of abundance, it sends a message to the universe about your generosity of spirit, therefore bringing more generosity back to you. Using this knowledge I've created this really simple birdseed spell for witches on the go on Imbolc. Place a handful of birdseed into a bundle—you can use a fancy fabric pouch or a simple paper envelope, just make it easily portable. Bless the bundle with this or your own words:

Seeds of abundance that I share today, blessings of abundance come back my way.

Carry the seeds with you into the world, casting them into a place where you usually see birds. Anywhere from a park to a parking lot, your generosity will feed them and be returned to you.

Melting Ice Spell

Imbolc is a season when we think about what is frozen in our lives and attempt to bring about a thaw. This spell on the go can be done with any ice, anywhere, anytime, so if you're looking for some quick yet powerful Imbolc magic on the go, this one is for you. All you need is a small piece of ice, a napkin, your hands, and your intention. The ice can be found in nature if you live where it's cold, or if it's above freezing where you are, a small piece of ice about half an inch in diameter from your drink or a vending machine will work just fine. It will melt quickly, so you'll have to have figured out what your intention is ahead of time.

What is frozen in your life? There's something that's been at a standstill and you need to break it free. Is it your finances, motivation to exercise, or a creative block? Put that image in your mind and focus hard on that aspect of life being figuratively frozen in ice. Pick up that piece of ice and visualize the ice as holding the one thing that you need to unfreeze right in the middle, stuck. Hold the ice in your hands; you can rub it, squeeze it, breathe on it, use your energy to melt that ice. Hold your hands over the napkin to catch any water as it melts. As the ice gets smaller and finally disappears, feel the image in your mind breaking free of the ice—it's a joyful feeling of hope. Dry your hands on the napkin and warm them up. You should notice new opportunities to achieve your now freed goals over the next few days, take them!

Wear Colors of the Day

Pick the colors to wear on Imbolc while considering what the colors mean and the energy you want to embrace on the sabbat.

White is the color that people used to dress corn dollies representing Brigid during Imbolc. During this sabbat, white can also represent the milk of the first ewes. White is a magical symbol of purity, new beginnings, healing, and hope.

Light green is the color of the tiny shoots that you have to really look for, but they are there. This is a color of new beginnings, growth, the promise of prosperity, and is also the color of the heart chakra.

Yellow is the warming sun that comes to melt the ice. Wear any shade of yellow on Imbolc to bring energies of the sacred flame, creativity, and communication into your life.

Sabbat on the Go Tips

Weather divination is a long standing tradition of Imbolc. Ages before Groundhog Day there were many folk rhymes about Candlemas Day and the weather, they all suggest that if the weather is bright and fair, watch out for an extended winter.

Bring a travel mug full of blackberry herbal tea with you today. Trace a pentagram or other magical symbol of your choice in the air over the cup then press it down with your palm, and pop the lid on. Now you have enchanted Imbolc tea to go.

For a special scent you can wear on Imbolc, try rosemary, basil, dragons blood oil, or if you don't have those, a drop or two of real vanilla extract.

Imbolc Ritual

JD Hortwort

As you prepare for your Imbolg celebration, set up a fire bowl or campfire outside, if possible. If not, use a large crystal bowl filled halfway with sand or rice. Set up at least as many candles as there are members in your group or one for every Sabbat of the year. Set it in the center of your ritual area on a table. This will be your Imbolc balefire.

Gather the following materials. Gather any ritual tools that are used in your group practice. Group members should also be encouraged to bring one or more of the tools they use at home. If you like, assemble the candles and herbs to be used for future rituals throughout this year. These can be bundled together and tied with ribbons or wrapped in tissue paper and placed in a basket at the altar.

You should have a basket or bowl of eggs for the member who will embody the Goddess Briget. Appropriate cakes and ale for grounding at the end of ritual would be egg-based breads, cakes or cookies plus cider, mead, or milk sweetened with honey.

Have a gold and white candle for this ritual. Have a small cauldron of water blended with juniper or cedar oil and a juniper branch for asperging members and tools. Appropriate herbs for Imbolg to use for smudging include pine resin, cedar oil, bayberry, and any white or yellow flowers in bloom for the season, like crocus or camellia or daffodils.

Begin the ritual. Everyone except a member representing Briget is inside the circle. Once the circle is cast, call your quarters or guardians as is your custom. At the House of Akasha, we usually call in this fashion.

North: *Spirits of the North, Spirits of Earth, Ancient Ones. Be with us and guard us for this, our Imbolg celebration tonight.*

East: *Spirits of the East, Spirits of Air, Ancient Ones. Be with us and guard us for this, our Imbolg celebration tonight.*

South: *Spirits of the South, Spirits of Fire, Ancient Ones. Be with us and guard us for this, our Imbolg celebration tonight.*

West: *Spirits of the West, Ancient Ones, Spirits of Water. Be with us and guard us for this our Imbolg festival tonight.*

High Priest (HP): *Lord Dagda, Lord of the wild wood. Newly returned to us this Yule. Be with us and guard us for this, our Imbolg celebration tonight.* (HP then lights the gold candle and the balefire. If the group is using a candle bowl instead of a balefire, the HP lights all the candles in the bowl.)

High Priestess (HPS): *Something is amiss. The Goddess, Briget, is not with us. How can we celebrate the return of the growing season without the goddess of fire, the goddess of fertility, the Goddess Briget, daughter of the Dagda. Briget, she of many names. Brid, Bridgit, Brigan, Brigantia, Lady of the Shores, Bride the Beautiful, Flame of Ireland. We have lighted and tended the sacred fire. We call you back to us.*

Lady Brid, She of the fire. Protector of the hearth. Inspiration of poets. Guardian of smiths. Be with us and guard us as we honor you tonight.

Briget rings a bell three times at the entrance to the east of the circle. **HPS** cuts a door in the East to let Briget in and says: *Welcome, Briget.* She closes the opening to the circle behind Briget, who enters with the basket of eggs. All members chime in, *Welcome, Briget.* The **HPS** lights the white candle.

Briget: *The days have grown longer. My rest has ended. It is time to return to this world.*

Briget begins to walk deasil around the circle, pausing in front of each member. The member holds her basket temporarily and charges the eggs with positive thoughts and energy for the coming year. As they do so, **Briget** continues to speak:

Imbolg is a time of renewal. All around us we see signs of that renewal. These eggs symbolize new energy, the potential for new growth, new possibilities. Even as Winter continues to chill our bones, flowers come forth as crocuses, daffodils, and more. We still see creatures all around us, frolicking in the tree limbs. The badger and groundhog stir from their dens to test the New Year.

The creatures of the farm that will sustain us with their wool, their milk and their meat are eager to return to the fields as they prepare for the next generation. While many trees are bare, we still see joy in life in the evergreens that surround us.

Even in the balefire, we see the illumination that will light our way to new ideas, new self-development, new goals as we go forward to greet the coming year. (Briget takes the basket of eggs to the altar. These will be made into an egg-based dish for the meal after ritual. She takes a place beside the altar.)

HPS: *Take a moment to contemplate Briget's words. Consider what they mean in your life.*

Silent meditation for at least a moment

HPS: *Everyone hold your ritual tools.*

HP lights a charcoal and sprinkles Imbolg incense on the coal. Using his hand, he smudges the group altar and ritual tools. He then proceeds around the circle to smudge the members' tools.

HP: *Imbolg is a fire festival. We have lit the balefire to bring the light back into our life. We cleanse our ritual tools of all the energies and associations from the past. We charge them with our positive energy for the coming year.*

HPS holds the asperging water and using the juniper branch, she sprinkles the altar and ritual tools. She proceeds around the circle to cleanse the member's tools.

HPS: *Imbolg is a time of new beginnings and fresh starts. We purify our ritual tools and cleanse them of any lingerings from the past.*

As the **HP** and **HPS** proceed around the circle, smudging and asperging members' tools, the group chants:

Welcome, Briget. Welcome the new year. We welcome you with gladness and cheer.

When they are done, the **HP** and **HPS** take the cakes and ale before **Briget** for a blessing.

Briget: *May this food and drink fill us with the hope and promise of the coming year.*

Cakes and ale are shared with the members. Everyone prepares to open the circle.

HPS: *Lady Briget, Goddess of the hearth, healing, and fertility. Thank you for returning to us and being with us for this, our Imbolg celebration tonight. Hail and farewell.*

HP: *Lord Dagda, Lord of the wild wood. Newly returned to us this Yule. Thank you for being with us and guarding us for this, our Imbolg celebration tonight. Hail and farewell.*

West: *Spirits of the West, Spirits of Water, Ancient Ones. Thank you for being with us and guarding us for this, our Imbolg celebration tonight. Hail and farewell.*

South: *Spirits of the South, Spirits of Fire, Ancient Ones. Thank you for being with us and guarding us for this, our Imbolg celebration tonight. Hail and farewell.*

East: *Spirits of the East, Spirits of Air, Ancient Ones. Thank you for being with us and guarding us for this, our Imbolg celebration tonight. Hail and farewell.*

North: *Spirits of the North, Spirits of Earth, Ancient Ones. Thank you for being with us and guarding us for this, our Imbolg celebration tonight. Hail and farewell.*

The circle is opened.

Notes

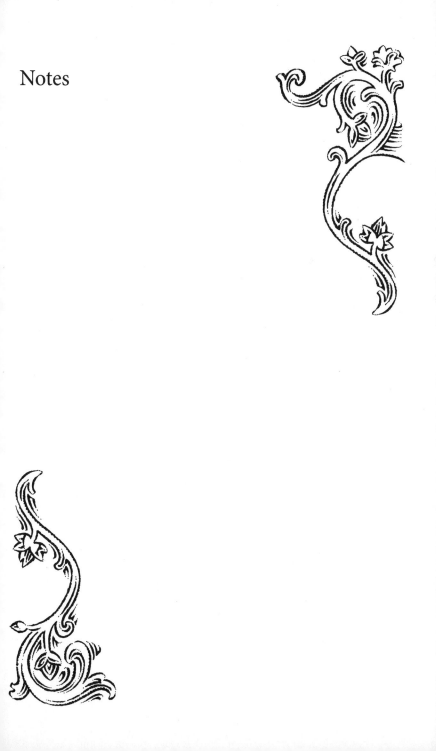

Notes

Ostara

Ostara Water Keepers

Dallas Jennifer Cobb

OSTARA, THE SPRING EQUINOX celebration, takes its name from the Great Goddess: Eostre, Eostra, Oestara, Ostara, Astarte, Ishtar, and Aset. A celebration of thawing, sprouting and rebirth, it marks a time when the earth is returning to vibrant fertility. Equinox means equal day and night, and is a phenomena shared by all of earth's inhabitants, a rare, common experience.

Ostara is a wonderful time to focus on water, and not just because water is one of the sacred elements. In the northern hemisphere Ostara is the time of snow melting, spring run off, and rains. In the southern hemisphere Ostara often coincides with the rainy season. But the real reason that Ostara is a good time to focus on healing the water is that it follows soon after the First Nations 13th moon.

For thousands of years Pagans have held water as a sacred element. To the indigenous peoples of the world, water is life. Water is the life blood of Mother Earth.

But, with the growing effects of climate change, global warming, and the increasing commoditization of this valuable natural resource, it's time for us to take action to protect and heal water. Using the unifying experience of equinox, Ostara is a powerful time to work with collective energy toward collective solutions.

Water Worldwide

Everyday there are news stories of water being polluted, diverted, bottled, sold, and even stolen. With Standing Rock still fresh in our minds, we know what is at stake here in North America. Our access to water is being limited, as it is being polluted and threatened on a mass scale.

Water is essential to human survival. When we are born our bodies are made up of about 78 percent water. As we age, we literally dehydrate. By one year of age we are about 65 percent water, as adults we drop to about 60 percent and are down to almost 50 percent in our elderly years.

The suggested amount of water a human needs to drink daily is 64 ounces, yet 783 million people worldwide do not have access to safe, clean drinking water, and 1 in 5 deaths worldwide of children age 5 and under are attributed to the lack of clean water.

It's easy to think that the water issue is something that is "over there" and affects only developing countries, but water issues are abundant here in North America. Recent research undertaken in Canada revealed that risky water systems pose a huge health threat to almost 33 percent of First Nations people living on a Canadian reserve. The United States is "on the verge of a national crisis that could mean the end of clean, cheap water…the situation has grown so dire the U.S. Office of the Director of National Intelligence now ranks water scarcity as a major threat to national security alongside terrorism." And, we have seen the results of environmental disasters as a result of gas and oil pipeline accidents affecting drinking water along their routes.

The Great Lakes

I live in Southern Ontario on the north shore of Lake Ontario. The beauty, majesty, and power of the lake affects me daily. In the summer I swim across the bay to the lighthouse and back, adrift in the magical underwater world. In autumn I walk the boardwalk entranced by changing colors, migrating geese, and falling leaves. In winter the ice forms volcanoes with icy lake water gushing up and out of them, forming a glistening world of ice castles nestled along the shoreline. And in spring, I wander in rubber boots, witnessing the inland waters rising high enough to burst through the beach, moving sand and rock, soil and plants, so the water can run through and join Lake Ontario.

Lake Ontario is part of the Great Lakes System, which is the largest collection of fresh water in the world, about one fifth of all the fresh water on Earth. In Canada 10 million people rely on water from the Great Lakes to sustain them, in the United States there are 24 million.

Of all the water in the world, only 1 percent is drinkable freshwater (from rivers, lakes, and streams) and there is another 2 percent frozen in the polar ice caps. The remaining 97 percent of the world's waters are salt water.

Understanding how valuable drinking water is can help people recognize the need to be aware of protecting and healing water.

A Water Keeper

I am part of a vibrant Pagan community that organizes and holds rituals. This spring I was invited to join a Tyendinaga First Nations ritual that took place on the Bay of Quinte, an inland body of water connected to Lake Ontario. When I received the invitation to join in a water ceremony, I leapt at the chance. I had heard about the First Nations water blessing ceremony, and wanted to take part. The ceremony is held at the thirteenth moon in late February or early March, and is always done at the new moon, a time of intention setting for the coming moon cycle.

The local ritual was linked to simultaneous rituals around the world in other communities concerned about groundwater protection. While this ritual was held on First Nations land, and there are many First Nations communities throughout North America who are engaged, the web of communities who are mobilizing to protect, bless, and restore groundwater health is vast, and not limited to First Nations people. It is time for all of us to get involved in the protection and healing of our water.

When I attended the ceremony, I took a pledge to heal and help the water. I urged my ritual circle to organize an Ostara Water Blessing ritual weeks later, which led to more widespread awareness and engagement throughout our community.

Let me tell you about Nibi Wabo, and maybe I can inspire you to become a Water Keeper too.

Nibi Wabo

In 2002 a ceremony was held in the Algonquin community of Kitigan Zibi in Northern Quebec. Thirteen grandmothers were gathered representing Algonquin and mixed blood women from four races. Twelve of the participants were asked by the thirteenth to pass the ceremony on to other women worldwide because in many countries women are the keepers, and carriers, of water.

In 2003, while a sacred fire was held in Kitigan Zibi, Quebec, groups gathered world wide in sacred ceremonies involving up to 3,000 women in Canada, the United States, Mexico, Jamaica, Guatemala, Brazil, Columbia, Germany, Italy, Holland, Senegal, Japan, and New Zealand.

In the years that followed, the ceremony grew and spread. In 2005 there were 9,000 women who gathered worldwide, at the same time as the thirteen Algonquin elders sang on the ice to the water. Feathers used in that sacred ceremony in 2005 were distributed to spiritual elders and healers around the world, that they would continue the work. The ceremony has spread and grown since then.

It is a simple ceremony. A sacred fire is lit just before sunset. It burns for thirteen hours throughout the night. Men may join the ceremony as fire keepers, bearing witness, being of service, remaining quiet, and supportive. If no men are available, women fire keepers are chosen and take on the task of keeping the fire fed and the women warmed.

Women gather around the fire and are smudged with a mixture of cedar and sage to purify them. The importance of water is discussed, and the origins of the ceremony are told. The structure is outlined and the words of the sacred water blessing song are taught in Algonquin/Ojibwa. (Note: This song is passed from woman to woman in verbal tradition, and is not meant to be written down or transmitted on the internet. While you can hear Nibi Wabo being sung in a video, I have been asked not to write the words here out of respect for the First Nations traditions.)

When darkness falls, the women go out on the ice and form a circle. They sing the water blessing song four times to each direction, turning to face the direction as they sing. Some women drum, shake rattles, or bang birch sticks together, keeping the time of the song. The versus are sung quietly, and the chorus is sung loudly, the varying volumes emulating the effect of rushing water. It is believed that the energy of the women heals the water through the song.

After singing, women return to the fire for a traditional feast, and spend the night together talking, sharing, and learning.

The originators insist that this is a woman's ceremony and it's meant to be fluid and not rigid, so it can be altered depending on who is doing it. What is important is the blessing of the water through song, so that the water absorbs the healing vibration.

Some groups bring water with them that they bless and offer as a gift to the body of water they stand beside. Other groups bring water and pour it into a large vessel, marrying the waters, and each woman takes some married water home to use in her sacred work.

The ritual I went to included learning a simple prayer:

> *I am sorry*
> *Please forgive me*
> *Thank you*
> *I love you.*

I later learned that it is called Ho'oponopono and is a practice of reconciliation and forgiveness from the Hawai'ian First Nations hakuna (priests and priestesses). *Ho'oponopono* literally translates as "to make right for all." *Ho'o* means "to make" and *pono* means "right." *Ponopono* means "making it right for all, ones self and others."

As with singing, we turned to each direction and repeated the prayer.

We were instructed to take the prayer home and say it every time we used water: to make tea, wash, bathe, or water plants. We were to pause, repeat the four stanza's, and remember the sacredness of water. We were encouraged to use the prayer to heal our relationships, especially with our children.

Since the ritual, I've become more conscious of my use and enjoyment of water. I often wrap my hands around a teacup and whisper. I wet my toothbrush and looking into my own eyes in the mirror, whisper the Ho'oponopono to myself.

Now that you understand the sacred and essential nature of water and have heard the song and learned the prayer, why not pledge to be a water protector in your community? Becoming more conscious of waters' use and power might just inspire you to get active and engaged. Whether you choose to take action locally, engage in your home community, join an international water protection group, or conduct a sacred water healing ceremony, you can protect and heal this sacred element.

Cosmic Sway

Charlie Rainbow Wolf

ONE OF THE MOST interesting aspects I see in the heavens for the spring equinox is what astrologers call a "yod," sometimes referred to as "the finger of God." This month it involves the Moon's North Node in Cancer, Jupiter in Sagittarius, and Venus in Aquarius. It all points to karma, to family and traditions and home life.

To get all astrological on you, a yod is an aspect where two planets or other power points working fairly harmoniously with each other are being pulled by a third planet (or point) with which either of them have nothing in common. In this instance, Jupiter in Sagittarius and Venus in Aquarius are playing reasonably nicely together. This sextile is creating a very impulsive and rather eccentric vibe, but then the inconjunct of the Moon's north nodes in Cancer is tugging at them. The individualistic and humanitarian energies are being weighed down by karma, tradition, and maybe some good old-fashioned feelings.

The yod creates frustration. It brings intense challenges, but also the chance for increased awareness leading to growth and improvement. The yod intensifies all of the angles—the sextiles and both inconjuncts—and points them like a laser. This month, that point is focused on the Moon's north node. Be ever vigilant when it comes to karma, because it's a key factor in how the next season unfolds.

The yod brings a period of adjustment. In this case—once again—it's karmic. There's little or no common ground when it comes to the influence of the Moon's north node on Jupiter and Venus, which could give rise to a critical point, or a call to action. In this case, it's karma that's demanding that the needs be met, disrupting the influence of Jupiter and Venus, and throwing consequences and repercussions at them. Whatever happens now is going to create residual energy to be dealt with at a later date, both on a personal and a larger scale.

As well as being caught up in that yod, Venus is a bit testy this month, making a square to Mars. They're both in fixed signs, Venus in the water bearer and Mars in the bull. Venus transits aren't long lived, so this is only really going to influence Ostara and either day around it. Temptations will be strong, and remember that Jupiter is in Sagittarius, where it rules, making a positive aspect to Venus and encouraging some spontaneous behavior. Venus in Aquarius is pushing boundaries and breaking rules, and Mars is adding fuel—and perhaps a bit of rebellion or sense of adventure—to all of that erratic energy.

At the same time, Jupiter is making a hard aspect to Mars. Mars in Taurus is frustrated anyway, because Mars likes to get ahead and Taurus is the king of routine. The very last thing Mars needs is Jupiter trying to push it into what it already knows it wants but just can't seem to attain, yet that's exactly what's happening. The overall energy of the first week of spring is likely to be frustrating and short-tempered, to say the least!

If the yod didn't bring us enough karma, once again Chiron is at a critical degree, this time at 0° Aries. Chiron felt rather at home in Pisces, but Aries? That's a whole new energy, and one that this planetoid hasn't seen since the 1960s! If you want a bit of insight as to what to expect, look back to the period from 1968 to 1970. While history may not repeat itself, you'll certainly see the influence. A lot of dreams—and perhaps even nightmares—are about to come through the void from the intangible to reality.

Remember that Saturn–Pluto thing we talked about for Imbolc? It's getting even stronger, now with only 3 degrees separating them. This brings a little bit of harmony to this aspect, provided that neither planet's energy gets too pushy. Less is more with this aspect, and when put to the test, it often flies out of the gate with a resolve and a tenacity to either find a way forward or create a new path. The potential to work with both innovation and discipline is strong, and that has the capacity to bring about very radical changes.

Saturn's also involved in a conjunction with the Sun as our solar system's star enters into Aries. It's vital to only focus on what's important. This aspect brings a deep awareness of challenges and difficulties but also an opportunity to find the resolve and discipline to deal with them. Every problem has a solution; this aspect, coupled with Pluto's influence, makes it easier to see.

Uranus has changed signs this month, too, moving out of Aries for the final time and starting its seven-year trip through Taurus. Yes, it dallied here for a bit last year, but now it's finished dancing across the cusp. The last time Uranus was in Taurus was around 1934–1941. Look back at events from that time period to see what potential this transit holds.

Taurus and Uranus are both stubborn, and there's more than a little opposing energy here. Taurus is fixed, down to earth, and practical. Uranus is wild, unpredictable, and often outrageous. The two don't make particularly good bedfellows. It may create a bit of a bumpy ride, so fasten your seat belts—this is a seven year voyage!

Ostara Celebration: Let the Laughter Echo

Ostara is one of the two times of year when night and day are of equal length. It's a time of balance, of recognizing harmony and equality. It's also a time of creating a bit of light-hearted fun, a time for play and celebrating life in all its many forms. This ritual is meant to be frivolous, and it's one where even the youngest members of the family or community can join in. If you work solitary, you can still do it—just remember to keep a smile on your face!

You will need:

Colored jelly beans or other colored candy pieces (we're rather fond of the malted or chocolate mini-eggs)

Gummy bears or jelly babies

A large chocolate rabbit

A glass of milk, cordial, soda pop, or something stronger.

Arrange everything on an altar or table, and decorate it with bright colors and other seasonal items. This ritual is best done at midday if possible, but any time will work. However, do bear in mind the sugar content, and don't let the high keep you awake all night! Also, please be responsible with this. If you know that you're sensitive to sugary foods, don't overindulge—and do remember to brush your teeth after the ritual!

At the start of the ritual, make sure that everyone has a good handful of the colored candies. We do it one candy of each color per person, so that usually means that everyone has four or five mini eggs. Cast whatever circle you wish, and invoke your customary deities, remembering to include Ēostre—it is her Sabbat, after all. I've given the instructions for doing this with a group; please adapt them if you're going to be working solo (it won't be hard).

Once your circle is cast, have each person in turn choose a colored egg, and shout out what it means to them. For example, you might say something like this for a yellow candy:

All hail the great yellow egg, the color of the Sun, which brings light and life on this day when the skies are equally bright and dark! All hail the great chocolate egg, with the dark and velvety sweetness that melts in the warm Sun. Get thee into my belly; you are most gratefully received!

Remember, this is supposed to be fun! Go through each color, and maybe make it a bit of a contest to see who can outdo the other, or who can create the most giggles. If you're doing this solitary, use your imagination. You might want to write down your words in a poem or a jingle before you start.

Now treat the gummy bears or the jelly babies in the same manner. We've had great fun doing mock screams if someone didn't bite the heads off first (always eat gummy bears and jelly babies head first, so you can't hear them scream), treating them as sacrifices to the great gastric gods. Create some hilarity around this. Laugh and play. There's no better cure for the doldrums than some good old-fashioned buffoonery, especially when there's candy involved!

Finally, bring out the sacrificial chocolate rabbit! You might want to dress it up on a platter or something. If you've got a ritual leader or a spokesperson, give them the task of proclaiming the rabbit honorable and worthy. If you're doing this by yourself, create your own words to verbally anoint the rabbit before it is consumed. You might want to say something like this:

Very well met, rabbit of delight, succulent sweetness of velvety brown. We honor your presence at our table. Symbol of fertility and growth, we ask that you allow our awareness, rather than our waistlines, to grow and expand as we indulge in your chocolaty goodness. Let my ears hear clearly!

Break off the rabbit's ears and eat them, then pass the rabbit to the next person. They might want to say something like "Let my eyes see distinctly," as they break off the rabbit's eyes and eat them; or "Let my legs run swiftly," or "May my back always be strong," or "May my belly always be full," as those body parts are eaten.

When the rabbit is consumed, pass around the drink. Toast each other, toast the sweet feast you've just shared, and toast the deities you've invoked for sharing in your merriment. Close your circle in your customary way, and keep the positive energies flowing!

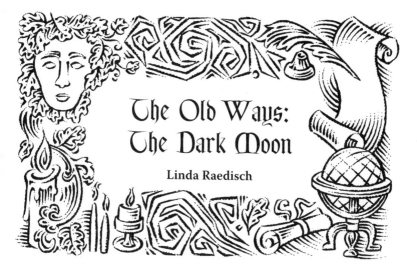

The Old Ways: The Dark Moon

Linda Raedisch

THE DEEP THROBBING OF the priests' drums at the dark of the moon would have been a familiar sound to all those living on the fertile plain between the rivers Idiglat and Buranum. The beating of the drums marked one of the smaller but no less important feasts of the Sumerians as well as the Assyrians and Babylonians who came after them. Idiglat and Buranum are the names by which the Sumerians knew the Tigris and Euphrates, the rivers having been christened by the even earlier marsh dwellers.

When darkness fell on the night of the new moon, the priests beat their drums to warn away unwanted spirits and to remind everyone to prepare their homes to be visited by the ghosts of the ancestors. This monthly Sumerian Halloween was called *ki-si-ga*, "that which is placed on the earth." It was a feast of the dead, held on one of the black nights at the end of the Sumerian month, an occasion for the living members of the family to fulfill their responsibilities to the departed—and not just the recent dead but also the distant ancestors along with whatever neglected spirits happened to be wandering by. Every wandering spirit was once clothed in flesh and was surely still wanted somewhere.

The atmosphere on the night of the ki-si-ga was probably not unlike that of the Jewish Sabbath: the gathering of the family, the flurry of activity before darkness fell, then, as the first star appeared, the lighting of the wicks in the little dishes of sesame oil. Cedar bark and seeds of wild rue were probably thrown on the brazier as the bread, water and pottage were passed round. Everyone would be wearing clean clothes: the men in sheepskin kilts from which they had brushed the dust and sand and picked the worst of the brambles, the women in woolen tunics freshly laundered in a lather of soapwort stalks. The Sumerians referred to themselves as "the black-headed people." On this night, the women would have combed and oiled their dark hair and braided it round their heads while the girls, having just come in from the pastures, might crown their black curls with chaplets of quivering aspen leaves and frothy pink tamarisk flowers.

But let's not forget the dead! It was for them that the barley cakes and a few spoonfuls of stewed meat and onions were placed upon the ground. The Sumerians must have realized how easy it was to forget the dead and how dangerous the dead could become if neglected.

One of the most troublesome demons to come out of this region began her life as an ordinary girl. Who knows what went wrong? Perhaps her husband spurned her shortly after the wedding night and she had no family to return to. Perhaps she died alone in the dry foothills without a grave or offerings to help her find her way to the Great Below. Whatever the reason, she's still wandering around, stirring up trouble. She has gone by many names. In the Kabala, she is "princess of screeching," in the Zohar "that Certain Woman" who seduces men by "the diminishing of the moon."

But she derives her more familiar name from a cameo appearance she makes in the Old Testament, in Isaiah 34:14, as "Lilit," which can be translated as "screech owl." Lilit doesn't do much in Isaiah; she is listed as one of the many wild creatures who will haunt the fallen-down palaces of the Edomites. Her presence there, along with satyrs, jackals and scavenging birds, is evidence of the complete devastation that will be visited upon the kingdom of Edom, of the irreversible wilderness that will overtake its streets and houses.

If you have heard only one thing about Lilith, as her name is now more commonly spelled, it's probably that she was Adam's first wife, exiled from the Garden of Eden because she refused to assume the missionary position. She had nothing against the position itself; she simply wanted to be the one on top. Having been shaped from the same slick, wet clay as Adam, Lilith saw herself as his equal and therefore entitled to straddle him whenever the mood took her. This was acceptable to neither Adam nor God whose secret name she shrieked aloud as she flew out the gates and into the wilderness. She was pursued by three angels who cornered her in a cave by the sea and pressured her to return. But Lilith never went back to Eden, never remarried, never had living children of her own. Instead, she preys on other women's children, stealing their spirits out of the womb or cradle and seducing the women's husbands in their dreams.

You can rifle through the pages of Genesis all you want but you won't find Lilith's story there. The account of Adam's first, failed marriage appears in the Midrash, a voluminous literature including many legends that had circulated in the Jewish community for generations before scholars started writing them down in the early centuries CE. There are actually several cautionary tales about Lilith in the apocryphal writings of the Jews. Some of these stories are at least as old as Genesis 2, while others may predate it by hundreds if not thousands of years.

The Eden out of which Lilith fled was probably in southern Iraq. The name "Eden" passed into Hebrew via Akkadian, another Semitic language that had replaced Sumerian for everyday use by 2000 BCE. The word *eden*, which originally meant an alluvial plain, probably came from Ubaidian, the language of those original marsh-dwellers, which had been replaced by Sumerian by 3500 BCE. We don't know by what names the Ubaidians called their own ghosts, but a Sumerian ghost was a gidim. When the Akkadian speaking Assyrians swept into the area, they introduced the term *lil*, which could mean "ghost," or more vaguely, "spirit."

The line between ghosts and demons was a fine one, easily and frequently crossed by the shades of the restless dead. Lilith must once have belonged to a close-knit family of ghost-like demons, the head of which was the lilu, a male spirit who embodied the southwest wind and preyed upon babies both in and out of the womb. The female was the lilitu. Unlike the lilu, who kept to the desert sands, the lilitu could enter a house through the window. These creatures were probably inspired by dust devils: small, whirling vortices of sand and the fine, dry sediments left behind when the rivers flooded. I've only ever seen a dust devil up close once on a New Mexico college campus. Everyone stopped and stared, even the kids who were used to seeing that sort of thing. Had we come from an older civilization, I'm sure we would have been terrified.

The third member of the family was the ardat-lili. In Akkadian, an *ardatû* is a "nubile young girl," so the ardat-lili is a "maiden-lili." She is the most anthropomorphic of the three, behaving very much like a bride left at the altar. She accosted young men and struck women barren. And she carried with her the askance-looking that the Sumerians had reserved for the ghosts of individuals who had died before their time and continued to roam the earth instead of lying quiet in their graves.

So whether you feast for the dead once a year, eight times, or at each new moon, be sure to leave a light and a little dish of food out for the spirit of the jilted bride Lilith. Because she's still out there...

Resources

Patai, Raphael. *Gates to the Old City: A Book of Jewish Legends.* Northvale, New Jersey: Jason Aronson Inc., 1988.

van der Toorn, Karel, Bob Becking, and Pieter W. van der Horst, eds. Dictionary of Deities and Demons in the Bible. Second Edition. Grand Rapids, Michigan: Wm. B. Eerdmans Publishing, 1996.

Feasts and Treats

Blake Octavian Blair

SPRING EQUINOX AND THE Ostara season conjure many visions of an earnest start to gardening and visions of green beginning to grow and show upon the land. Fertility is a pervasive theme and seasonal symbols of birth, growth, and abundance are everywhere in our celebrations. Eggs are a virtual seasonal must and fresh ingredients with flare are favorites on the culinary docket. Of course, what is Ostara without sweets? This menu includes a sweet treat with a springtime herbal flare! Prepare for a festive feast and spruce your feast table with festive adornments such as dyed Ostara eggs, statues and figurines of the classical symbol of the rabbit, and pastel candles to remind us of the colors of the spring blossoming!

Spring Dandelion Green Salad

I think many of us have nostalgia associated with dandelions appearing in springtime, bright cheerful yellow beacons that symbolize sunny days to come. Dandelions are in fact a popular culinary ingredient, and this salad makes them into a star on your Ostara feast table. It's balance of textures and bright flavors make it a delightful addition to this equinox menu of exotic flavors. Of course, it also integrates the popular Ostara symbol of the egg.

Prep time: 10 minutes
Cook time: Approx. 30 minutes
Serves: 4-6

For the salad:
2 hardboiled eggs, sliced
¼ cup toasted slivered almonds
½ medium red onion, sliced
½ lb dandelion greens
1 11-ounce can mandarin orange slices
½ cup dried cranberries
8 ounces goat cheese

For the dressing:
2 tbsp diced red onion
¼ cup white wine vinegar
Juice of 1 orange
1 pinch salt
1 pinch cracked black pepper
1 tsp sugar
1½ cup extra virgin olive oil

Begin by placing the eggs into a pot of water, about one inch coverage over top of the eggs. Bring to boil. When water comes to a boil, immediately remove from heat, cover, and let stand 10 minutes. Remove eggs from hot water and place in ice water. Allow eggs to cool, then peel and slice the eggs.

Add slivered almonds to cold dry skillet and turn on to medium heat, stir frequently until aromatic and slight golden brown color and glistening appearance is achieved. Remove from heat.

Slice the red onion into strips.

Tear dandelion greens into a large mixing or serving bowl. Add in the mandarin orange slices, sliced red onion, slivered almonds, dried cranberries, and sliced hardboiled eggs.

To prepare the dressing, place onions in vinegar and let soak for five minutes. Then add all other dressing ingredients except for the oil and whisk until well combined. Then, while whisking, slowly drizzle oil into bowl with salad ingredients.

Once dressing is added to salad bowl, toss until salad and dressing is well mixed and salad is evenly coated in the dressing. Crumble goat cheese over the top and serve.

Egg Báhn Mì Sandwiches

Báhn Mì is a Vietnamese sandwich that has its origins from the French colonization of Vietnam. It features homemade pickled vegetables, a fresh produce element, and a protein. One of the various traditional proteins is fried eggs. What would an Ostara celebration be without venerating the symbol of the egg?! All this is served traditionally in a French baguette, although, here a more readily accessible alternative is offered for individual servings.

Prep time: 15 minutes
Cook time: 40 minutes
Serves: 4

For the pickle:
1 medium bell pepper
1 small sweet onion
3 medium carrots
1 cup water
1¼ cup apple cider vinegar
1 tbsp salt
1 tbsp sugar
1 tbsp pickling spice
1 small cucumber
⅓ cup cilantro leaves

For the sandwich:
¼ cup mayonnaise
2 tbsp sriracha sauce

6 large eggs
2 tbsp butter
4 small hoagie rolls or hamburger buns

The first step is to make a pickle of green bell pepper, onion, and carrot. Cut the onion into slices and the pepper into strips. Cut the carrots into sticks approximately uniform size to the strips of onion and pepper. This can easily be done by quartering a small to medium carrot and then cutting the pieces to appropriate lengths.

To prepare the pickling brine, combine the salt, sugar, water, and apple cider vinegar into a medium saucepan, add pickling spice in a metal tea ball. Put pepper, onion, and carrot into the brine and cook on medium heat for about twenty to thirty minutes.

Now prepare the fresh cucumber by cutting it into similar size sticks to the other vegetables, set aside.

Pick cilantro leaves off of stems and place aside in a small bowl.

In another small bowl, mix the mayonnaise and sriracha sauce and combine well to make a sriracha aioli. You can adjust the quantity of sriracha according to your preferred level of spiciness and heat. Dress rolls or buns with desired amount of the aioli.

When ten minutes time is left until the pickle is finished, proceed to prepare the scrambled eggs.

To make the scrambled eggs, crack six large eggs into a large bowl. Combine with a pat or two of butter, and whisk until well combined. Heat a skillet over medium heat, and then add the egg mixture and stir slowly but constantly.

When the eggs are set up to desired consistency, add to the rolls, top with desired amounts of pickle, cucumber, and cilantro to each sandwich. Serve and enjoy!

Lavender Cookies

It pays off to have an all-purpose basic cookie recipe that is easily adaptable in your magickal kitchen cauldron of tricks. Here we use one to create a delightful springtime lavender treat.

Prep time: 10 minutes (and about 2 hours to chill dough)

Cook time: 10 minutes

For the cookies:

1 egg
¼ cup granulated sugar
¾ cup packed brown sugar
2 tsp vanilla extract
1 stick butter (8 tbsp)
2 cups all-purpose flour
2 tsp cornstarch
1 tsp baking soda
½ tsp salt (adjust to taste)
Lavender buds (to taste)

In a large bowl, combine the butter, egg, sugars, and vanilla. Proceed to beat until the mixture is light and fluffy. This should take approximately five minutes.

Then add the all-purpose flour, cornstarch, and baking soda. Mix to incorporate.

Now add the lavender buds, and briefly mix until just incorporated. One minute or less. Note: while you can add the lavender to taste, I caution against adding too much. The lavender in moderation has a delightful light taste. When too much is added, it takes on a soapy flavor.

Place dough in refrigerator for 1½ to 2 hours to chill.

When chilled, either use a cookie scoop or form small balls approximately two inches in diameter, placing them upon a greased baking sheet. Slightly flatten the mounds as you place them onto the sheet. Place the mounds approximately two inches apart from each other to allow expansion during baking.

Place cookies in a 350 degree preheated oven.

Bake approximately ten minutes, until the edges have begun to set and the top appears mostly done. If the centers seem just slightly underdone, still remove at ten minutes as they will continue to set as the cookies cool.

Place cookies onto a cooling rack or tray. Allow five to fifteen minutes to cool. Then add icing while cookies are still slightly warm.

For the Icing:

3 tbsp confectioners' sugar
1 tsp rosewater (You can substitute plain water with a few drops of vanilla extract added)

Combine all ingredients in a bowl and whisk together until well combined.

Icing may be applied in any way you desire. I like to put in a pastry bag and drizzle onto the cookies. If you do not have a pastry bag, simply put icing into a plastic zip top bag and snip a corner to create a makeshift pastry bag.

Once iced, serve and enjoy!

Crafty Crafts

Natalie Zaman

SPRING IS THE BRIEFEST (and maybe the most long-awaited) of seasons, so much so that you just want to bottle it—and you can! Spring is a time of renewal, and there's nothing as revitalizing, refreshing—and exfoliating—as a salt glow.

Sparkling Spring Flower Salt Scrub

A quick tutorial on how to glow with salt: After you've bathed (in the shower or bath), take a scoop of salt scrub and gently work the salt into your skin. Use as much as you need to cover your entire body. The salt exfoliates, the essential oils leave a lovely scent and the base oil softens and moisturizes. You can apply the salt with your hands or a washcloth. Try not to use a brush or shower scrubbie; let the salt do the exfoliating. Rinse the salt off thoroughly before patting your skin dry. (Note: The scrub we're making for this craft is for your body. Facial salt scrubs use lighter oils and scents as well as a finer grain of salt.)

A necessary supply needed to perform this bathing ritual is a salt scrub. Infused with flower essences, buds and scented herbs, this delicious mixture can be used for both practical and ritual cleansing. Use it as a part of a weekly self-care regimen to brighten and renew your skin all over (you shouldn't salt glow every day), or incorporate it into a magical bathing ritual—extra decadent when coupled with a spring time milk bath! (See the suggestions at the end of Imbolc's Crafty Crafts.)

Time Lavished: Prepping the salt scrub takes practically no time at all, maybe a half an hour, if that. This does not include drying time for the lavender (or any other herb or flower you might be using). You will also need to allow some time for the flowers, herbs and essential oils to infuse into the salt, at least twenty-four hours.

Coinage Required: I found that I spent the most money purchasing essential oils. I got lemon balm leaves and lavender buds from my garden, recycled a jar and had the salt and base oil in my pantry. If you have to purchase all of the ingredients to make your salt scrub, you'll probably spend between $20 and $25.

Supplies:

2 cups of coarse sea salt. (If you want to really splurge, use Himalayan pink salt. The pink color is pretty, and the Himalayan salt has greater amounts of trace elements—calcium, magnesium and iron—and also has esoteric properties: strength, healing and grounding respectively.)

About ¼ cup of an unscented or lightly scented oil such as almond, jojoba, or sunflower. Coconut oil will work, but you'll get a hint of coconut scent in your salt.

A handful of lemon balm leaves

1 cup of dried lavender buds

Lemon balm oil (Remember to dilute and test all essential oils for sensitivities and allergic reactions!)

Bowl

Spoon

Measuring cups

Mason jar or recycled jar

Lavender and/or light green powdered glitter. If you choose to use it, do so sparingly for a shimmery glow. Lavender and green together make for a lovely fairy-like sheen! (Note: omit glitter if you have any skin sensitivities!)

Pretty labels

One 6 × 6 inch piece of cloth

Ribbon or raffia in a coordinating color

I chose the lavender and lemon balm combination for several reasons: Both of these herbs are readily available in my garden, I love the scent of these herbs (clean and bright like springtime), as well as their healing connotations (cleansing, uplifting and nourishing). Try other spring flowers and essences such as lily of the valley, peony, camelia and nature's astringent witch hazel.

The labels, cloth, and ribbon are optional for capping your jar—a nice touch if you're giving the salt as a gift!

Before you begin putting the salt scrub together, prep your plants. Tear or cut the lemon balm leaves into little pieces and remove the lavender buds from their stalks. (Save the dried lavender

stalks. They smell just as good as the buds, and you can bind them with string to make smudge sticks or tie them in bundles and dip them in beeswax to make fire-starters.)

In a large bowl, combine the salt, lemon balm leaves and lavender buds thoroughly, then give the mixture a sniff. It might be aromatic enough without adding any essential oil (you can always add some later). Next, add the base oil a little at a time. You want the mixture to be more packable than crumbly, but not soaking. If you add too much oil, don't worry. Simply add more salt a little at a time until you get a drier consistency. You can also add more leaves and buds, but the salt should be the main ingredient.

Next, add the essential oils if needed. The amount you use (if any) is really a matter of taste. Add a few drops at a time until you're happy with it. Lastly, add the glitter if you're using it. (Keep in mind that when you use the scrub, the oils will ensure that bits of glitter will adhere to your skin even after you've rinsed off.)

Pour the salt mixture into the jar, cap it, then shake it up to mix it a little more. Technically the salt should keep anything from spoiling, but I still like to store homemade and handmade bath products in the refrigerator and use them within a month or two of making or opening. I also find that keeping the salt in the refrigerator helps in maintaining a more solid consistency. If you're giving the salt as a gift, cover the lid with the square of fabric and tie it with the ribbon.

Just as with the milk baths (see Imbolc's Crafty Craft, page 106), the salt scrub ingredients can be adjusted per the season. Try infusing salt with clove, orange peel and cinnamon oil for a spicy autumnal or winter glow. Again—and I can't say it enough—remember to dilute and test any essential oil before using it on your body, especially with a salt scrub as it will exfoliate your skin, making for greater sensitivity.

Portable Magic

Mickie Mueller

WHEN OSTARA ARRIVES, IT'S really starting to feel like spring is here and winter is behind us. My husband, Daniel, and I were married on Ostara, so in addition to celebrating the spring equinox, we've usually got some kind of anniversary plans as well that makes a bit of magic on the go a great addition to the day. So how do you celebrate the spring equinox in the middle of the week? It's okay if you're busy—I've got some easy ways that you can use to add a nice balance between the magical and mundane to the day no matter where you are or what you have to accomplish today. As you go about your day, take special care to pay attention to any flowering plants or buds waiting to burst forth that you may see, the tender light green shoots spring forth from the warming earth, animals are abuzz with plans for new life to come. These signs of spring can be seen all around, whether you're living rural, in the suburbs, or even in the city. During this exciting time of new possibilities, embrace the idea that magic doesn't have to be on a fancy altar, it's in your heart and it goes along with you everywhere.

Seeds of Light and Abundance

Purchase a pack of seeds for herbs or flowers that are easy to grow from seed. For example, you could try basil, sunflowers, sweet peas, zinnias, or any that speak to you being sure to check to see which ones grow well in your area. Draw a simple egg with a star inside somewhere on the packet. Carry the seed pack in your pocket or in your purse. Throughout your day you will notice signs from the universe that the seeds will grow abundance for you, you'll see signs of growth, money, wealth, plenty. Every time a sign grabs your attention, think of your bundle of seeds that you carry, and imagine the seed packet glowing with golden light. Feel warmth from the pack. Every sign you see for abundance will charge your seeds. When your day is done, place the seed pack somewhere safe until you're ready to plant them.

Rabbits, Hares, or Serpents to Go

When I want to bring the spirit of the spring equinox with me, I love to wear my little primitive rabbit pendant; it's carved from wood and it's leaping full of energy. It's a cool little piece that I found ages ago and I only wear it on Ostara, so I immediately go into that mindset when I put it on. Rabbits and hares are symbols of abundance and fertility because they breed like, well, like rabbits! You can usually find jewelry with rabbits or hares on them this time of the year, some will be cute and pastel for fun, but if you look around you can sometimes find a more elegant style for not too much money. Check second-hand stores or handmade marketplaces and see what you can find. If fuzzy creatures aren't your style, don't despair; this is also the time of the year when serpents come out of their earthen burrows to warm themselves in the sun. Snakes shed their skin, making them a perfect symbol of rebirth and renewal.

Once you've found a piece of Ostara jewelry that you like, hold it in some sage or incense smoke to spiritually cleanse it. Then hold it in your hands and focus on the themes of the spring equinox: rebirth, fertility, new life—fill the jewelry with that energy. Wear it on Ostara and take that magic to go while you honor the sabbat.

Inner Strength Tarot Meditation

You'll need your favorite Strength card from one of your tarot decks and a 3 × 5 inch rigid plastic sleeve, to protect your card. You can find plastic sleeves wherever you can get baseball cards or gaming cards, or pick up a pack online—they come in really handy for tarot spells and meditations. Place the card in the sleeve and place in on the table so you can meditate on the image over breakfast. Look at the card and ask yourself how it illustrates strength. Ask your Higher Spirit to help you see those qualities in yourself throughout the day. As the earth finds the strength to burst forth with life, the Strength card will show you that you have everything inside you to face the challenges of life with grace, wisdom, and strength. Watch for the evidence of your own inner strength as you go about your day with mindfulness.

Wear Colors of the Day

Wearing the colors associated with Ostara can help you connect spiritually with the energies of new life as the inertia of winter is shattered and the world around you bursts with new activity.

Green is a great color to wear on Ostara because it's the color of abundance, growth, and rebirth. Green is appearing everywhere now; some trees and shrubs even have a few leaves bursting forth, and it's so welcomed after the long winter.

Light blue reminds me of the return of the clear sky this time of the year; it's a color of joy, expansion, and opportunity reflecting the magic of Ostara. Another spring association with the color blue is robin's eggs. It's one of my favorite colors for Ostara eggs and robins are one of the first signs of spring singing of renewal across the land.

Light shades of purple like lavender or lilac are seen in nature as flowers bloom. Purple is also a color of balance, a mixture of warm red and cool blue adding to its spiritual associations and emotional healing during the spring equinox when day and night are in balance.

Black and white is a perfect color combination for those who just don't rock the pastel look. The spring equinox is a time of balanced light and dark, so wearing black and white on Ostara can help you bring your energies into balance.

Sabbat on the Go Tips

Bring a hard boiled egg, egg salad, or quiche for lunch. For vegan celebrants, a tofu quiche is a perfect option. Whether you eat eggs or not, include a spring green salad for your Imbolc lunch and sprinkle it with crunchy seeds, sesame, sunflower, and /or poppy seeds. As you enjoy these Ostara treats, think about how they will impart growth and new beginnings in your life.

Oils to wear today include primrose, orange blossom, lilac, or any floral scent.

If you work in an office or someplace where you can have flowers, bring in a vase of spring blooms either picked yourself or purchased. Even better, enjoy potted blooming bulbs like tulips or jonquils, then you can plant them later.

Ostara Water Blessing Ceremony

Dallas Jennifer Cobb

WHEN PREPARING, CONTACT THE local First Nations people. Speak your intention and invite collaboration. I live near Tyendinaga First Nations. The Mohawks of the Bay of Quinte also live on Lake Ontario and the adjoined Bay of Quinte. While organizing, we worked with a Mohawk woman who suggested the use of the "water blessing words" from the *Haudenosaunee Thanksgiving Address*. View the full Address here: nmai.si.edu/environment/pdf/01_02 _Thanksgiving_Address.pdf

In addition, invite representatives from water protection organizations and groups active in your area. Working together, we weave powerful magic.

Invite participants to bring about one ounce of water in a resealable container—water from somewhere meaningful to them: their well; a nearby stream, spring, river, or lake; the tap in their home; or even bottled water. Water is not hierarchical, so lake water is not better than tap water for the purpose of this ceremony.

Ask people to consciously gather their water, asking permission from the water and promising their care. This raises awareness, creating a conscious relationship between person and water.

Completing these small conscious acts raises the energetic vibration of their water, the molecules imprinted by individual energy, words, sounds, and thoughts.

My ritual group consists of six priestesses. You may have fewer or more, and they may be mixed gender. The ritual can be divided up among you in whatever way feels right.

Entering the ritual space, participants hold their water in both hands. They're cleansed and blessed by two priestesses: one dips a cedar bough in water and flicks a fine spray around the participant, cleansing their energetic field; the other wraps their hands around the participants hands and water, repeating the water blessing stanzas from the *Haudenosaunee Thanksgiving Address* (in translation).

Priestess: *We give thanks to all the waters of the world for quenching our thirst and providing us with strength. Water is life. We know its power in many forms—waterfalls and rain, mists and streams, rivers, and oceans. With one mind, we give our greetings and our thanks to the spirit of Water. Now our minds are one.*

Participants enter and assemble in a circle, standing.

Priestess: *The circle is cast as we pass this blue ribbon, linking person to person. Holding this ribbon, we are between the worlds, and what happens here affects all worlds.*

Four priestesses call in directions, each greeting a body of water which lays in that direction, locally. A priestess calls in the center and the ancestors: *Let us invoke Grandmother water.*

Priestess one: *Today is Ostara, spring equinox. Equinox literally means "equal night"—the day and night are equal length. The earths' axis is not tilting toward nor away from the sun. The equator is temporarily in the same plane as the sun that travels in its annual journey from the southern hemisphere to the north. The world is unified in the equality of day and night, just as we are unified in our purpose. We gather to bless the waters of the world—steam, mist, rain,* *puddles, ponds, streams, rivers, lakes, oceans, tears, and the waters of our living wombs.*

Priestess: *The ribbon symbolizes the water that moves through all of us. Hold it with your left hand, the receiving hand, and hold your water in your right hand, the giving hand. A walking meditation is done in silence. We walk in contemplation of our gratitude for water, and send blessings to it. We'll move slowly, deliberately and silently. Match your footsteps with the person in front of you. Let us walk as one. We walk withershins* (counterclockwise) *to symbolize that we are trying to undo the damage that has been done to the water.*

When it is your turn to add your water to the cauldron, silently add your blessings too. Keep your small bottle, you will need it later. We will leave the cauldron and walk deasil or (clockwise) to symbolize that from here forward we walk with water. As you walk out, raise your eyes and look at the faces that pass you, knowing we are all in this together.

One Priestess slowly leads the participants withershins around the circle, spiraling inward toward the cauldron. After emptying her bottle, she changes directions to spiral out. Another Priestess is at the other end of the ribbon. When she returns back to the circle, she speaks.

Priestess: *Please hold onto the ribbon that keeps us all connected, so we can stand in unity. Place your bottle by your chair. Pause until all are ready, standing in a circle. We stand together tonight as water bearers joined with women worldwide. We bring water from our individual lives, adding it together to create "waters of the world." We have water from many sources, many people and many bodies of water. All mixed together. She motions toward the cauldron, her hand circling.*

Like the water we are all connected. (She motions to the people, her hand circling.) *This water is blessed water.* (Motions to the cauldron.)

These people are blessed people. (Motions around the circle.)

*This water is magical water. (*Motion.)
*These people are magical people. (*Motion.)
We have charged this water individually, now let's raise our en-
ergy and charge it collectively.

Another Priestess leads the chant:
We all come from the Goddess
and to her we shall return
Like a drop of rain
flowing to the ocean

Drumming accompanies and slowly builds the tempo and volume, raising the energy. Then ending the chant. Please sit down,
still attached to the ribbon.

Priestess: *I want to teach you Ho'oponopono, an indigenous Ha-*
wai'ian practice of reconciliation and forgiveness. It includes repen-
tance, forgiveness, gratitude, and love. Please say it with me, and as
we repeat, send your message to the water on the altar.
I am sorry
Please forgive me
Thank you
I love you

This is repeated many times.

Priestess: *In the book* The Hidden Messages of Water, *Dr. Ma-*
saru Emoto photographed water molecules and showed that water
changes shape as a result of being spoken to, and exposed to music,
prayer and meditation. His research provided visual images of how
intent shapes reality.
Tonight, we individuals unite. Our individual water is united
into "waters of the world." Our individual energy is united into col-
lective magic. We move from the mundane world into the magical
world. As we prepare to go back to the mundane world, alone, let
us take some collective magic with us. The "waters of the world"
represents us all, together. We've used chant and prayer to charge

it magically. Gather your small bottles, and hold them before you, ready to receive some of the magic of unified action. As your bottle is filled, know that you receive the powerful magic of the collective, the will to protect and heal all water.

Priestesses move around the circle carefully filling each individual bottle from the cauldron. When the bottles are filled, the chalice is passed.

Priestess: *We seal our work with the blessings of the chalice. Please chant with me:*
We bless this water, we bless the ground,
we bless this chalice that we pass around.

Each participant takes a small stone from the chalice. When you return to where you came from, use this magical water to heal your waters, your people, your relationships and your lives. Magically charged water can be used in any way that water is used: to drink, cook with, for people and pets, for plants and gardens, and even for beauty and hygiene. Add a few drops to your tea, ingesting the sacred water and being nourished spiritually. Add it your family members drinks or food and talk to them about the importance of water conservation, protection and healing. Bless your pets, your gardens and your homes. Place this stone on your altar to remind you of your solid promise to the earth: to protect and heal her waters.

The directions are released and the ribbon is passed back, rolling up as the circle is opened.

Priestess: *Please sing with me and then let us feast:*
The circle is open but unbroken,
May the grace of the goddess be ever in your heart.
Merry meet, and Merry part,
and Merry meet again.

Each participant has magically charged "waters of the world" to take with them to use in the continued work of water conservation, healing, and protection.

I have used this water in my rain barrels, planters and gardens. I have offered magical water to the great Lake Ontario and the smaller lakes where I enjoy backcountry camping praying for their healing. When I use them I whisper Ho'oponopono:

I am sorry,
Please forgive me,
Thank you,
I love you.

Notes

Notes

Beltane

The Great Mother: Queen of May

Suzanne Ress

WHEN I OPEN MY front door early in the morning at the start of May, I hear the music of many dozens of birds, singing while they busily work to collect food for their newly hatched young. I see the bright green grass in the pastures, soft and sweet, it seems to grow from one hour of the day to the next. And I smell the honey-scented perfume of the black locust trees (Robinia pseudoacacia) blossoming throughout the surrounding woods. This lovely springtime fragrance lures millions of honeybees to gather the copious nectar of the trees' racemes of white flowers. Already at sunup I hear the bees happily buzzing in the trees.

The word *Beltane* comes from old Gaelic and means "blazing fire," for May Eve (April 30) and May Day (May 1) was a major festival time for our ancient Celtic predecessors, and it was a fire festival. Great bonfires were lit on the evening of April 30th and fed to burn through the night and into the next day. Sometimes animals were lead between two fires, for it was believed that the heat and smoke would purify them and increase their fertility, as it did the land. A few brave humans jumped over or ran between the fires for the same reasons.

Beltane was second in importance only to Samhain in most of the Celtic world. In parts of Wales, May 1st (Calan Mai) was even more important than Samhain. The Welsh believed that on that day a doorway opened into fairyland. The Welsh were the probable originators of the May pole dance tradition, while the rest of the Iron Age Celtic tribes were still dancing deasil around the bonfire.

Beltane was, and still is, a solar festival celebrating birth, fertility, and the blossoming forth of all life, represented symbolically by the union of the great Mother with the sun god at this beautiful time of year.

The ancient Greeks worshipped the goddess of the hunt, wild animals, virginity, and childbirth in the name and form of Artemis. Many of the ornaments, statuettes, and carvings that archaeologists have found that were connected to the Artemis cult took the form of a bee, or a female head on a bee's body. The Greeks believed that honey came down from heaven onto flowers and trees to be collected by bees, the messengers of souls.

The Beltane Buzz

On the island of Crete, in ancient times, the father of the nymphs who raised Zeus was called *Melisseus* which means "the bee man". Melissa (literally, "bee") was one of the nymphs who raised Zeus, feeding him on milk and honey. It was believed that the muses and the bees brought the gifts of song and poetry to humankind, while honey mead brought song and prophecy. Nectar and ambrosia, the food and drink of the gods, were names for mead and honey.

One day, in late April or early May, while the black locust bloomed everywhere, I lay down on an outdoor garden bench to rest for a few minutes after lunch. Predictably, I fell into a deep sleep. The air temperature was so pleasant, and the birdsong so soothing.

I was soon and suddenly awakened by a loud buzzing noise, something like dozens of flying drones hovering over my head. I sat bolt upright, realizing immediately what it was, and ran to my bee yard. In a wide, cloud-like formation above the hives, what appeared to be hundreds of thousands of buzzing bees glittered in the sunshine. A swarm! I stood and watched, willing them to land on a very low branch of a small cherry tree.

But my will was not strong enough, for they chose to alight on a thick branch of an old cherry tree about eighteen feet off the ground. I watched for about twenty minutes, until most of them had settled into the form of a long thick brown beard hanging from the branch.

It is believed that the wood on which a swarm has landed becomes imbued with magic power, and is then an excellent choice for making wands and other tools. Certainly it is true that a swarm leaves something on its branch, for once one swarm has chosen that spot, others that issue afterward will often chose the same one.

I left them alone and tended to other business: I prepared a lightweight Styrofoam swarm box with four wax frames and tossed in a cotton pad scented with lemon grass essential oil, and then I set it under the cherry tree in the sun to warm. I gathered wild *Silene vulgaris* and dandelion greens from the edges of the pasture to cook for dinner, and I picked a tender head of lettuce and a hand full of fresh chives from our garden for a salad, then I went to the chicken coop to gather the eggs our hens had laid that day.

Finally, I pulled a big heavy ladder out of storage and dragged it into the pasture where I set it up to lean next to the swarm on the high tree branch.

Then I put my protective bee suit on over my clothes, and, carrying the swarm box under one arm, I slowly climbed the ladder. In my pocket were two long coiled utility straps.

With quite a bit of difficulty, swearing, and trying not to lose my balance while looking up with my hooded mask on, I finally managed to hang the swarm box from the branch, using the utility straps, so that the bottom tip of the swarm beard was inside the box.

Just as I finished, I saw my husband walking up from the large vegetable garden he had been planting at the bottom of the hill.

"Need any help?" he called to me.

"I think it's okay," I said from up on the ladder.

"Maybe in a little while, if they all go in, you can help me get it down."

He passed on by, and I climbed down the ladder. Seeing all of our horses lined up on the other side of the fence watching me, and lustily eyeing the spring grass, I decided to let them into the pasture for an hour to graze. But before I went to them I took off my bright yellow bee suit and flung it on the grass at the foot of the ladder for when I'd need it later.

Just before opening the gate for the horses, I saw my husband pass by again. He noticed the yellow suit sprawled out on the ground at the base of the ladder, and, mistaking it for me, ran toward it at full speed!

The horses and I, watching this drama from the other side of the fence, had a good laugh when he got to the suit and realized it was empty.

A colony of bees will swarm around Beltane, either because it has outgrown its hive or because its old queen is faltering in her egg laying. In both cases a new, virgin queen is deliberately created by the colony, by nourishing an ordinary female egg/nymph on royal jelly. The swarming bees follow either the old queen or the virgin queen out of the hive, to form a new colony. From one colony come two: this is the honeybees' way to populate. A swarm is a joyous celebration, on their part, of fertility, a new virgin queen, and the blossoming of nature.

An old folk rhyme, which has a variation in just about every European language, is:

A swarm of bees in May
Is worth a load of hay,
A swarm of bees in June
Is worth a silver spoon,
A swarm in July
Is not worth a fly.

Just before swarming, all of the bees that intend to leave the original colony load their stomachs with honey. They produce a wonderful pheromonal odor similar to lemon grass essential oil, and they all rush out of the hive together, usually between 2 and 4 p.m. on a sunny day. Because their stomachs are so full and their minds are on swarming, they don't go far, and they rarely, if ever, sting.

Once a swarm has been captured and hived into a swarm box, if their queen is a virgin, the bees must wait a few days while she makes her mating flights and returns to start laying eggs. After 21 days, the first eggs will have become bees, but it will take several more weeks before the hive has enough mature forager bees to produce honey. A July swarm doesn't have enough time to produce any honey before summer's blooms come to an end, so it is considered worthless to a beekeeper.

Cave art discovered in Spain, near Valencia, has shown us that humans were already collecting honey from wild beehives in late Paleolithic times, more than 12,000 years ago. Early humans had realized that not only was honey delicious to eat, but it could be used for healing and curing various ailments, and as a preservative for food and other things. And when honey became fermented into mead, drinking it could make one feel like a god.

Mead was the first fermented drink, before both beer and wine. Most certainly the first mead was produced by accident when a too-runny, unripe honey was left and forgotten in a warm place. Whoever unsuspectingly slurped up some of that first fermented honey and became inebriated must have been truly amazed at honey's power.

The ancient Egyptians were amongst the first beekeepers. To them, the honeybee was a symbol for the human soul and rebirth. They believed that bees were made when the sun god, Ra, wept upon the Earth. His tears turned into bees that worked the flowers and trees to make honey and wax. Wax was used in sorcery to form candle likenesses of animals and humans for spell casting, and it was used to mummify the dead.

India's oldest sacred book, the *Rig-Veda* (1500–1200 BCE), written in Sanskrit, is full of allusions to honey and bees. The gods Vishnu, Krishna, and Indra were known as "Madhava"—the nectar-born ones. Their symbol is a bee.

From the *Rig-Veda*, Agni, the messenger between gods and humans, addresses both when he says:

I have partaken wisely of the sweet food
That stirs good thoughts, best banisher of troubles,
The food round which all gods and mortals,
Calling it honey, come together.

Around 900 BCE when the Biblical Proverbs were written, number 24:13–14, compares honey and honey comb to the knowledge of wisdom:

My son, eat thou honey, because it is good, and the honeycomb,
which is sweet to thy taste: So shall the knowledge of wisdom be unto
thy soul: when thou hast found it, then there shall be a sweet reward,
and thy expectation shall not be disappointed.

In present day Italy where I live, the month of May is known as "Mary's month," or the month of the Madonna. This is a remnant from the long ago Roman times of Diana (Artemis) worship, when Beltane and the month of May were times to celebrate both the virginity of the new queen and the fertility of nature. And it is certainly not by chance that international Mother's Day is celebrated everywhere on the first Sunday in May.

As a beekeeper, it is impossible for me to experience Beltane without being aware of bees, blossoms, and honey. It is this awareness that brings me closer to the old Celtic ways and the Beltane festival celebrating the great Mother, rebirth, and the blossoming of new life in all of its forms.

Cosmic Sway

Charlie Rainbow Wolf

BELTANE INTRODUCES US TO three retrograde planets: Jupiter, Saturn, and Pluto. Pluto is far enough out there that his retrograde really isn't going to have that much of an impact—not like Mercury, who insists on dancing backward through the skies every three months or so! However, Jupiter and Saturn both need a bit of attention in order to avoid potential problems later on. Let's start with Jupiter.

Jupiter turns retro every thirteen months or so, and it's backwards journey through the skies lasts approximately seventeen weeks. When a planet turns retrograde, start to focus on the "re" words; review, rethink, reconsider, reunite, respect, reconsider, regret, and more. Jupiter is the planet of growth and expansion. It's possible for things—even good things—to happen too fast. Jupiter's regular retrogrades give you time to reflect and catch your breath.

This is an excellent time to take inventory of your life and make sure that you're headed where you truly want to go. Challenges may arise, challenges that make you question whether you need to adjust your priorities, or maybe change tracks altogether. Because this is a time of "re" words, make sure you're only reflecting on what you want to see happen, and that you're prepared for it when it does.

Problems that have been growing out of hand are easier to tame when Jupiter is retrograde, giving you a less expansive energy so that you can control them. It's all about finding a balance; and Jupiter retrograde is a good time to reassess things.

Saturn is also retrograde this month, and like Jupiter, it makes a regular jaunt backwards, occurring approximately every year and lasting somewhere in the region of eighteen weeks. Saturn's title of "The Lord of Karma" is well earned, and when it turns retrograde, that's emphasized and magnified. Karma isn't any great cosmic force; it's basically just the laws of cause and effect. If you've made a mess of something in the past without taking responsibility for it, it's going to catch up with you at some time or another. Likewise, if you've been paying your dues and learning your lessons, that's going to catch up with you, too—in a good way.

Saturn retrograde demands that you look at your priorities and examine your current obligations. It asks you to slow down and evaluate things, and if you don't heed this request, then it will turn into a demand with challenges being thrown at you until you are forced to stop for one reason or another. While this may seem like a stumbling block, it's actually an asset. Once you've paused and assessed the situation, you'll be able to move forward with more determination and progress once Saturn turns direct again.

The problem with these enforced reflections is that if there was already a bad mood or a negative mindset before Saturn turned retrograde, this is now going to be amplified. Now there's a chance to look the issues straight in the eye and plan how to deal with them. It's a good idea to do this voluntarily, without having more trials thrust in the way before the lessons are learned!

It's important to face these challenges and get a plan of action formulated before Saturn turns direct again. Once Saturn stations and starts backtracking over previously covered ground there's a chance to put some of what's been learned to work, and progress and productivity should return. Saturn comes off as a hard taskmaster, but that's because it's discipline is firm. What loving father doesn't chastise his child to keep them on the straight and narrow?

So, what's the big deal—why spend so much time looking at Saturn? Well, for one, it's going to be around awhile and for two, it's still making that opposition to the Moon's north nodes—yet another karmic force in the heavens. It's also still conjunct Pluto, although it will pull away a bit because of the retrograde.

And if all this wasn't enough, Mars in Taurus is really challenging Saturn this week. There's a great potential for tensions among authority figures or against them. The best plan of action is to tend to the immediate issues first and then focus on revising the long term goals. Responsibilities may be imposed on you. If haste is applied (Mars), it has the potential to create even more consequences (Saturn). Take it day by day, step by step moment by moment. Fortunately this transit only lasts about five days.

Mars is also throwing it's weight around in an opposition to Jupiter. There's a lot of enthusiasm and a lot of energy here, but it's scattered and unfocused. It may be hard to choose just what path to follow or what you truly want. The fact that Jupiter is retrograde is actually an advantage with this aspect, because it tames some of that expansive energy. This is frustrating for Mars, which wants to get ahead, but it's in the best interests in the long run. The retrograde motion of Jupiter creates a space to examine what's truly worthwhile, and what's just a pipe dream.

Beltane Celebration: Spin Some Positive Energy

Beltane was originally a fire festival, and many still celebrate the flames of fertility at this time. It's not unusual to use fire to purify and to protect. Today, people aren't as wary of supernatural forces as our ancestors were, but it's still appropriate to use the fire as a purification or to banish something that's unwanted. There are many ways to do this, such as writing down something unwanted on paper and burning it in the fire, jumping over the fire to protect yourself from the darker side of society's traits such as prejudice or discrimination.

A simple ritual to get the energies changing in your life in a good way involves a candle, and a few moments of your time. While it's appropriate to do this at Beltane, this little trick can be used any time you're having a bad day—and I've even used it without the candle, too. All you need is a candle and about three minutes of your time. If you're doing this as a Beltane ritual, it's best to do it at sundown. Simply light the candle, and start to sing the "I'm a Little Teapot" nursery rhyme.

As you start singing, slowly spin around and around in a counterclockwise motion—or clockwise if you're in the southern hemisphere. You're winding up the energy you want to change or get rid of when you do this. Don't spin too fast or you'll make yourself dizzy!

When you get to the word "out," simply jump out of the vortex of energy that you have created. It's okay to hold onto something (or someone) so you don't fall! This isn't just a symbolic gesture, either. Just like water makes a whirlpool in the bathtub when going down the drain, you're making a cyclone of energy with your twirling. When you jump out of it, you're leaving it behind.

When you've finished, simply pinch out the candle. Trust that the flame has burned up the energy that you have hopped away from, and that things will get better. If you need to do this again in a few days, or even a few hours, go right ahead. It's effective without the candle, and very portable because there are no tools needed for it to be successful. I've even done it in the ladies room at work before today—although if you do it where people can see you, they may think you're a bit weird!

It's easy to make this a group activity. Light a small bonfire—and I stress small! If this is a large gathering, put some of the fire in a bucket, cauldron, or other fireproof container. One by one have the participant's twirl and jump the flames. Two people need to assist the jumper, one either side, to ensure that they're safe from falling. When everyone has jumped, let the small fire burn out. Participants should take a cinder from the fire to keep in a safe place, and at a later time when they need to repeat the ritual individually, they can simply jump over the cinder.

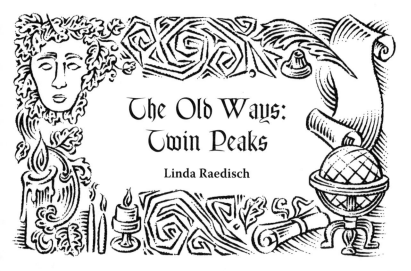

The Old Ways: Twin Peaks

Linda Raedisch

IT'S BEEN HALF A turn of the year's wheel since Halloween. Tonight is Walpurgis Night, and in some parts of Europe, little girls will be dressing up as witches again to celebrate the old belief that on April 30 witches from all over the map mounted their broomsticks and flew to the Brocken, a grim mountain in north-central Germany, for the biggest sabbat of the year. So this seems like a good time to ask: What were they wearing?

The witches of medieval folk and fairytale wore kerchiefs or nothing at all, but many of today's Walpurgisnacht celebrants will be wearing pointy hats. In a nineteenth-century engraving of sixteenth-century Scotsman John Fian's coven, the witches flying round the churchyard are wearing pointy hats too. Had such a coven actually existed, they would certainly not have been, for the high-crowned, broad-brimmed black felt hat did not become a cutting-edge accessory until the early 1600'.

In her portrait of 1616, Rebecca Rolfe, a.k.a. Pocahontas, signals her acceptance into English society by wearing the Geneva or Pilgrim's Hat, as it was known. Though high in the crown, Rebecca's hat has a flat top. In the waning days of the black felt hat's popularity, the crown was shortened, and the brim turned up at the sides, giving us the hat we are now used to seeing on the Quaker Oats man. By the 1700s, the only people still wearing the classic pilgrims hat were the Welsh and a handful of old crones living in the backwaters of North America, the very women most likely to be suspected of witchcraft, though the drive to torture and execute them had finally waned.

Witches and Hats

To this day, Mother Goose wears a pilgrim's hat dressed up with ribbon, buckle and white, frilled cap. While Mother Goose's conservatism makes her merely quaint, the witch figure is an unkind exaggeration of the old Puritan woman living alone on the outskirts of town, eschewing merriment in all its forms and scowling at passersby. Just as her character was exaggerated, so was her hat: the rim grew as broad as a cake plate, while the crown rose so high that the only logical outcome was that it should come to a point.

And at this point, dear readers, some of you will have risen from your comfortable chairs and tossed this book aside in order to defend the great antiquity of the witch's hat. A handful of you might even be asking, flabbergasted, "What about the Three Witches of Subeshi?"

For those of you still seated, the Three Witches of Subeshi is the name given in fondness to the remains of three ladies who were buried in a hilltop cemetery in the Qizil-tagh, or "Flaming Mountains," of Western China, sometime between 500 and 300 BCE. The area now belongs to the People's Republic of China, but most of its population are Turkic-speaking Uighurs. We don't know what language our so-called Witches spoke because, while their bones and personal effects have been preserved by the merciless aridity of the sands, they left no written records.

The Flaming Mountains are just northeast of the Tarim Basin, one of the driest regions in the world. In our witches' day, before the rivers changed course, it would have been a little easier to make a living here in the foothills. Our Three Witches could have kept their sheep and goats close by instead of having to drive them up into the mountains each summer. They also raised wheat and millet and exchanged some of their goods with the footloose nomads who trickled down into the valley. Some of those nomads decided to stay, taking up farming but retaining their own peculiar fashion sense as they merged with the descendants of the Ayding Lake People who flourished here in the late Bronze Age.

Unfortunately, our witches are not as well preserved as some of the older mummies of the Tarim Basin. They are not much more than well-dressed skeletons, but their initial resemblance to Halloween witches is striking. A pouch containing a humble cosmetics kit accompanied the Hightop Witch, as I like to call her. She wore short, pale leather boots, the kind of moccasins worn by the Navajo and Apache of America's Desert Southwest. Once she had pulled on her hightops, she could have used the pointed stick of kohl to outline her eyes, reddened her cheeks with the ochre and even whitened her face either for ritual purposes or to make it look as if she had not been out minding the sheep all day in the bright sun. She had a comb, too, for combing the legions of nits out of her long hair before she bound it up inside a black yarn hairnet. Netting covered the brim of her charcoal-gray hat as well: a hat that, at almost a yard in height, had to be placed beside her in the grave. The crown, which tapered to a rounded point, was held up by sticks jammed inside it.

The Mitten Witch was buried in a fleece-lined cloak thrown over the shoulders of her brown wool blouse and a skirt woven in narrow horizontal stripes of red, blue, purplish brown and mustard gold. Her delicate leather slippers were stitched to her woven stockings, to save time in dressing, I suppose. While the crown of the Mitten Witch's hat was only about two feet tall, it culminated in not one but two emphatically pointed peaks. Soft-brimmed, the Mitten Witch's hat is more like a hood than a hat. And, oh yes, she wears what appears to be a falconer's mitten on her left hand.

The Winter Witch was the proud owner of yet another double-peaked hat, this one with a sort of veil hanging down from it and covering her face. Her grave contained a generous array of personal and household objects as well as a husband. The couple were both bundled up against the cold in jackets and boots and most likely died in winter.

So what is the history of these "witches' hats"? Back in the Bronze Age, people with distinctly Caucasian looks had wandered into the Tarim Basin, probably from the west. They wore a variety of molded felt caps that rose to soft peaks and were festooned with red and yellow cords and little bunches of feathers. They were more like the Phrygian caps known to the ancient Greeks than witches' hats. Though the people of Subeshi were probably in part descended from these Bronze Age wanderers, they were neither Caucasian nor East Asian, but something in between, like many Central Asians today. Our Witches' exaggerated crowns were more directly inspired by the headdresses of the Saka, a complex of tribal peoples who represented the eastern end of the cultural spectrum which ended with the Scythians in the west. The Sakas' distant, literate cousins, the Persians, divided these roving bands into the "Haoma-worshipping Saka," the "Saka from over the Sea" (Scythians) and the "Pointed Cap Saka."

Our Witches were the contemporaries, or near contemporaries, of the "Ice Princess" who lived to the north and west of Subeshi, on the other side of the Altai Mountains. The Ice Princess was laid in her wooden coffin with a three-foot-tall plume of black felt held up by wooden rods and was just one of a number of "princesses," "warrior priestesses," and "Amazons" who wore their unwieldy headgear into the emerald pastures of the afterlife. The Ice Princess was also sent off with golden ornaments and a tunic of wild silk.

Though by no means wealthy, the Three Witches of Subeshi were certainly women of high standing, possibly priestesses and probably not "witches" at all. So, is there anything to be said for the Great Antiquity of the Witch's Hat? The putting of tall, pointy hats on the heads of important people was an established practice among early Indo-European-speakers such as the Hittites, Persians and Scythians. Europe lies at the far western end of that cultural horizon. Could some memory of the pointy hat have persisted in the English-speaking world into the nineteenth century? Maybe.

Resources

Barber, Elizabeth Wayland. *The Mummies of Ürümchi*. New York: W. W. Norton and Company, 1999.

Mair, Victor H. "Mummies of the Tarim Basin," *Archaeology*, March/April 1995.

Mallory, J. P., and Victor H. Mair. *The Tarim Mummies: Ancient China and the Mystery of the Earliest Peoples from the West*. New York: Thames and Hudson, 2000.

Feasts and Treats

Blake Octavian Blair

THE ARRIVAL OF BELTANE usually brings with it the variable weather of late spring, where the weather can range from cool and breezy to hot and sunny. It brings the challenge of preparing a menu that can stand up to either case. The dishes in this line up should satisfy the appetite of either occasion. With lovely Mediterranean flavors, fresh vegetables, and both bright and decadently rich flavors, this menu brings a hearty but not heavy feast to the table. Dress up your Beltane feast table with beautiful seasonal flowers and garlands that remind us of the maypole and that spring is indeed in full swing!

Fresh Springtime Strawberry and Spinach Salad

This salad brings a lot of classic fresh spring and early summertime ingredients together in a combination that creates a bright and refreshing dish. It has enough body to serve as a light meal perfect for warmer days when served in larger portions, or makes a wonderful starter to a full feast menu when served in smaller portions. You can serve it with or without the tempeh, however, it adds a nutty flavor and a nice dose of protein that I feel really round out the dish when served as an entrée. Kick off your Beltane with the bright sweetness of strawberries!

Prep time: 20 minutes
Serves: 2–4

For the dressing:

¼ cup balsamic vinegar
1 tsp Dijon mustard
Salt (to taste)
Cracked black pepper (to taste)
½ cup olive oil

For the salad:

3 tbsp sunflower seeds
2 tbsp olive oil
8 ounces tempeh, sliced into strips
10 ounces spinach
3 tbsp blue cheese
5 ounces strawberries, sliced
¼ red onion, chopped

Begin by preparing the balsamic vinaigrette dressing. First add the balsamic vinegar, Dijon mustard, salt, and cracked black pepper into a large medium sized bowl. Mix ingredients until well combined. Next, while whisking, drizzle the olive oil into the bowl until well combined with ingredients. Set aside.

Next, add the sunflower seeds to a cold dry skillet and turn on to medium heat, stir frequently until aromatic and a slight golden brown color and glistening appearance is achieved. Remove from heat.

To cook the tempeh, add the olive oil to a medium sized skillet and preheat over medium heat. Add the tempeh strips into preheated skillet. Cook for approximately 5 minutes, turn strips over, and cook second side for another 5 minutes or until golden brown color is achieved.

Now, into a large salad or serving bowl, add the spinach, blue cheese, strawberries, red onion, sunflower seeds, and tempeh. Pour dressing over top and toss until thoroughly coating all ingredients. Serve and enjoy!

Steamed Artichokes

A favorite simple dish in our house is steamed artichokes. They can stand alone as an entire meal, or they can be a wonderfully fun appetizer, just adjust the portion size. A classic *beurre blanc*, or white butter, is a classic French sauce made with equal parts white wine and white wine vinegar, but this adaptation imparts a unique flavor for a decadent holiday treat of feasting caliber! There is some work to eating artichokes; it is what I call an interactive food. You'll want to put a "graveyard" bowl on the table for the inedible portions of the petals to be tossed in during eating. However, there is no combination quite like butter and artichokes.

Prep time: 10 minutes
Cook time: 25–60 minutes (~half inactive)
Serves: 2–4

4 large whole artichokes
3 tbsp all-purpose seasoning

For the beurre blanc
1 tbsp diced onion
¼ cup cooking sherry, mead, or other alcohol
¼ cup apple cider vinegar
1 lb butter cut into 1 tbsp pieces
Salt to taste
Cracked pepper to taste

Begin by placing a few inches of water into a large cooking pot with a steamer basket placed inside. Bring water to a boil and add artichokes into the pot. Cover and let steam until tender. This will take anywhere from 25–60 minutes depending on the size of the artichokes. This is a popular dish and has been cooked many times in our house. The cooking time has varied, so be sure to test before serving for doneness. This is easily achieved by seeing if you can pull off a petal and taste. If it isn't done, you'll have extreme difficulty removing the petal, and further the edible portion will not be tender. When done, serve with beurre blanc in a bowl for dipping.

You can prepare the beurre blanc while the artichokes are steaming. To prepare the beurre blanc, place onion, alcohol, and vinegar in a medium saucepan and reduce by three quarters to a syrup. While whisking continuously, add butter 1–2 pieces at a time. Do not add more butter until what has previously been added has completely melted. Adding all the butter will take approximately 15–20 minutes. Strain through a fine mesh to remove the onion chunks, season with salt and pepper. A little added garnish and seasoning of white pepper makes for a pleasing presentation. Serve immediately.

Note: For those of you who may have never tried eating a whole artichoke before and want to give this a shot, it can be a little mystifying, but really it's quite easy. You pull the petals off and scrape them between your teeth to pull off the fleshy edible part, and you discard the unedible portion of the petals. At the end, you're left with the artichoke heart. You'll find a hairy looking part on top. Don't eat the hairy part! That's called the choke and it'll be most unpleasant to eat. Scrape that part off with a fork or spoon, then cut up the heart and dip in the buerre blanc to eat.

Mediterranean Inspired Pasta

Our shamanic and druidic sister, Susan, is fairly famous among her loved ones for a simple delicious pasta dish that uses ingredients easy to stock back into the pantry. The whole dish comes together fairly fast, and yet it tastes as though the flavors have been melding for hours. She happily bequeathed me her recipe and allowed me to develop it further into my own variation. When I was designing menus for this book, she and I both thought a variation would be a lovely fit for a summer Beltane evening!

Prep time: 5 minutes
Cook time: 20 minutes
Serves: 5–6

1 cup sliced green olives
1 8-ounce jar of sun dried tomatoes in oil
1 14-ounce can diced tomatoes
⅓ cup capers
1 lb rotini or other pasta
Olive oil (to taste)
8 ounce log of goat cheese

In a medium saucepan add the green olives, sundried tomatoes, diced tomatoes, and capers. Set on medium low heat to warm. Bring a large pot of water to a boil and then add pasta and cook until al dente, 9–12 minutes. Drain pasta in colander.

Add in the vegetable mixture from saucepan and the drained pasta back to the pot and mix until all ingredients are well combined. Add olive oil as needed to get an even coat of the entire mixture. Note: how much you will have to add varies and it's up to your culinary judgement. There will be some oil existing from the sun-dried tomatoes.

Serve into bowls and place goat cheese on table so that diners may add the desired amount on top of their dishes.

Chocolate Strawberry Milkshake

Beltane in many areas of the globe can have quite warm weather. There is nothing better than a cold sweet treat on a hot day. This chocolate strawberry milkshake fits the bill for Beltane quite nicely. Frankly, Beltane should have sexy foods. It's a fertility holiday for goddess sake! Strawberries and chocolate both make that list. Is it a standalone treat? Is it a desert? Can it be served alongside the main feast? The answer to all of these questions is of course, yes! Actually, I think it makes a really creative drink for cakes and ale ceremonies during the sabbat ritual, but be sure to pop them into the freezer beforehand and pull them out just before so they don't melt!

Prep time: 5 minutes (per milkshake)

Serves: 1

½ cup frozen strawberries
3 large scoops chocolate ice cream
½ cup milk (more as desired for consistency)
2 tbsp chocolate syrup

Add all ingredients into a blender. Blend until desired thickness and consistency is reached. If your mixture is too thick, add additional milk to thin to desired consistency. Serve and add additional frozen strawberries and chocolate syrup to top as desired. Serve in a glass with a spoon and straw.

Crafty Crafts

Natalie Zaman

CORN DOLLIES: THEY'RE NOT just for the harvest anymore—at least, when they're made from something other than corn. Flowers lend themselves to "dollery" just as much as wheat sheaves and corn stalks. This craft combines the concept of the corn dollie (a human figure made of natural materials that symbolizes spirit, or, in this case, the Goddess) with the traditional voodoo doll or doll baby.

Voodoo dolls are sewn and stuffed with personal items, or pinned with trinkets and photos making them highly personalized and powerful magical tools. Doll babies are rubber or ceramic figurines submerged in a charged brew of oils, herbs, trinkets, and more likely than not, glitter, and sealed in a jar. Our Goddess doll baby will combine a bit of all of these elements: seasonal, natural materials, intentions, glitter (needed for the doll baby aesthetic!) and wax to hold it all together and seal it. The result is a charming effigy bound with your intention that you can send to the universe on Beltane's goodly fire (or in any bonfire ritual).

What follows are instructions to raft a basic doll baby. You can make them with pretty much any kind of plant or flower (or combination thereof). Refer to the table for help in determining what herbs and colors to use for specific intentions. You can also use your favorite reference, and more importantly, your own intuition and feelings. Magic is always most efficacious when it comes from the heart.

Time Lavished: A Goddess doll baby making session will take some time, especially if you're growing and drying your herbs and flowers (this can take 2-3 weeks). Actual construction will last about two hours and that includes time for the wax to melt and cool. If you're creating these dolls as part of a ritual, allow time for the creation of sacred space and any other preparations your tradition dictates.

CoinageRequired : You can buy flowers and herbs to use for this Craft, but consider wild harvesting or growing them. Besides being frugal, this extra step adds magical potency to your work. If you purchase everything, supplies will costs about $20–$25.

Supplies

Dried herbs and flowers
Essential oils
String or cord for binding
Heat-proof receptacle to melt candle wax. Never melt wax in a microwave or over direct heat—it's a fire hazard!
Bees or soy wax
Tongs
Glitters

Begin by dripping drops of essential oil onto the plants you'll be using, keeping in mind the purpose of your doll. Refer to the chart on the next page to create dolls for specific intentions:

Intention	Plants	Oils	Glitter and Wax Colors
Psychic Development	Lilac, mint, mugwort, honeysuckle, rosemary	Frankincense, myrrh, patchouli, peppermint	Purple and White
Fertility and Creativity	Dandelion, red clover, raspberry leaf	Sandalwood, patchouli, cinnamon, clove, vanilla	Red and White and/or Orange
Love and Passion	Basil, catnip, daisy, dandelion, violet, thyme, rosemary	Rose, lilac, ylangylang, neroli, patchouli, vetiver	Pink (Red for passion)
Prosperity and Growth	Basil, honeysuckle, juniper	Patchouli, mint, cinnamon	Green and Gold
Cleansing	Sage, Lavender	Lavender	Blue and White
Protection	Basil, barley, blackberry, calendula, catnip, clover	Patchouli, tea tree, cypress, eucalyptus	Black

Gather the herbs and flowers into a bunch. Trim the stems so that the length from flower tip to stem tip is about six inches. Bind the bundle near the flowered end to form the doll's head. Alternatively, you can bind the doll about an inch below the cut stems and make that the head; the flowers below will form the fullness of the doll's skirt. If you choose to craft the doll this way, trim the stems after you bind them so that they are even.

Take some of the plain stems that you just trimmed and gather them into a bundle; these will be the doll's arms. Lay them on your

workspace and then set the doll on top of them so that together they form a cross. The bottom of the doll's head should sit just above the arm bundle.

Bind the arms to the body with a piece of cord. Slip the cord behind the doll underneath the first binding that you made. Criss-cross the cords in front of her, then wrap them around the back to do the same. Wrap the cords several times around the body and arms to secure them, then knot the cord off. Trim the arms so that they are neat on the ends and even on both sides.

Melt the beeswax in a container that will allow you to dip the entire doll into it. Allow the wax to cool slightly before dipping your doll in the wax using the tongs (Even slightly cooled, liquid wax can burn!). You may need to dip her several times to cover her completely. If you don't have a container that's deep enough, use a ladle or spoon to pour the wax over the doll. Roll or sprinkle the doll in the appropriately colored glitter and your Goddess Doll Baby is ready to burn!

The intentions in the chart provided were designed with the spirit of Beltane in mind, however, you can make Goddess Doll Babies for any intention: clarity, contentment, friendship and healing…the possibilities are endless. Use your favorite reference (and your own intuition and experience) to determine the plants and colors to work with.

Portable Magic

Mickie Mueller

IT'S BELTANE AND LOVE is in the air during this lusty month of May! I know many of us would rather be dancing around a bonfire in a field or weaving a maypole to celebrate this sabbat of love, growth and abundance. Instead it's the middle of the week and we're running to the bank, sitting in traffic or waiting in line at the post office. We live in a different world than our ancestors did, but that doesn't mean that we can't honor the sabbat on the actual day. I've been blessed enough to have enjoyed a few Beltane's with a large group of Pagans in the woods, drumming, drinking mead, and sharing fellowship. Even though life demands that I can't do that every year, (and certainly not on a weekday) I try to come up with ways to make it a special day by taking my magic along with me even if I have mundane activities to do far from the fires of Beltane.

Florida Water Spritz

Flowers are an important part of any Beltane celebration. Florida water is not named after the state but comes from the Spanish word *florido*, which means flowery or "full of flowers." If you can't go around throughout the day in a crown of flowers this Beltane, Florida Water may be the next best thing. This scented water has been used in home remedies and many magical traditions since the 1800s. It's great for stress relief, good luck, protection, and clearing away negativity. There are many recipes to make your own—I created this one ages ago after experimenting with several recipes and ingredients I already had or could get locally. I love this one; I use it regularly to clear negativity in a room or in my aura. This has become a staple at my house, and I do think you'll love it too. You'll need a spray bottle to keep it in. Fill the spray bottle about three-quarters with bottled spring water. Add six drops of each, rose oil, lavender oil, bergamot oil, one drop each of frankincense and clove oil if you have it. Add one tablespoon of lemon juice to the mixture. Now fill it the rest of the way with vodka. Shake it up and spritz yourself with it on Beltane morning. Shake it and use it any time you need to de-stress or clear away negativity.

Abundance Honey

You can usually find honey straws at your local farmers market, produce stand, or health food stores. I've seen them from time to time at grocery stores or big box stores too; you'll need only one honey straw for this spell. Honey is a very magical ingredient and is produced of course by bees, some of the most productive creatures in nature. This honey spell is meant to bring good fortune and blessings of abundance your way on Beltane. Place a honey straw in a jar full of coins overnight, it's ok if the coins don't entirely cover the straw, just add all the coins you have on hand. Set the jar outside in the evening on Beltane eve so that the spirits of the land may impart their blessings on the honey. The next morning grab your honey straw when you're on your way out the door and carry it along with you on Beltane. Enjoy it with lunch or for a snack, as you do, let the enchanted honey feed your cells and become part of you. Upon returning home, leave one of the coins under a tree or somewhere in nature as a gift to the spirits, a bit of honey from your honey jar would probably be an appropriate offering as well.

Heal Your Heart with Rose Quartz

Beltane is a sabbat we think about when we think about love; whether you're already in a relationship, looking for that special someone, or happily single, our hearts are important for our well-being. Rose quartz is a wonderful stone to carry in order to open your heart, not just to romance, but every kind of love, including the all important love for yourself. I really appreciate the energy of rose quartz for healing and opening your heart which is a really appropriate way to honor the sabbat of Beltane. If you have any rose-quartz jewelry, break it out to wear on Beltane. If not, it's pretty easy to find a stone. I've seen them at metaphysical shops, gem shops, even craft stores and big box stores sometimes have rose quartz jewelry if you don't have other options. Run your rose quartz under running water to cleanse it of any residual energy, and visualize it washing away. Hold it to your heart and ask the stone in your own words to heal your heart and open it to love. Hold it there as long as you wish. Now wear it or carry it with you on Beltane. Every time throughout the day that you feel warmth in your heart, no matter the reason, recognize the magic of Beltane working through the rose quartz.

Wear Colors of the Day

Clothing was always an important part of Beltane, many people wore their best finery to May festivals, bright cheerful colors for celebrating. Although you don't have to wear your finest clothes, think about the colors you choose and the energies they impart on Beltane.

White is often associated together with red on Beltane. Wearing white on Beltane symbolizes the cleansing, purifying, and clearing of your personal energy field.

Red is the color of vitality, passion, and strength, a perfect color for your Beltane wardrobe. It was traditional to jump over a fire for purification on Beltane, if there won't be any bonfires in your area to leap, wear some red to represent fire and renewal.

Pink may seem a sweet and romantic color, or like a color of self love, but it's also related to sexuality and passion. Decide your purpose and wear some pink on Beltane to work with the energies of the day.

Green is a great Beltane color to wear—it's the color of fertility, and this sabbat takes it to a whole new level. Celebrants used to "Go a-Maying," or "Green the Fields," which meant running off to have sex outside, blessing the land with fertility. Wear green on Beltane to honor the spirits of nature, growth, fertility, and abundance.

Sabbat on the Go Tips

Carry the Empress tarot card with you in a 3 × 5 inch rigid plastic sleeve. Meditate on her power of fertility, inner and outer beauty and, love of self. See if you can bring her Venus energy into your day.

Have a spa day, or at least a spa hour. Even picking up a facial mask or pedicure kit on your lunch break or on the way home can be a lovely way to celebrate love for yourself and tap into the beauty vibes of the day. Want to really splurge? Check out your local massage therapy school—they usually offer really affordable massages.

Before you leave for the day, run your hands over the grass to gather a bit of dew and wash it over your face. According to tradition, Beltane dew imparts beauty.

Beltane Ritual: The May Queen

Suzanne Ress

THIS RITUAL IS TO be performed after sunset on the evening of April 30. All participants should read through and become familiar with the ritual a day or more beforehand.

In a safe and private outdoor location, build two bonfires, leaving a space of at least eight feet between them. Build these up well ahead of time so that when the sun goes down and participants begin to arrive the fires are blazing steadily. Make sure to check local fire ordinances and obtain a fire permit if necessary.

You will need to assemble the following items:

Four beeswax candles and a lighter
Honey, and a tiny spoon. Raw, local honey is most suitable.
A chalice
A bottle of mead
Some wood from a branch where a swarm has landed. If this is not obtainable, a stick from a hawthorn tree can be substituted.
A small triangle of paper for each participant.
A hand full or more of dried bay and hawthorn leaves.
After-ritual refreshments to make a light meal. Suggestions: things to cook on skewers over a fire, such as hot dogs, veggie dogs, sausages. Salads, and cold dishes. Honey cakes.

Participants shall be instructed to arrive just after sunset, dressed in brightly colored festive clothing and adorned with tassels, bells, ribbons and flowers.

One participant shall be elected Queen, and she shall lead the ritual. The others will follow her in dance and song.

Set up an altar at least eight feet away from the two bonfires but balanced evenly between them. On the altar place the four beeswax candles, one to the east, the south, the west, and the north. At the center place the lighter.

Participants shall stand before the altar, with the two bonfires burning behind them. One participant will hold the bottle of mead and the chalice, and another will hold the jar of honey and the spoon. The Queen stands at the altar, facing the others and the bonfires. She lights the four candles, starting with the one representing the east, and says,

I light and call upon thee, element of air!

Then, moving clockwise to the south, she will say, or sing out,

Come amongst us, oh, element of fire!

Light the candle. Next, she will light the western facing candle, and exclaim,

Element of water, I invoke thee with this flame!

And finally, she will light the northern candle, and say,

I light and call upon thee, element of earth!

The participants will all say in unison,

Queen of all blossoming nature and all of the elements, great Mother Earth, to thee we pay homage, bringing nectar and ambrosia.

The participant who carries the bottle of mead and the chalice will step forward and offer these items to the Queen, who will take them and place them at the center of the altar.

Then the participant who holds the honey and the spoon will step forward and offer these things to the Queen's outstretched hands.

All participants will form a circle around the Queen and the altar, and they will hold the palms of their hands facing upward to her. Using the small spoon, the Queen will move deasil around the circle, anointing each participant's palms with three drops of honey, saying,

The gift you give to me will come back to you threefold.

When she has finished, the Queen steps back behind the altar, and places the honey and spoon in its center, then fills the chalice with mead. She now carries the chalice to the participants, saying,

Let us drink together of nature's wisdom.

Each participant shall take a small sip of mead, and, after she has served the last one, the Queen herself will drink what is left in the chalice. Participants now say in unison,

We work together, toward a sweet and useful result, and always while working we sing and dance and enjoy the scents of flowers and the warmth and the sunshine. We support you, our Queen, great Mother Earth, knowing that what is good for you is good for us as well.

The Queen now begins to dance, and, as she dances, she sings out,

Full of honey may the flowers be!
Rich in honey may our earth be!
Rich in honey may our lives be!

Everyone will follow her in dancing, and singing, and whosoever wishes may invent some new song or chant or dance, or otherwise praise the earth in whatever way she desires.

The magic branch, whether it be a branch from a swarm, or a small hazel branch, may now be consecrated by the Queen moving it briefly above each of the candle flames and anointing it with three drops of wax, three drops of honey, and three drops of mead. It shall be left on the altar for the remainder of the ritual.

The Queen will now distribute a small triangle of paper with a few crumbles of dried leaves in its center onto the outstretched left palm of each participant. Everyone shall close their eyes and spend some moments of silence visualizing whatever it is they need most at that time in their lives flowing toward them like a river of honey. These needs can have anything to do with fertility, happiness, or purification. The Queen can lead participants in this visualization if desired, describing in detail the beautiful golden flow.

When enough time has elapsed, participants crumble the triangle around the dried leaves, wiping the drops of honey onto the paper, and, one at a time, step out of the circle and approach one of the bonfires and toss their packet in.

Now, whoever feels so inclined may take off all or most of their clothes and finery, and dance between and around the two bonfires, chanting, singing, laughing, whistling, or whatever she sees fit to do.

When this merry making begins to wind down, the Queen (who certainly may participate with the others if she chooses), shall call down and close the quarters, and blow out the candles, starting at the north, then the west, the south, and the east.

Refreshments should be served at this time. The party after the ritual may go on for as long as desired, into the next morning, but make certain to put out the fires safely after leaving the place.

Notes

Notes

Litha

Kosmesis for Summer Solstice

Deborah Castellano

KOSMESIS IS THE ART(E) of adorning one's self, and there are examples of it through out mythopoetic history as well as in real life customs. We'll get into those, but my favorite examples are from pop culture. Think makeover montages: my personal favorites are Wonder Woman because Diana is not an idle doll-like recipient, and complains about functionality of World War I fashion and St. Trinian's because Annabelle gets a makeover from all the school's factions and she keeps the parts she likes best from each, making a new fashion statement.

But kosmesis and the makeover montage have existed for a while. A long while. Like, since *The Iliad* from 760 BC and Hesiod's *Works and Days* in 8th century BC, so this is far from a new idea. In *The Illiad*, Hera was so pissed off that Paris called Aphrodite the prettiest she was willing to go to war about it. Literally. She constantly supported Greece because she didn't like the Trojans and Paris. She gets Athena to agree to help her because Paris, and by default, all his friends, spurned her too. *The Illiad* is sort of a SyFy soap of its time, so there's lots of fighting and changing sides, deity involvement and glory, but in order to be sure that those of us who like more of a soapy romance/betrayal sort of storyline keep tuning in, there's a separate book called T*he Deception of Zeus,* which was really scandalous for its time. Like little Rory Gilmore's actress from *The Gilmore Girls* going onto be a badass gender traitor on the mini series version of *The Handmaid's Tale*. And what they do to her for being a gender traitor, which, spoiler, was horrific.

Anyway, eventually Zeus is like "knock it off!" No more gods in this mortal war. I can't deal with all of you doing all this crazy crap all the time. Hera's like, challenge accepted, husband. So Hera does a full makeover montage (kosmesis) where she makes herself extra sexy for Zeus—she does her hair, her makeup, she puts on the perfume he likes, she puts on the dress Athena made her/said she looked hot in (...for her dad) and goes to Aphrodite and is like, *look*. Do you like men telling you what to do? Because I sure don't. Also, I don't like not being allowed to touch this war because we started it and we should be allowed to finish it too, am I right? And Aphrodite, in response, says I'm 110 percent not in favor of being told what to do by Zeus. But also I'm still the prettiest. Hera's, frustrated, has a plan. So she seduces Zeus and Aphrodite puts him to sleep so they can go about their war business and not be bothered. Hera's team, Greece, wins the war and she gets to have both the satisfaction of being a successful warmonger and the knowledge her husband still wants her.

Pandora is also a story of kosmesis. She may have started out as a goddess, but research about such matters gets a little shaky because this was a very, very long time ago. If she was a goddess, she was probably some kind of fertility demigoddess. Either way, mythos decided to make her human, and that's the version we kept. In this particular version, she became the gods' Barbie doll, where everyone wanted a chance to play with her. They named her, they adorned her, they gave her a bath, they gave her great hair, they gave her deception, and they gave her a mission. Pandora's mission was to be the all-giver. Which meant that she was to be all giving of both misery and hope. Meanwhile, Promethus is getting a bad vibe from this whole crazy makeover party happening and he tells Epipmetheus not to mess with any gifts from Zeus. Epimetheus agrees, but then Pandora is like, hey, Epimetheus. And Epimetheus says, hey Pandora. I like your hair. Let's get married. And Pandora is like, it's great, right? Yeah let's tie the knot, babe. Oh by the way, I'm going to just dump out the contents of my jar all over the place so humans can have the full spectrum of experience. You're welcome! Fear is fun, right? I'm just going to keep hope here in my jar though. For today, let's say humans still have hope.

Kosmesis was often used as a way to mark a rite of passage for women historically. When a bride would get married during ye olde Illiad days, there were strict rules about bathing before getting married. The water always had to come from a running water source and hauled back to where the bride was getting ready. It was such a process that the brides often kept the vase (*loutrophoros*) used to bring the water to her on her wedding day as a souvenir. While bathing is a lot easier in this day and age of indoor plumbing, it's still often part of our modern kosmesis rites, partly because we're really into hygiene as a modern society and partly because there's still hints of magic about the process of bathing.

In daily life, there are actually intricate rules that guide what we wear to what and what we don't wear to something. It can be argued that while our bodies are ours, all cultures have some form of adornment; there are few cultures where nudity is accepted with no jewelry, body paint, or some form of adornment. As such, while our bodies belong to ourselves, what we put on our bodies to make them socially acceptable belongs both to ourselves and our cultural norms, which we use as markers to determine what to do when we want to blend in and what to do when we want to stand out.

We make these decisions on nearly a subconscious basis of what we know by our cultural markers regarding what's appropriate to wear where and if we want to stand out or blend in. For example, if you work in a very rigid corporate environment, you are probably not going to wear a corset and leather pants to work. Conversely, if you are going to a nightclub, you probably are not going to wear an immaculately pressed business suit. Think about what you would wear to a job interview, as a wedding guest, as a funeral attendee, at the bowling alley, at a cocktail party where there are people you want to impress, dinner with friends, dinner with your in-laws. Think about what you would wear to make a statement in each of these events and what you would wear to each of these events to not be noticed. Dress "code" is so important it tends to take on a moral ethic. When people describe how someone is dressed, words associated with morality are often used. Impeccably dressed. Badly dressed. This heavy amount of social pressure in how we are perceived in society by our dress leads most of us to feel embarrassed if we are underdressed because it illustrates that we don't know how to behave in society; if our garments are stained it makes us seen as ill-kempt, or if our underthings are showing when we would not want them to be, we are inadvertently exposing our potentially naked bodies for unintended view by others. Because of the moral aspect to dressing, it is far more likely that you will feel self conscious about being somewhat under dressed because of the societal shame associated with it rather than being somewhat overdressed, which will feel conspicuous but also gives us an air of societal superiority. If we are too overdressed, however, we will loop back around to shame because, again, it shows that we did not know how to behave in this particular environment.

Think about the common stress dream that many people have about being completely unadorned (and naked) in front of a classroom or a boardroom. The dreamer often feels shame in those dreams because adornment is so finely and subconsciously linked to one's sense of self. While just about everyone dresses unreflexively to do basic mundane tasks like running errands, taking your kids to after school activities, going to bed with a long term partner, this simply balances the scale for when we need to dress very deliberately for an important work event, for a new group of friends, for a first date. It's also about context. Think about the example of a first date. What would you wear when you already have butterflies for this new person and want to impress them? What would you wear if you want to see how the date goes but aren't sure if you want anything intimate to happen? What would you wear if you were going on this date out of politeness and definitely didn't want anything intimate to happen? There would probably be some differences there, even if they were small like putting on more deodorant (or not), washing your mouth with mouthwash (or not), what scent you would chose to wear, what underthings you would chose to wear (or not), if you wore make up (or not), how you did your hair, which t-shirt or dress you would chose to wear, and if you would iron it or lint roll it first. There could also be larger differences involved going between those possibilities such as how revealing or tight your clothing choices are, how fashionable with the current trends you chose to appear, or if you intentionally dress "lower" than you usually would. Are you trying to match the other person in some way so that they feel closer to you (she always wears black, so I'm wearing black, he always wears a tie so I'm going to wear a tie)?

So, we've got the mythos and we've got the historical context. That can only leave witchcraft. Kosmesis is the first part most modern occultists want to ditch. But why? If you are practicing witchcraft in the twenty-first century, you are already doing something that's scoffed at by the majority of society; why would adornment be the straw that broke your camel's back? You're already wearing robes, buying crystals, chanting, using spices not for their intended purposes, making up symbols and getting together with a bunch of fellow witches to do these things together, but somehow you feel that this knife fight that we call magic only requires the knives that you feel comfortable with already. Because as we all know, witchcraft is totally dependent on feeling safe and comfortable and never stepping outside your comfort zone or doing things we find strange and difficult to get the results we want.

Right.

If you've tried any version of kosmesis, you know how powerful it can be, and here's an opportunity to learn how to really just get in there with it. If you haven't tried a version of kosmesis before because you think that's crap girl magic (regardless of your gender), then now would be an excellent time to challenge that preconceived notion.

Let's talk summer solstice. It's the first day of summer, the last hoorah of the light part of the year spilling over with fertility, abundance, and celebration. The air is awash in the heat of the festival season.

It's also here in this heat, in this bounty of fresh strawberries, honey, elderflowers, and lavender that we start to welcome the return of the dark, every day becoming shorter from this day until winter solstice. We'll be back in the belly of the beast of winter before we know it, it's the last holiday on the light side of the year. Everything will begin dying soon.

But not yet.

It's a bit of a head trip if you spend enough time really considering this tenuous bit of the tightrope we walk together as we circle the wheel of the year. So let's use kosmesis to really dive into it.

Cosmic Sway

Charlie Rainbow Wolf

LITHA KICKS OFF WITH some interesting planetary weather. Saturn is still retrograde, still making that wide conjunction with Pluto, and still creating a double dose of karma. Jupiter and Pluto are also retrograde, and Neptune joined them just a few hours ago.

Neptune retrograde (until November 26) isn't really something that's going to have particular significance because it's an outer planet. However, it is in its ruling sign of Pisces at the moment (2012–2025), so that puts a bit more oomph to its movements, especially if it's making an important aspect to one of your natal planets during this time.

Neptune turns retrograde every year, and this lasts for just over five months. If you consider that Neptune spends approximately 40 percent of its time retrograde (as do Uranus and Pluto, so it's not that rare), compared to the inner planets who are retro less than 10 percent of their travels. Neptune in Pisces brings a shift in consciousness. It's been around 165 years since we've seen it, so if you want to get an idea of what impact this transit has on society, read up on a bit of history.

It's not surprising that there were so many doomsday prophesies around 2012; Neptune in Pisces does open the door to a great cosmic shift in the way that mankind might perceive things. It's a very spiritual transit, and this has the potential for a lot of soul-awakening and renewal. If you think about it, it's during these years that a lot of healthy eating and spiritual practice has gone from the eccentric or the arcane and come out into the open, more accepted by the masses.

Retrograde Neptune—and bear in mind, this happens for nearly half the year, every year—has the capacity to strip away any area where delusions have taken hold. That's often a harsh but necessary reality. It could well feel like a loss until it's passed and there's been time to reflect on what's been gained. It stands to reason that the larger the delusions and misconceptions, the bigger the shock it will be to see the truth clearly. Just as Jupiter and Saturn were times for reflection, so is this. Let's face it: all of these planets are retrograde simultaneously, so why not welcome the opportunity to chill out and review your plans, revising what you'd really like to achieve this year, and this lifetime.

All of this reflecting may bring up some stuff from the past that's been buried, or that resurfaces after it's been supposedly dealt with. If that happens, face it. Neptune rules "hidden enemies," anything or anyone who is liable to do something unexpected, and with potential consequences. It's important to acknowledge the source of the pain, and deal with it—because often the first and sometimes strongest instinct is to hide or to run.

It's important to resist the temptation to wallow in this heartache, another one of Neptune's traits. Often, Neptune retrograde will blow this up out of all proportion. However, if everyone is feeling hurt, anxious, or worried, then it will have a knock-on effect, rippling through society as a whole. Tenacity and striving for improvement are vital, because those who don't believe in astrology or who aren't aware that this is happening won't be paying attention, and the fear-mongering or selfishness will run rampant if given half a chance. Neptune is also making a trine to that karmic north node;

between Neptune and Saturn and the nodes there's a lot of karma flying around this month!

Venus is making its presence known, with a passing glance off Neptune just before Midsummer's Day. Running up to Litha, it's a good idea to avoid dealing with loud and aggressive people if at all possible, and seek out those who are amiable and optimistic. This isn't a time to be a people-pleaser, nor to overindulge in anything. The rose-colored glasses have to be removed so things can be seen as they really are, rather than how they ought to be.

A few days before Litha, Mercury is making an opposition to first Saturn and then Pluto. The Mercury–Saturn aspect might create some situations that seem frustrating, but look farther ahead. This wrench has been thrown into the works to enforce discipline and focus on long term goals. Stubbornness and poor communication easily arise out of this transit. The key is to find the balance between being dedicated and being obstinate, and working through things one step at a time.

The Mercury–Pluto transit encourages the vocalization of likes and dislikes. This may be confrontational, but it also has the possibility to bring forth some incredible insights into your own thought process as well as that of others. People might push your buttons at this time; the key to successfully navigating this is to find out why, for that's what the lesson is there for. Once the reasoning is understood, a way to disentangle the situation can be found. Like Venus, the effects of the Mercury transits are only going to last for two or three days, but because the rest of the cosmic weather is so full of karma, what happens during this period may have later repercussions.

Litha Celebration: Midsummer Prayers

One of our favorite activities for Litha is to make prayer ties. Many different cultures do this, or something similar, from the Welsh clouties to the Tibetan prayer flags. This can easily be done in solitary or in a group. To make Litha prayer ties, you'll need the following:

Scraps of cotton fabric, 4–6 inches square. This is best if it is an old t-shirt or something that belongs to you, something that has your energy on it, but any cotton will do. It must be cotton, though, not a manmade fabric. Seasonal herbs—gather up what you like the most, herb leaves or flower petals. You can wild harvest these, or purchase them. Cotton string—again, it needs to be cotton, not manmade. A Litha candle (because Litha is a Sun festival, working with a candle helps to embody the Sun's light and energy). Choose a warm sunny color, such as yellow or orange.

At sunrise on the solstice, or as soon as you get up if sunrise isn't possible, light your Litha candle. Do this after you've bathed, but before you've had anything to eat or drink. If you want to cast a circle or welcome any deities, now is the time to do so.

Next, take a pinch of your herbs and put them in the center of one of your scraps of fabric. Tie the pouch shut securely with the cotton string, leaving a long tail of at least 6 inches. As you fill and tie the bundle, say your Litha prayer. This can be anything from asking for what you need, to thanking the deities or spirit beings for their presence, or just a phrase of gratitude to the universe.

Continue making your prayer ties, saying your requests or prayers as you do so. Make one, or make several. Pray for yourself, or for your loved ones, or for world issues. There's really no wrong way to do this. Keep making your prayer ties until you're finished, and all your herbs and fabric has been used.

Now pinch out the Litha candle and go on with the rest of your day. At sunset, take your prayer ties and, using the tails of the cotton string, attach the prayer ties to a fence, gate post, or tree. Choose somewhere they won't be disturbed, somewhere the Sun will fall on them easily. It's important that they're not disturbed and that they're exposed to the elements of nature. As the Sun shines on them, the rain falls on them, and the wind blows them, they'll gradually disintegrate, and as they do, your prayers will be taken deep into the elemental kingdom, and heard. This is why it's necessary to use cotton; manmade fibers won't decay with the elements.

The Old Ways: Midsummer Stars

Linda Raedisch

SEVERAL OF OUR WITCHES' sabbats once bore the names of Christian saints. St. Bridget is still going strong in Ireland while St. Walpurga perseveres pretty much in name only. St. Michael, whose feast day coincides with Mabon, has been forgotten even by the Catholics I've spoken to, but June 24 is still known as St. John's Day in most of Europe. Rather than suffering from the indelible stamp of Christianity, it remains one of the most important dates in the Pagan calendar. In ancient days, Midsummer Eve probably eclipsed Yule as the solar event of the year. After all, the winter solstice is just a promise, but at Midsummer that promise is made good.

In the more northerly latitudes, it won't get dark at all tonight. Witches and fairies enjoy the sunshine as much as everyone else, so they'll probably want to come and dance around the bonfire too. As long as they don't forget their crowns of summer blossoms, they'll be able to blend right in with the crowd. Whether you know it as Litha, Midsummer, or St. John's Eve, the summer solstice is one of the easiest Sabbats to observe at home: all you need is flowers.

If, on the other hand, you prefer to go abroad, one of the best places for a Pagan to celebrate the year's longest day is the Lithuanian countryside. Join the throngs of people on one of the flower-dotted hills on the bright evening of June 23 to watch the Lithuanians celebrate Midsummer Eve, or Ligo, in ancient style. Lithuanian is the oldest living Indo-European language. In other words, if you already speak Lithuanian, you'll have a leg up on learning the Bronze Age liturgical language of Sanskrit, should you ever choose to do so. Many of the Lithuanian gods and spirits have direct counterparts in Vedic Hinduism, for these were the gods worshipped by the cattle-driving Indo-Europeans before they parted ways on the steppes of Central Asia thousands of years ago. Because the Lithuanians did not officially adopt Christianity until 1387, much of the old religion that has been lost elsewhere in Europe survives in Lithuanian folklore and festivity.

The name Ligo means "to sway," and to sway while singing is a sign of joy. Along with swaying, singing, and bonfire-feeding, flowers carry the day at Ligo. The men wear wreaths of green oak leaves while the women and girls weave chaplets of blue cornflowers, red fern fronds, and whatever else they happen to pick along the way: elder blossoms, vervain, purple vetch, and the foamy white corymbs of wild carrot. Most important are the daisies, which, to the Lithuanians are "little suns" or "wheels."

No, you can't beat Ligo for ancient Paganism in action, but the Lithuanians don't have a monopoly on Midsummer flowers or Hansblumen as they are called in German. In Germany, it was supposed to be good for the eyes to view the St. John's fires through a bouquet of larkspur. There, Johannestag was also known as Holdertag, Elder Day, as in the elder shrub, *Sambucus nigra*. "Nigra" refers to the purplish black berries that appear in the fall, but at Midsummer, the elder is still a-froth in white blossoms. For a Midsummer treat, Germans dip the umbels in a thin batter and fry them like pancakes.

At this time of year, it was only practical to add corn flowers and corn poppies to one's Midsummer bouquet. Though strikingly pretty, the sky blue Centaurea cyanus and scarlet Papaver rhoeas are really just weeds and best yanked out of the "corn" or grain fields where they like to grow.

The fern fronds that Lithuanian women like to weave into their flower crowns bear no flowers of their own; baby ferns are achieved by the broadcasting of tiny spores, not flower seeds. Nevertheless, at midnight on St. John's Eve, ferns were supposed to burst out in golden blossom, a belief that must have had more to do with Midsummer drunkenness than the sober observation of nature. Even ordinary plants had magical properties if picked at midnight on the twenty-third or noon on the twenty-fourth, and magical plants were twice as potent.

If a young swain wanted to know how he and his girlfriend would get on in the coming year, he could plant two shoots of orpine, aka Johnny, Orphan John, Midsummer Men, or *Sedum telephium*, side by side at midnight on St. John's Eve, one for her and one for himself. If the shoots twined around each other, they would marry. If one of the shoots died, it meant that person would not live to see another Midsummer.

In parts of Spain, Midsummer Eve is known as Verbena after the purple vervain, *Verbena officinalis*. In appearance, vervain is about as exciting as statice, but its reputation precedes it. The ancient Greeks used it to clean their altars, and the Persians used it as a sacrament in their solar rituals. The Romans liked to burn it in their temples, and the Druids treated it with almost as much reverence as the mistletoe. The Druids did not simply pick it. First, an offering was made—no need for a human sacrifice; a little honey would do—then a circle was drawn around the plant with a knife or piece of iron. Only then could the plant be dug up, and only with the left hand.

So what makes vervain so special? I'm sure a hardcore herbalist, perhaps even a Druid, could tell you, but I am at a loss. Only one of the go-to practical herb books I keep in my library even mention it, and that one informs me that it is regarded as a "pernicious weed" in much of the United States. According to this source, *verbena* means "sacred herb" in Latin, but my dictionary argues for "green shoot." Elizabethan writer Thomas Lodge says that "veruen" is like "poyson one waye and pleasure an other," so it's certainly an herb to treat carefully.

St. John's Wort, *Hypericum perforatum*, is no mystery at all. My herbals were all clamoring to tell me how this plant, taken as a tablet or a tea, lifts the mood, a boost I need more during the dark days of Midwinter than at Midsummer, but perhaps summer is the time to start. And if picked at midnight on Midsummer Eve, it ought to make me twice as merry! St. John's Wort, like vervain, is also considered a weed outside its native Eurasia. If you do make its flowers part of your Midsummer celebration, be sure to leave a few of them unpicked so you can enjoy watching them turn into pinkly blushing berries in the fall.

It's easy to see why St. John's Wort was named for the season in which it blooms. The golden yellow petals and long filaments resemble the rays of the sun whose special day this is. If you can't get your hands on *Hypericum perforatum*, any summer-blooming flower that resembles the radiant sun will do as a sacrament: feverfew, chamomile, arnica, daisy and even dandelion. For the center of your bouquet, consider the "king's candle" or mullein, which is also in its glory on Midsummer Eve. And the frosted velvet leaves of the wormwood plant can add a little touch of Faerie to a crown.

According to an old English folk rhyme, "Vervain and dill/Hinder witches from their will," but vervain was also supposed to be a key ingredient of witches' flying potions. Likewise, daisies, chamomile, and pretty much any member of the Asteraceae or "starry" family were supposed to be deterrents against witchcraft, but none of the witches I have spoken to have had a problem with them.

Feasts and Treats

Blake Octavian Blair

THE SUMMER SOLSTICE SEASON is upon us! Though we are celebrating the height of the sun and the longest day of the year, we are also likely trying to stay cool and beat the heat! As the summer heat ramps up, we look to cool menus of refreshing foods. In the warmer months, I'll often plan meals I can cook on the stove top or with as little heating as possible. These recipes will fill your belly but won't heat up your kitchen, so you can keep cool as you celebrate the solstice! Dress up the feast table with bright summery colors in honor of the bright sunshine and reminders of your favorite summer activities, such as seashells in jars of sand from the beach and beautiful summer flowers.

"Fire and Ice" Cucumber Sandwiches

This is my own personal adaptation on a classic favorite teatime snack of the English. However, it works well as an appetizer or snack at summer gatherings too. My version has a slight kick to it but doesn't read as too spicy with the cooling effect of the cream cheese and cucumber. Here is the perfect use for those plump cucumbers appearing in abundance at local farmers markets!

Prep time: 10 minutes
Serves: 4–6

8 ounces cream cheese
1–2 tsp powdered cayenne pepper (to taste)
1 tsp paprika
1 tbsp lime juice
2 tbsp fresh dill (to taste)
1 large cucumber
8–12 slices sandwich bread

Remove cream cheese from the fridge about ten minutes prior to making this recipe so as to allow it to soften slightly.

Place cream cheese into a bowl with 1–2 teaspoons of powdered cayenne pepper and a teaspoon of paprika. Add a tablespoon of lime juice. Add fresh dill to taste. Mix until ingredients are well combined. I find a fork works well for mixing.

Cut a large cucumber into sixteen equal coin shaped slices.

Spread desired amount of cream cheese mixture onto each slice of sandwich bread.

Arrange four coins in a single layer on top of half of the slices. Then top with remaining slices of bread.

Cut each sandwich into quarters and serve.

Midsummer Muffuletta

This pressed sandwich is simple yet classy for those hot summer days. It is easy to prep, fun to make, and big on flavor. The Muffuletta sandwich has its origins in New Orleans, a notoriously hot and swampy place. The version I'm offering here takes on a bit of a Mediterranean flair, however. It's like a fresh breath of cool Mediterranean air on a hot summer's day! Be sure to use a really good, high-end bread here. It needs to be strong enough to resist some pressure. Look for bakery artisan style breads in the bakery department of your supermarket.

Prep time: 10 minutes
Cook time: 70 minutes (10 minutes active, 60 passive refrigeration)
Serves: Approx. 4–6

1 large boule bread loaf
2 tbsp olive oil
Portobella mushroom caps, sliced
Salt (to taste)
Cracked black pepper (to taste)
8 ounce jar roasted red peppers
Sliced Green or black olives
6 ounces fresh spinach leaves
12 ounces fresh mozzarella cheese, sliced
Artichoke hearts

First prepare the boule loaf by slicing off the top and hollowing out the middle.

Next, in a medium to large skillet (I prefer cast iron, but it is not necessary) heat the olive oil over medium high heat.

As the skillet heats you can prepare the portobella mushrooms for cooking. If they did not come pre-sliced, remove the stems, de-gill the underside with a spoon, and peel top skin if desired, and slice into ½" thick strips.

Add sliced mushrooms to the preheated skillet and season with salt and black pepper as desired. Cover and cook for four to five minutes or until golden color begins to appear on the side touching the skillet bottom. Then turn once, season as desired, cover, and cook second side of mushrooms similarly until golden color begins to appear. When finished, put mushrooms on a plate and set aside.

While the mushrooms are cooking you can begin on the prep of the other ingredients such as the roasted red peppers, olives, artichokes, and spinach. If they are not already, slice the roasted red peppers into strips, slice the olives, cut artichokes into uniform pieces, and slice the mozzarella if it is not pre-sliced. You can set these ingredients aside in bowls or leave them momentarily on your cutting board.

Now, arrange the portobellas in a single layer in the bottom of the hollowed out boule loaf. Start with a single layer, and if you cover the entire bottom of the loaf and have mushrooms remaining, feel free to layer deeper as desired.

Next, layer desired amount of the spinach leaves into the boule, creating the next layer. Follow with the mozzarella, roasted peppers, artichokes, and olives to create more layers. Continue layering until the boule is packed full.

When the boule is full, place the lid on the loaf and proceed to wrap tightly in plastic wrap. Then, place the filled loaf onto a cookie or baking sheet and press the loaf by placing heavy objects on top of it. Large canned goods work or especially effective and my preferred method, is to place a couple of cast iron skillets on top of it. Make room in refrigerator and place weighted sandwich into refrigerator for at least an hour.

When ready to serve, remove sandwich from fridge, unwrap, and slice into wedges.

Note: Use the amount of each ingredient you desire, there is a lot of flexibility with the recipe and plenty of room for substitutions. Often, you may have many of the listed ingredients or alternatives that would work in your pantry.

Skillet Summer Squash Duo

This is a quick and easy summer side dish that pairs well with the Muffuletta or other hot weather dishes. It's equally fast and easy on the stove top as it is on the grill and full of color making for a beautiful presentation on the plate. A great way to integrate seasonal produce into your Midsummer feast!

Prep time: 5 minutes

Cook time: 10–15 minutes (maybe longer depending on volume of squash)

Serves: 4

2 large zucchini, sliced into coins
2 large yellow squash sliced into coins
2–3 tbsp olive oil
Salt (to taste)
Garlic powder (optional)

There two cooking method options for this dish:

Preparation Option #1: Stove top.

Spray a skillet with cooking spray. Arrange the coined zucchini and squash in a single layer in skillet. Sprinkle with salt as desired and then drizzle with olive oil. Cook on medium high heat approximately 7 minutes or until golden brown color begins to develop on the underside. Then flip coins, season with salt and olive oil, and cook similarly to first side. Depending on the quantity of coins you have and the size of your skillet, you may need to cook these in batches. If so, you can keep them hot by wrapping the cooked squash in aluminum foil until serving.

Preparation Option #2: Grill

If you are having an outdoor cooking, this dish converts well into skewers for grilling. Simply place the squash coins onto skewers, season with salt and drizzle with olive oil, and cook on the grill until color and tenderness develops. Cooking time will most certainly vary so you will want to judge doneness based on color.

Note: You can substitute many varieties of summer squash and easily adjust the quantities up or down depending on the size of squashes available and the number of people you plan on serving.

Crafty Crafts

Natalie Zaman

I WAS THRILLED WHEN the Powers-That-Be at the New York Botanical Garden decided to host a display of Frida Kahlo's work. (It's a lot easier for me to get to Brooklyn than Mexico City!) I left the exhibit with a new understanding of just how much Frida loved plants. Her house and studio, partially recreated for the exhibit, was filled with native herbs, flowers, and cacti. Her extensive wardrobe, which I read about obsessively later, contained many botanical themed pieces.

Frida (Kahlo)'s Fantastic Flower Crown

Several images of Frida—photographs and portraits—feature her wearing a crown of flowers in her hair. Many of the plants she wore and painted have symbolic value; fertility was a favorite theme. In much of her art, Frida Kahlo expressed the precept that life is organic, changing and impermanent, as is this crown of living plants. Wear them to celebrate her spirit, the summer season and connect to the creative power of nature.

Time Lavished: Assembling the flower crown won't take long, perhaps half an hour. That said, allow time to gather the flowers that you'll be using. Obtaining crafting materials is more than a trip to the store or a rifle through the pantry. Every step is important and can be an enlightening and enriching experience. Consider wild harvesting rather than buying the flowers and herbs you will use for this craft. Besides the idea that acquiring your materials is just as important as the making itself (see Beltane's "Crafty Craft," page 182), flowers and herbs in bloom now embody the spirit of the season.

Coinage Required : You can buy flowers, but why not be a locavore? Wild harvest your flowers (and other plants and herbs). After that, all you need is some stem wire (wrapped floral wire) and a roll of floral tape, which all told comes to less than ten dollars. (And that allows for a little glitter, too!)

Supplies

Wrapped floral wire (stem wire). You can use a regular headband, but floral wire is considerably lighter, and the fact that it does not lie close to the head on it s own allows more room for the plants and floral tape you'll be attaching to it.

Floral tape (or clear scotch tape in a pinch)

Spray bottle with glycerin and water

Seasonal flowers and herbs.

Glitter (Is it really optional?)

I used rosemary, honeysuckle, and lavender to make my crown, but they can be substituted with any combination of flowers and herbs. Try to use the plants as soon as possible after they've been picked. Otherwise, keep them in water and refrigerated to keep them fresh for your crafting session. Note that the crown and accompanying projects can be made with flowers or with silk flowers and greens, but one of the things that I love about summer is the fragrance—not just of the blooms, but the abundance of herbs that overflow in my garden. Look to all the plants of summer when crafting your crown.

Rosemary, honeysuckle, and lavender are summer plants that can be found throughout my home area, the northeastern United States. Visit https://www.americanmeadows.com/wildflower

-gardening#america to find what wildflowers are in bloom in your area. The plants I suggest are ones that I use in my own garden and what I can find in the wild. Substitute whatever flowers and/or herbs that you wish, but try to use hardy plants. Case in point: I also grow lemon balm in my garden. The scent is wonderful, but once picked, the leaves get soft and droopy very quickly without water, so they wouldn't be a good choice for a crown. On the other hand, the stems of the rosemary, honeysuckle, and lavender are not as delicate and hold up better over time.

Begin by fitting the piece of stem wire to your head (or the person who will be wearing the crown). Bend the wire around your head so that it fits comfortably. Don't make a circle with the wire; keep it open like an Alice-style headband. A standard piece of wrapped stem wire will fit an average adult's head without having to trim it.

Pick your flowers and herbs, wash them if necessary, and trim the stems and any dead leaves.

Starting at one end of the band, lay your first plant, lining up the end of the stem with the end of the band. Secure it with a piece of floral tape. Place a piece of tape every 2–3 inches until the entire stem is secured to the band. Repeat on the other side of the band. The stems may overlap—this is okay as it makes for a fuller crown. (If you want your band to look like Frida's, secure the bulk of your plants at the top, or crown of the band. The flowers will sit at the top center of the headband and extend about 4 inches out from each side.)

Add each new plant in the same way, covering blank areas, or where the band could be fuller, and tuck blooms and greenery in. Once you have a few stems taped to the band, you may be able to weave flowers and herbs in rather than taping them. Play with pattern; use all of one type of flower or herb, or vary the placement of the flowers by size and color. You can add plants randomly, but I like to add them one type at a time, filling in empty spaces as I go along.

When all the flowers and herbs have been attached, give them a little sprinkle of glitter. Just a hint. You know you want to!

Store the crown in the refrigerator to keep it fresh until you're ready to wear it. Spritz the flowers with the glycerin water to freshen them up.

When you're finished with the crown, remove the plants and leave them at the base of a tree or toss them into running water as an offering. Everything else can be reused to make a new crown except for the tape. You can also use the crown as a means to dry flowers and herbs for later use in magical workings.

Flower Bracelets, Torques, and Anklets

Did I mention flower crowns (and other jewelry) are perfect festival wear? The same method can be used to create more living accessories.

Measure a length of stem wire that will comfortably fit around your neck (or wrist, upper arm, or ankle). Starting at one end of the wire, lay your first plant, lining up the end of the stem with the wire-end. Secure the stem with a piece of floral tape. Place a piece of tape every 2–3 inches until the entire stem is secured to the wire. Continue to add flowers, herbs, and greenery until you're happy with the fullness.

If you wish, leave a bit of empty space (1–1½ inches) at the ends of the wire. Thread a small bead or crystal on the end of the jewelry, then bend the wire to secure it. Each piece—a torque for around your neck, a bracelet, arm band or anklet—is open for ease of adjustment and removal. Don't forget to sprinkle them with glitter!

Use natural materials to create other seasonable headpieces and jewelry; evergreen and mistletoe leaves and berries (holly tends to dry out quickly) at Yule, wheat sheaves and multi-colored leaves for an autumnal crown, or bare branches (tipped with glittery frost) for winter festivals.

Portable Magic

Mickie Mueller

LITHA IS THE LONGEST day of the year—a time of abundance, light, and plenty—also known as Midsummer. Our family has had some great summer solstice days at the lake when it fell on a weekend; we played in the water and the sand soaking up rays and each other's company. Many of us will be celebrating Litha on the weekend, but since the summer sun will be at its zenith on a Friday during the workday, perhaps some fun ways to recognize the day and take advantage of the magical energy are in order. When the sun is at its pinnacle, it's the perfect time to work magic for success, prosperity, and good fortune. I have some creative ways that you can harness that powerful sun energy no matter what you're doing today or where you are. Here are some bits of Midsummer magic that you can take with you on the go.

Summer Solstice Compact Mirror Success Spell

Here's a mirror technique I developed that you can apply to all kinds of situations. I feel like it's just perfect for the summer solstice. A compact mirror can hold magic energy and intentions inside it when it's closed. Energy can be stored inside because the two mirrors face and reflect each other. You can charge the mirror like a battery ahead of time and release it at a predetermined time so that your spell work can culminate exactly when you want it to and wherever you happen to be by simply opening the compact. It's a game changer, right?

Determine your goal. This is a success spell, so what do you want to channel that success energy toward? Your career, overcoming personal adversity, a new project, whatever your goal is break it down into a couple simple words so that you can focus on it. At some point before the summer solstice, maybe the weekend before, set up your altar space with an open compact mirror, a yellow or gold candle anointed with clove, cinnamon, or bergamot oil (olive oil works great too). Carve a sun shape into your candle. Surround your candle with symbols of success like cinnamon, tiger eye, citrine, acorns; you can also include symbols of your specific goal. As you light the candle, let it fill the space with its energy of success as you visualize your goal. Hold the compact mirror horizontally behind the candle flame so that you can see the flame reflected in both mirrors at the same time with the actual flame in front creating a triangle. Stare at the base of the flame of the candle and simply repeat your goal stated in as few words as possible over and over. When you feel the energy rise to the pinnacle, visualize the energy going into the compact and snap it closed. Don't open it, but leave it next to the candle until it burns out. You'll take it with you on the day of the summer solstice.

Decide if you prefer your spell to culminate with noon in your time zone or with the time of the astronomical summer solstice, which you can look up on the internet for your time zone. I like to set an alarm on my phone so I don't get busy and forget. When the time comes and the sun is at its zenith, simply open the compact, even if you're on a bus, in a classroom, at work, it won't seem odd to anyone, just open it and the energy will release to manifest into the universe. To anyone else it will look like you're just checking your hair. Now that's power!

Sexy Tea to Go

It's Litha, it's hot out, and you could use a magical way to cool off as you go about your business. I have three words for you: raspberry sun tea! It's so easy to make, you can find tea bags in most grocery stores or your local health food store. Just put a couple bags in a big jar of water along with some sugar, stevia, or honey to sweeten if you like. If you're busy on Litha, you can make it the day before, put your jar out in the morning the day before Litha in a place where the sun will hit it most of the day, take it in when you get home and stick it in the fridge. The next morning fill your travel mug with tea and some ice, what a great way to drink in the summer solstice and make the day special.

Raspberries are a very sexy fruit, and they're also very tough with all those brambles, so they're just like you, sexy and tough. As a bonus keep in mind that they're in season right now so if you want to get really fancy you can freeze some fresh raspberries in ice cubes the night before to add to your drink.

Midsummer Lunch With the Fairies

Stop by your favorite park on midsummer if you have time during your travels, maybe on your lunch break. Spend a bit of time under a tree that calls to you. If you don't have much time, you'd be amazed how much just ten minutes in nature can do. Talk a bit to the fairies and spirits of the land. Listen with your heart, you may hear the wind rustling the leaves, feel the sun on your face, share your heart with the spirits. At the end of your visit make a wish if you feel moved to do so. Leave a bit of bread or a cookie as an offering before you depart and return to the hustle and bustle of the world.

Wear Colors of the Day

Think about the colors that you wear within your energy field on Litha, there's great power in the air, and choosing the right colors is a smart way to harness that power.

Wearing gold or yellow on Litha can help you connect with the solar energy of the day. It can also boost a positive outlook, remove negative thinking, and get you into a creative mindset.

Deep green is the color of the Green Man, the personification of growth and the earth. Wear green on midsummer for prosperity, good luck, connecting with the natural world and the spirits that protect it.

Red can also represent the power of the sun as well as strength and courage. Adding red to your wardrobe on Litha boosts your motivation, highlights your leadership qualities, and bolsters self esteem.

Sabbat on the Go Tips

Carry a tiger eye or citrine with you today for the energy of the sun and success.

Enjoy a snack of sunflower seeds, you can charge them with the suns energy ahead of time if you wish. Ask the spirit of the sunflower to help you follow the sun the way they do, let it cast it's light of success on your face, and to always face that light even when clouds are overhead.

Hang a sprig of fresh rosemary from your rearview mirror, the heat of the day will release the oils and fill your car with its blessings.

Carry the Sun tarot card with you in a 3 × 5 inch rigid plastic sleeve. Meditate on the blessings in your life and focus the energy from past successes onto future events.

Kosmesis Summer Solstice Ritual

Deborah Castellano

THE RITUAL ITSELF WILL happen late afternoon; in the drowsy hours of the warmth of the day you will do the magical act. But the ritual truly will not be complete unless it's followed by a dark act of decadence during the evening; a smoky bonfire, a luminous opera, a club where you can feel the bass run through you like the universal heartbeat. The perfect gin martini in a velvet surrounding. A visit to a faraway lover. When selecting the activity that will follow your ritual, think about the intention you are setting with your kosmesis and plan accordingly.

First, set your intention. Much like Hera and Pandora, you have a job to do. What are you attempting to accomplish with your kosmesis? Be clear, be succinct. Now is not a time for fear. Ask for what you want and then just a little bit more. Kosmesis is not for the meek and the circumspect. You are asking for the Aztec four hundred divine rabbits who preside over parties and drunkenness—too much is never enough.

Then, select everything that you will wear: purse/wallet, underthings/lingerie, pants/skirt, top/dress, jewelry, scent, skin care, cosmetics (a little eyeliner never hurt anyone, all genders included). Don't be afraid to try things on. This can be your personal makeover montage. When you have selected your adornment in its entirety, lay it out. Put on a robe.

Select your spirits, ancestors, and goddesses that you would like to guide you on this adventure. They don't need to be traditionally associated with kosmesis—it's more important that they are game and you have a relationship already with them. Arrange your altar, ideally a vanity table or bathroom sink, with representations of your goddesses, spirits, and ancestors. Bring any offerings you would like to make to them and make them. Invite them to be a part of your kosmesis. Speak from the heart and go with what inspires you in the moment. Give your intention. If you don't know what to offer, incense, bottled water, flowers, sweets, and candles are rarely offensive. Consecrate your altar by sprinkling rose water on it. Let everyone know that the altar will stay in place until the next morning.

Next, prepare food for yourself. A bit of decadence will help set your intention for you if you prepare and eat mindfully.

Suggested Menu for Inspiration

Bread

Honey (sweetness to your life)

A cordial glass full of St. Germain or Elderflower soda (the essence of summer solstice)

Fresh strawberries (to attract in your intention)

Dark of the Night Yogurt: Plain yogurt with olive paste and lavender Breton gray salt (olives for success, salt to keep you grounded in reality, lavender for anything can happen and any wishes)

Honeyed Solstice Bread

1¼ cup hot water (as hot as it gets from your tap)

1 tbsp honey

1½ cups bread flour

1½ cups whole wheat flour

1 tsp salt

2 capfuls of olive oil

1½ tsp active dry yeast

Add ingredients to your bread machine in order as they are listed here. Set your bread machine to the smallest loaf, regular whole wheat setting and lightest crust. As your bread machine is mixing, check to make sure the bread is mixing correctly (is it too sticky? Too dry? Add more bread flour or water as needed).

Dark of the Night Yogurt

1 container plain Greek yogurt

Pinch of lavender

Pinch of salt

A spoonful of black olive paste (or purchased olive tapenade if you are being lazy about it)

Kosmesis Recipes

Next, plan how you will accomplish the bathing aspect of the rite. Will you take a bath or shower? What kosmesis goods will you use? Be sure to hold your intention while performing your kosmesis.

Here are a few simple recipes you can enchant while making them by infusing your intention into them:

Lovely Litha Bath Tea

1 tsp quick oats

1 tsp dried milk

1 tsp dried rose petals

1 tsp powered honey

1 tsp flax seeds

4 tbsp pink Himalayan salt

Small mason jar

Small muslin bags

Mix ingredients together in the jar and let sit out uncovered overnight. Mix again and then cover. To use, spoon into a muslin bag for a (mess-free!) bath.

Luscious Lips Scrub
1 tbsp honey, warmed
1 tsp sugar
2 drops peppermint essential oil
Toothbrush
Small jar

Mix the honey and the sugar together; pour in small jar. Use the toothbrush over your lips with the honey and sugar mixture. Rinse from lips and from toothbrush.

Cooling Summer Facial Toner
¼ cup witch hazel
2 tbsp rose water
6 drops rose essential oil
4 drops cucumber essential oil
Small spritz bottle

Mix ingredients together in spritz bottle. Screw on cap and shake. Use after washing your face but before moisturizing.

Brightening Strawberry Face Mask
10 fresh strawberries
3 tbsp honey
1 tsp lemon
1 egg white
1 tbsp coconut oil
5 drops rose essential oil

Mix ingredients in a blender until smooth. Apply to your face and leave on for 15 minutes. Rinse it off with warm water.

Final Kosmesis

Dress while making eye contact with yourself in the mirror. Consider each piece's significance to your kosmesis and your intention as you put it on. Adorn yourself in cosmetics, scent and jewels as you see fit, continuing to hold your intention and your own gaze. Kiss the mirror. Go to the place that you have chosen for the evening. In the morning, thank your spirits, ancestors, and deities. Draw an omen using whatever divination you would typically use. Dismantle your altar. See what the dark of the year will now bring you.

Notes

Notes

Lammas

Lughnasadh Games

Melanie Marquis

AS THE FIRST OF three harvest-themed sabbat celebrations, Lughnasadh can get a bit lost in the crowd. It's important for me as a Pagan to feel a genuine connection with the energies of each special season, and I've found that focusing on the unique aspects of each sabbat helps me to remember exactly what I'm celebrating, and why. One unique aspect of Lughnasadh is that it has roots in ancient funeral games that were held in honor of Tailtiu, whom legends held was the mother of Irish king turned god-figure, Lugh. Tailtiu was said to have died from exhaustion after plowing all the fields of Ireland in order to make them ready for agriculture. In honor of her sacrifice, it was told, Lugh had initiated the first-ever Tailteann games to celebrate her selfless contribution to the welfare of her people. Solemn rituals were held to honor the dead, but following these rites, it was customary to have more festive celebrations. These celebrations often took the form of large community fairs and festivals that included competitions of athleticism, artistry, oration, and many other games and sports. These events came to be known as funeral games, as they were associated with the fairs held in honor of Tailtiu.

Such Lughnasadh fairs were held for centuries in Ireland, with some historians claiming an origin that dates back all the way to 1600 BCE. Horse racing and chariot racing were prominent aspects of the games, along with tests of speed and strength including racing and wrestling. There were also creative competitions to showcase skills in poetry, storytelling, and other types of artistry.

Although I'm not typically a very competitive person, and certainly not at all athletic, I find that enjoying a little friendly competition at Lughnasadh helps me to connect with the traditions practiced at the ancient celebrations. There isn't a whole lot of specific information out there regarding the precise details of traditional Lughnasadh games and sports, so I've had to formulate my own modern adaptations based on what we do know about the general nature of the competitions held so long ago. The games we play at Lughnasadh are definitely different from the games played in Ireland centuries ago, but they still afford us an opportunity to test our speed, strength, and other skills just like the ancients did.

Tests of Speed

One thing we know about Lughnasadh celebrations is that tests of speed, such as foot races and other cross-country style events, were often among the chief sports. I'm definitely not a champion runner, but I still enjoy such competitions, since it's just for fun and no one expects me to be great. I invite my friends and family to join me, with promises of small prizes such as money or tasty treats to the winners. We begin with a simple foot race around the block followed by a fifty-yard dash to see who truly is the fastest. After that, I like to add some twists to help even the playing field. The sack race is one of my favorites. My local coffee shop always has a free supply of large burlap sacks in which their coffee beans are delivered. They're big enough for an average sized adult to stand in, covering most or all of the legs so that the top edge of the sack can be held at upper thigh or waist level. We hop with all our might, racing from one side of my backyard to the other. I may have been a kangaroo or jackrabbit in a past life, because for some reason I excel at this. I'm destined to lose nearly any other even semi-athletic competition that we have, but when it comes to the sack race, I know I may have a chance to actually win.

We also do some team races, from three-legged races to relay races. One of the most fun and festive team races we've devised is the corn-shucking competition. At one end of the yard, we place two equal piles of fresh corn, unhusked with leaves and cornsilk still intact. Between the two piles, we place a trash can to collect the leaves and cornsilk that will be stripped off from the fresh ears of corn. On the opposite side of the yard, two large empty boxes are placed to collect the corn that each team manages to husk.

The participants are divided into two teams, and each team is asked to line up behind one of the corn collection boxes. When the race begins, the players will one by one race to their team's pile of corn, grab an ear, and shuck it as quickly as possible. The leaves must be completely removed and tossed into the trash can. The ear of corn is then raced back to where the rest of the team is waiting, and is thrown into the team's corn collection box. The next team-mate can then follow suit. Whichever team manages to shuck their pile of corn the quickest wins. Many of my family and friends are not very athletic, but by adding such twists to the traditional foot race, we can all have fun together in a fast and frenzied fashion and experience that same rush of speed and hustle that the runner feels when approaching the finish line.

Horse Competitions and Chariot Racing

From horse races and chariot races to equestrian swimming competitions, horses were a big part of ancient Lughnasadh games. I don't have horses, or a chariot, but I've found some ways to celebrate Lughnasadh in a similar vein, nonetheless. Figuring out how to mimic a chariot race was admittedly a bit of a challenge at first. I wouldn't even know where to find an actual chariot, except maybe at a museum. The car could certainly be seen as the modern version of the chariot, but we all know that street racing is extremely dangerous, illegal, and just flat-out dumb, so that was absolutely out of the question. Then it came to me. There is indeed an easy way to enjoy a vast variety of virtual street racing experiences safely, which involves zero gas and is a lot more fun. We simply choose a car racing game from our vast collection of video games, pin a large piece of poster board to the wall on which to keep track of the stats, and let the competition begin. Sure, it's not the same as the exhilarating experience of driving a chariot across an open field, dust flying and horses' hooves pounding the earth, but did the chariot drivers of the past have the opportunity to travel over roads that look like rainbows, or to transform their vehicle into a completely new contraption at the push of a button? Video game racing has its advantages!

I'm not opposed to getting my dogs in on the action, either. They might not be as impressive or as large as horses, but my chihuahua and poodle–dachshund mix can both run faster than lightning. I would never force them to play along if they didn't want to, of course, but I've devised a simple way to have the dogs compete in an enjoyable and humane way. We place our bets for "top dog," then toss dog treats out in the yard one by one, seeing which dog gets to the treats first. Naturally, the "loser" ends up getting just as many treats as the winner, but it's fun for us humans to watch them dash for the dog biscuits and cheer them on. We might also have a fetching contest, seeing which dog can fetch a ball or a stick the fastest. I know it's not exactly like traditional Lughnasadh horse racing, but it nonetheless is reflective of the inclusion of animals that was common in the "old ways" of celebrating the holiday.

Tests of Strength

Tests of strength were another common sport at Lughnasadh fairs and festivals. In Ireland, for instance, hurling competitions were popular. We get into the spirit with a couple sacks of potatoes. One ten-pound bag and one five-pound bag are all we need. Each bag is placed inside a pillowcase which is tied around the top with a ribbon.

This is to ensure that the potatoes don't fall out and spill all over the place, as the plastic bags they come in are prone to breakage. First, we compete to see who can hurl the five-pound sack of potatoes the farthest. We mark each contestant's throw with a small length of ribbon or a stick. Next comes the ten-pound bags. After a round with both potato sacks, we repeat the competition using our non-dominant hands to hurl the potatoes. The winners receive potatoes as prizes. It's pretty silly, but it's definitely a workout that gives us a fun way to put our strength and power to the test.

Another game we like to play tests strength as well as endurance. I buy several twenty-five pound bags of dog food, and participants are asked to stand in a line, side by side. Each participant extends their arms straight up beside their ears, and at the same time, each person is given a bag of dog food to hold above their head. Then, we wait. As arms begin to tire, competitors drop their bags and thus drop out of the contest. The last person standing with their dog food still held high above their head is the winner. For those who don't have quite that much athletic prowess, we might have a simple push-up contest, seeing who can do the most consecutive push-ups before collapsing in an exhausted heap—without overdoing it, of course!

Artistry, Storytelling and Bardic Games

Not all the games common to Lughnasadh were athletic. Some competitions were more artistic and cultural in nature, with storytelling and bardic contests being particularly popular. We like to play a game that combines recitation skills with creative storytelling skills. Everyone sits around in a circle, and the first person starts a story, saying only one sentence. The next person in the circle has to then recite that first sentence exactly, and add on their own, new sentence to the story. The next person in the circle then has to recite both of the preceding sentencing, and add on their own sentence, and so on and so on until someone in the circle inevitably fails to remember what has been said, or fails to come up with a new sentence. That person is then eliminated, and a fresh round is started. The last player left is deemed the champion. We also like to have more traditional storytelling competitions, where participants take turns telling their best stories in different categories. There is a ghost story contest, a funny story contest, a sad story contest, and a strange story contest. Everyone votes on their favorites anonymously, and winners are awarded with blank journals in which to create their next award-winning stories. For the more art-minded among us, we also host an arts and crafts competition. Each participant can enter a craft of their choice in the contest, be it a painting, a crocheted piece, textile arts, a handwoven basket, or whatever else they might like to create. Participants are asked to vote for their favorites by putting quarters into small cans that are placed next to each of the art pieces. As our Lughnasadh games are wrapping up, the quarters are counted and the art piece with the most votes wins all the quarters.

The Serious Side of Games

We might typically think of games and sports as mere entertainment—fun enough, but essentially rather pointless. However, there is a deep and meaningful connection between the games of Lughnasadh and the underlying spiritual tides of the season. Just as Tailtiu was said to have pushed herself past her limits for the benefit of Irish agricultural, just as the grains must give up their lives in order to be harvested, ground, and baked into bread, we simple humans have our own challenges that we, too, must face. Engaging in competitive sports and games forces us to be our best, to try our best and to go beyond our limits. To be rewarded with a fruitful harvest requires skill, effort, sacrifice, and luck, and by playing games at Lughnasadh, we experience the intertwining of those factors firsthand. I probably won't win a single event (with the possible exception of the sack race, if I'm lucky), but competing to the farthest extent of my abilities regardless will remind me to always give my best, just as the earth gives us her best in the first fruits of the harvest celebration of Lughnasadh.

Cosmic Sway

Charlie Rainbow Wolf

THE FIRST HARVEST SKIES keep going with the karmic theme that has been present for most of the rest of this year. Saturn is still retrograde, still opposite the Moon's north nodes, still making a wide conjunction to Pluto—which is also making a wide opposition to the Moon's north nodes. Jupiter is also still retrograde, and making that hard angle to the nodes in Cancer. Neptune also continues the backward dance, making a positive aspect to the Nodes. All of this is old news, just the continuing theme.

What is interesting for Lammas is the stellium in Leo that includes Venus, the Moon, the Sun, and Mars. Venus, the Moon, and the Sun are conjunct, and that's going to create quite the mix of energies. It's moody, creative, independent, and perhaps a bit self-indulgent, too. There's a quest for recognition, on a personal and a global scale. There's the potential to get a lot accomplished, but it's not an influence that will be long-lasting. All of these are fast moving planets (although the Sun and the Moon aren't technically planets), so it will be here and gone in a day or two.

The main player here is the Sun, which is the ruler of Leo. It's at this time of year people tend to draw attention to themselves. Many are starting new classes at school or new terms at college. A Leo Sun brings spirit, warmth, and amicability. Of course, it is possible to have too much of a good thing, and when that happens, show offs and narcissists have a field day!

Coming into Litha, the Sun made a square to unpredictable Uranus. Unexpected issues may have cropped up, bringing with them surprise and change. This doesn't have to be a bad thing. The Sun brings the tenacity to stand fast and see what happens, both personally and on a much larger scale. Expect disruptions in the present state of affairs, and be diligent when it comes to what you're able to change and what you can't. Some things are going to be out of your control, no matter how determined you are that they need to be different. Avoid unnecessary friction, and remember that you may not be able to change the world, but you can certainly change your world.

Leo's vibe is generally honest and respectful, but it does like its own way. There could be too many people wanting to take the lead this month. Expect grand gestures and leadership opportunities. During this stellium in particular, the bossy ones will easily upset those who are more timid or reserved. Compromise is the key, and that may be hard to find.

The Moon in Leo brings a sense of pride and backs up the Sun wanting all the attention. Throw Venus in the mix, and there's a need for affection, recognition, and adoration—and hurt feelings when it doesn't happen. Insecurity leads to swagger and unnecessary attempts to show off. This influence will soon pass, but not before it's had the chance to bruise some egos!

In other news, Mars in Leo is making a hard angle to Neptune in Pisces. Mars in Leo has the capacity to bring a bit of a daredevil attitude. This is usually a good thing, risks that are calculated have the potential to create a favorable impression. However, when this energy gets backed into a corner, or when someone points out that errors have been made, ego and bravado are likely to come out fighting rather than simply admitting the wrong and trying to figure out what to do to fix things. In a group situation, this can cause a lot of hard feelings.

The harsh aspect to Neptune—which is still retrograde—asks for honesty and transparency when it comes to motives and intentions. It's a caution to diplomacy. Another side of this transit gives rise to feelings that come out of nowhere, and they're sometimes overwhelming. The important desires of life may become elusive, creating frustration when it comes to moving ahead.

Then there's Saturn again. Mars recently hit a challenging aspect with the Lord of Karma, and the repercussions are still influencing things. Inconjuncts are such pesky aspects, because there's simply nothing in common. Once again, authority issues arise. The emphasis is on the little things and the more immediate headaches, rather than where it needs to be—on the long-term situation. More haste really does mean less speed at the moment, and will do so for the next few days.

Mars is also in a disharmonious tangle with Pluto this month. These are some pretty intense energies, and could have an impact on what's going on globally as well as personally. There's a power play, here, some blind determination to get what's desired no matter who gets stepped on in the process. People are more inclined to fight back than make peace, and compromises are few and far between. On a personal level, try channeling some of this volatile energy in a sport or other physical activity. On a global level, hold your breath, for it's a fairly fleeting aspect and will be out of orb within 5 days or so. This transit can teach a lot about what's really wanted and what's not that important if people just pay attention.

Finally, let's take another look at Chiron, now retrograde again—and will be for the rest of the year. Like the outer planets, this retrograde isn't particularly influential unless it happens to hit one of your natal planets or power points. Chiron still means karma; yes, it may open up some pain from the past, but it also brings a chance to heal it, once and for all.

Lammas Celebration: A Feast of Grain

With Lammas being the festival of the first grain. Flour and cereals are taken for granted today, but it wasn't long ago that if the grain crop failed or wasn't gathered in time, it made for a long and hungry winter. Lammas actually means loaf mass, and it's traditionally the first harvest celebration. What better way to mark this occasion than by using the grain to make a loaf?

There really isn't any right or wrong way to do this. In our Lammas festivals of the past, we've had three different bread doughs featuring different grains braided together in one loaf, we've had everything from hand-me-down sourdough starters to bread machine loaves, and more! As with all rituals, it's the intent, rather than the outcome, that is the most important. Over the last few years, our Lammas loaf has been a beer bread. My husband makes traditional beers and ales, and of course, they involve the grain, too. It seems fitting that the cook and the brewer marry their skills for this harvest festival!

The ritual below is for a group, but it's easily adaptable for solitary practitioners. I suggest that you bake your own bread for the Lammas loaf. You can make this lighthearted by baking the bread in the shape of a gingerbread man, to represent the god Lugh (who gave his name to Lughnasadh, an alternative word for Lammas). If you've not got time, any loaf will do, even gingerbread itself! You'll also need the following items:

Ale, or another beverage of your choice
Straw
Cotton string
Beads, colored thread, markers, scraps of cotton fabric, and other
    means of decoration
A Lammas fire. This can be anything from a bonfire to a candle; it's
    whatever works best for you.

Cast a circle or open the festivities in whatever way your tradition uses. Give each participant enough straw to tie into a small human shape, using the cotton string to tie the bundles into arms, legs, body, and head sections. Everyone should make their own doll, and decorate it to resemble themselves.

When all the dolls have been made, circle the fire in a counter-clockwise motion, gaining speed to raise the energy. Once you've reached the level of energy you desire, all the dolls should be thrown onto the fire, along with the statement of what that person promises to get rid of in the coming year. All residual energy should be directed toward the burning doll, too. This is a banishing fire, to get rid of what is holding you back from being everything you can be.

When all the dolls are burned, it's time to sacrifice the grains by ripping apart the loaf, and drinking the ale or other beverage. Don't forget to feed some to the flames, and remember that—while fun—this celebration is a sacred promise. As the grain is sacrificed and cut so that the harvest may be gathered, you are going to have to sacrifice aspects of yourself in order to keep your pledge you made to the Lammas fire.

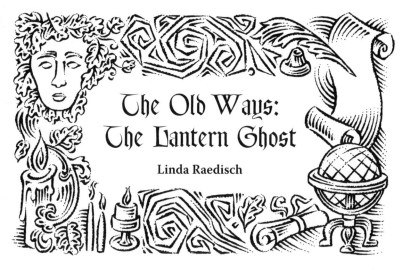

The Old Ways:
The Lantern Ghost

Linda Raedisch

IT'S HARD TO IMAGINE Halloween without jack-o'-lanterns. Nor would the Japanese festival of the dead, Obon, be Obon without an array of paper lanterns. Obon was originally celebrated during the seventh lunar month. Some towns and cities still celebrate it in July, but since Japan's switch to the Gregorain calendar in 1873, it has been more common to hold it in August. It remains to be seen if the old "Bon in July" will survive, as our Old Christmas and Old Hallowmass have not. Like the Catholic All Souls' Day, Obon originated in the Buddhist Ullambana but, like our Halloween, it has absorbed many of its accoutrements from native Paganism.

Obon is a three-day festival and candles burn throughout. Lanterns are hung inside the home, at front doors and gates and in the cemetery. Their glow lights the way for the departed souls to follow out of the realm of the dead and back again. Prettily arranged offerings of flowers, sandalwood incense, and vegetables are placed on the family's Buddhist altar to welcome them. The Japanese wouldn't dream of shouting their ancestors out of the house at the end of the festival as the ancient Greeks did at Chytroi. Instead, they are lovingly ushered away along a path of lights. The departing spirit might even be provisioned with a snack of rice balls packed in a little straw boat with a tiny paper lantern at the prow.

Lanterns in Japan come in all shapes and sizes, culminating in the huge painted lanterns-turned-parade floats of the Nebuta Festival that precedes Obon in the Aomori Prefecture. But the lantern that concerns us here is the humble round or egg-shaped chochin. Some are painted with Chinese characters, flowers, and ornamental grasses, but the most basic chochin is the plain white of the paper from which it is made.

To qualify as a chochin, you must be portable, and you must be one 100 percent collapsible, otherwise it would be impossible to light the little white candle mounted in your base.

This is how you are made: Your form exists before you do, for you are shaped around a mold composed of wooden slats, each resembling the silhouette of a banana. Each slat fits into a notch in a Tinker Toy-like cylinder at top and bottom. This is your temporary skeleton. Now, the master lantern-maker winds a thin, continuous strip of bamboo around and around your skeleton. He spins it quickly, for he is a master, but not too quickly for he must make sure that the bamboo strip sits in each of the grooves carved in the outer edges of the slats. This ensures that the empty spaces in between will be even, and you will have a smooth, regular surface.

When your new bamboo skeleton is complete, it's time to give you a skin of white paper and glue smoothed on with a horsehair brush. When you're all dry, your old wooden skeleton is collapsed with a twist and pulled out. Now you can be fitted with a lacquered ring at top and bottom, a handle and a tassel.

But, of course, you won't remember any of this. You're just a paper lantern. You won't become a sentient being for another one hundred years. If you can make it to your one hundredth birthday without mildewing, bursting into flames, or disintegrating in the rain, you will become a chochin-obake. We've already defined "chochin," but what is an obake?

I once taught an evening course called "Magical Origami" in which we folded figures from Japanese folklore: a talking spirit fox, a raccoon-dog hat, and a model I adapted from a kimono into a ghostly, hooded figure. I called it an "obake." I have since learned that this was incorrect. Although *obake* is usually translated into English as "ghost," it is the yurei who appears in white burial kimono to haunt the living. An obake, on the other hand, is not the spirit of a dead person—at least, not usually—but a monster, a shapeshifter, a supernatural being that might appear as something other than what it really is, like a fox, a teapot or, you guessed it, a paper lantern.

The Chochin-obake belongs to a special class of obake: it is a tsukumogami, a household object that, having attained the ripe old age of 100, has acquired a spirit of its own. Some tsukumogami are dangerous, but the Chochin-obake is more of a buffoon. He likes to stick his tongue out through the tear in the paper that has become his mouth and roll his single eye at startled visitors.

That said, the woodblock printer Hokusai (1760–1849) has left us a horrifying depiction of a Chochin-obake. When I first saw it, I mistook it for a creature that was half lantern, half severed head. It was actually a portrait of the famous ghost Oiwa, who liked to haunt her faithless husband in the shape of a paper lantern.

Here's what happened: The beautiful Oiwa was married to the good-for-nothing rogue samurai Iyemon. With the collusion of his wealthy mistress, Iyemon killed Oiwa by putting poison in her cold cream. Had she died immediately, Oiwa might have gone quietly to the underworld, but before she expired, she glimpsed the hideously scarred half of her face in a mirror. She haunted Iyemon for the rest of his miserable life until his brother-in-law finally killed him. A movie about Oiwa is still shown on Japanese television during the festival of Obon, just as the old black and white *A Christmas Carol* is still shown in English-speaking countries in December. Her hauntings continue to this day.

But if you, humble lantern, are still hoping to become a Chochin-obake, I'm afraid the odds are against you. Your smooth finish will not protect you from the elements forever. And there's always the risk that the grandchild of whoever bought you in the first place will pull you out of a closet one day, pop you up and say, "Hey, this lantern's looking pretty beat up. Must be really old. Better throw it away before it turns into a Chochin-obake." But if you do get tossed on the rubbish heap, you will not be entirely without recourse. Some household objects who find themselves broken or discarded at the age of 99 are so peeved they manage to turn themselves into tsukumogami by sheer force of will.

Because it is made to last, a good chochin does not come cheap. The fragility of its materials requires that it be made by hand, so it's worth every yen. If an authentic chochin is beyond your means, dear reader, there is another way that you, your friends and family can celebrate the dead this August. You can host a Hundred Ghost Storytelling Party, a popular summer pastime in Japan in the days before air-conditioning when the heat and humidity made sleep impossible. Here's what to do: light as many tea lights as you have ghost stories to tell. It doesn't have to be "one hundred," which in Edo period Japan could be interpreted as "a lot." After each story is told, put out one of the candles. As the night wears on, the room will get darker and darker, the stories more terrifying.

In Japan, the spookiest part of the night is the Hour of the Ox, which is actually two hours, 1:00 am to 3:00 am. Somewhere in there you're going to want to break for a snack of tofu over shaved ice or maybe some cold orange slices. Look out the window. Is that the moon shining out from the dogwood tree? No; it's a paper lantern. I wonder who could have put it there...

Resources

Ross, Catrien. *Supernatural and Mysterious Japan; Spirits, Hauntings, and Paranormal Phenomena.* Tokyo: Yenbooks, 1996. (Warning: There is a photo of a pre-posthumously mummified monk on page 95. I have glued a piece of paper over it. I recommend you do the same.)

Feasts and Treats

Blake Octavian Blair

THE FIRST HARVEST IS upon us! The season of the corn harvest, celebrations of the Great Mother in her form as the Corn Mother, and some of the hottest days of the year are likely upon us as well. The aim of this menu, like many summer menus, is to provide a zesty and refreshing line up of flavors that will not only satisfy your diners but also honor the first harvest. I have aimed to include dishes that feature ways to honor grains in ways that are in my experience often overlooked at many Lammas celebrations. Honor the season in its fullest and decorate your feasting table with some Indian corn, wheat stalks, and an image of the Great Mother in a form that speaks to you!

Bean Salad Salsa

For many of us, the August heat can be just brutal. A nice cool snack that is fast and easy to prepare and doesn't require any hot pans or ovens is always appreciated. This super easy, cold creation fits the bill! Serve it as a cold salsa for dipping tortilla chips, serve it as a cold salad before your main meal or as a side dish. It's sure to please and it coordinates well with the other treats present in this line up of Lammas delights!

Prep time: 10 minutes
Cook time: 30 minutes refrigeration
Serves: 5–10 (depending on portions)

1 14.5-ounce can diced tomatoes with green chilies, drained
2 11-ounce cans Mexican corn, drained
1 15.5-ounce can black beans, drained and rinsed
⅓ of a medium sweet onion, finely chopped
2 tbsp lime juice
1½ tsp chili powder

Begin by chopping the onion and placing in a bowl. Add lime juice and allow to sit for 5 minutes. The lime juice really is essential, do not omit it. It acts to eliminate any over-powering "raw onion" taste, balances the heat and adds the perfect amount of acidity. It marries into and brings out the flavors of the ingredients really well as the dish sits.

Meanwhile, open and drain canned goods as directed in ingredients list and then combine into a large bowl.

Now add chili powder and mix well. You can adjust the quantities of the lime juice and chili powder according to your taste preferences. Refrigerate at least 30 minutes to chill.

Serve as a cool and refreshing side salad or it is also delightful with corn tortilla chips as a salsa. Optionally, if you're feeling fancy, slightly warm/bake the corn chips.

Summery Fish Tacos

These tacos, dressed with a homemade slaw, make a nice refreshing summer dish that provides a fun way to incorporate honoring the grain harvest through the use of a bread often overlooked during this celebration…tortillas! These tacos have a flavor that is both fresh and bold simultaneously, and they are an entrée that sits light with your diners yet are satisfyingly filling. Since this recipe has a few different components to be made, I'll walk you through step by step. No worries though, it's all super simple!

Prep Time: 10 minutes
Cook Time: 15–20 minutes
Serves: 2–3

For the Slaw:

9 ounces shredded cabbage slaw
½ cup mayonnaise
2 tbsp lime juice
2 tbsp apple cider vinegar
½ tsp powder cayenne pepper (to taste)
Cracked black pepper to taste

If your cabbage is not already shredded into slaw, begin by chopping it to your desired consistency to create the slaw. Place the cabbage into a large mixing bowl.

Add the mayonnaise, stirring to combine well and coat the cabbage. Then add the lime juice and apple cider vinegar. Mix well. Now add cayenne pepper and black pepper. Continue to mix. When all ingredients appear well combined, give it a taste test. You can adjust the heat and acidity to your liking by adjusting the cayenne, black pepper, and lime juice to your taste.

Refrigerate until use.

Fish Preparation:

3 tbsp canola or olive oil
1 tsp ground cumin
1½ tsp curry powder
1½ tsp chili powder
8 medium size flour or corn tortillas
14 ounces tilapia fillets

To create a seasoning for the fish filets, in a small bowl mix the ground cumin, curry powder, and chili powder. Set aside.

Now, if you are comfortable doing so, you can prepare the tortillas parallel to cooking the tilapia fillets. If you feel your cooking management would be better not doing so, go ahead and prepare the tortillas now prior to moving on to cooking the fish.

Preheat a skillet or griddle on medium low heat. Proceed to warm the tortillas on the griddle until they achieve a bubbly texture from the air pockets and begin to get a slight bit of brown toasting. As they finish warming, place warmed tortillas under a clean kitchen towel on a plate to keep warm until all tortillas are ready or it is serving time.

Add canola oil to a large skillet and preheat on medium heat. Add tilapia fillets, carefully, to the preheated skillet. Sprinkle top of each filet with desired amount of the spice mixture that you created earlier. Cover and cook for 3 to 4 minutes. Then, flip filets, sprinkle with seasoning, cover, and cook an additional 3 to 4 minutes.

When finished cooking, remove tilapia fillets from the pan, place in a medium size bowl, and use a fork to flake apart the fillets.

Distribute the fish evenly into each of the warmed tortillas. Top with the slaw, and serve!

Note: Cooking times for fish can vary depending on how hot an individual stove runs, material of skillet, the thickness of the filets, and other variables. Your cooking time may run a couple minutes shorter or longer. Keep an eye on it to achieve the proper level of doneness.

Fresh Jalapeño Cornbread

Many traditions celebrate the harvest of corn at Lammas time, and yet, Lammas menus often seem devoid of this wonderful grain! Having grown up in the Midwest, I simply couldn't resist sharing a delicious corn based recipe to integrate into your Lammas festivities. Of course, this isn't any old pedestrian cornbread; fresh jalapeños bring brightness to the savory sweetness of the cornbread. Not too spicy, but with a little kick to add just the right amount of dimension! Serve with your feast dinner and even as ritual cakes!

Prep time: 10 minutes
Cook time: 40 minutes
Serves: 8–10

2 small jalapeño peppers, seeded and diced
1 tsp flour (for the jalapeños)
4 tbsp butter
1½ cups cornmeal
½ cup all-purpose flour
1 tsp salt
1½ tsp baking powder
½ cup sugar
2 eggs
1 cup milk, more if needed

Begin by removing the seeds of and chopping the jalapeño peppers. Next, in a small bowl, mix the jalapeños and flour and set aside.

Now add butter into a 10-inch cast-iron skillet or in a 9-inch square baking pan. Place pan into the oven and preheat the oven (skillet inside) to 350 degrees F.

Note: Cast iron is quite traditional for cornbread. However, if you do not have a cast iron pan, use a 9 × 9 baking dish.

Now, in a large mixing bowl, combine the cornmeal, flour, salt, and baking powder. In a separate small bowl, combine the sugar, eggs, and milk, and mix to combine. Then add the wet mixture to the dry ingredients. Integrate until you achieve an even texture using as few strokes as possible. If the mixture seems dry, add additional milk as desired. Up to 6 tablespoons may be required.

Now stir in jalapeños, again, with only the number of strokes required to evenly integrate them into the mixture.

When the oven is preheated and the buttered skillet is hot, carefully remove the skillet from the oven, add the batter CAREFULLY and smooth the top using a heat-resistant utensil such as a silicone spatula. Return skillet to oven. Bake about 35–40 minutes, or until the top is lightly browned and the sides have pulled away from edge.

You can test the doneness by sticking a toothpick into the center. When done, the toothpick will come out clean.

This corn bread is a delicious side or even as a desert. Further, it's perfect for use in a cakes and ale ceremony during your sabbat ritual! While it tastes good at room temperature, this cornbread is absolutely delightful served warm and lightly buttered.

Crafty Crafts

Natalie Zaman

THE BURNING MAN—a human figure made out of wicker, straw, or twigs, built hollow so that offerings can be put inside him—is a very old tradition that we know little about. The ancient people who first made them didn't write about their practices. The first person to actually record anything about Burning or Wicker Men was Julius Caesar, who wrote that the Celts created huge, human-shaped wicker figures, into which small animals, grains, and slaves (yes, people), were placed inside to be burned as offerings. His description, a part of his record of the Gallic Wars, included not only his experiences but those of others, so his is not an eye-witness account of a Burning or Wicker Man ritual. We're not 100 percent sure why Burning Men were built, at what times of the year they were burned, or what was really placed inside them, but we can make elements of this tradition work in a positive way.

The Burning Man

Effigies have been burned for thousands of years and usually for the same purpose: to send a message (usually to the "person" being burned) and so promote change. A Burning Man can be a means of sending a message. When he is lit, the intentions, requests, and offerings inside him are sent out into the Universe. Our Burning Man is crafted from recycled cardboard and dressed and crowned with grains and glitter. He's a John Barleycorn-come-Lugh through whom your wishes, intentions, and messages of gratitude will be "brought to light" at Lammas.

Time Lavished: You might spend an hour or two constructing and embellishing your Burning Man, but time must also be allowed for the glue that holds his elaborate outfit in place to dry. If you're making him for a ritual, build him at least a day in advance.

Coinage Required: If you buy everything on the list, a Burning Man build will cost about $25–$30. Please, please, PLEASE don't purchase boxes! I didn't include these in the cost as cardboard boxes are readily available almost everywhere. If you have none in your recycle bin, ask at your neighborhood shops; they'll be happy for you to take them off their hands.

Supplies

2 recycled boxes. One box will be kept intact to make the body and the other will be cut up to make the arms, head and feet. You can use any size box, but it's probably best to work with something of small to medium size (8 × 11 or 11 × 14 with a depth of 4–5 inches). Unless you're hosting a gathering in which hundreds of people will be stuffing their intentions into the Burning Man's belly, he doesn't need to be huge.

Scissors and/or a craft knife

Stapler

Craft glue

1–2 bunches of wheat sheaves

Masking tape

Recycled newspaper, paper bags, etc. for covering your work surface

Paint brush

Grains such as rice, oats, cereals, and wheat

Glitter

Small pieces of paper

Pens

First, prep the box you've chosen as the body. Stand it up vertically (so that it's taller, rather than wider), then cut a small window (mail-slot sized) in the front—this is where folks will put their intentions inside the Burning Man before he burns. Don't seal the box up yet, as you might need to maneuver your hands inside it to attach the feet and arms.

From the second box, cut a rectangular piece of cardboard that has a length that is approximately three times the width of the body (when it is standing up vertically). The width of the arm piece should be no more than the depth of the body box. (Example: If your Burning Man's body is 8 inches wide by 14 inches tall by 5 inches deep, you'll need an arm piece that is about 24 inches long and no more than 5 inches wide.)

Once cut, center the arm piece along the top of the body box. Bend the "arms" down to either side of the body box before tacking it in place with the stapler. (Staple it as many times as you need to; it will be covered with the grains and glitter.)

Cut two circles that will serve as the wicker man's feet and glue them to the bottom of the box.

To assemble the head, cut out two identical cardboard circles with 3 inch by 3 inch tabs on the bottom (see illustration). Proportion the size of the head to the size of the body. Smaller is better as the head will have some weight once you add all the embellishments—you don't want it to flop over!

Glue or staple wheat stalks around the edge of one of the circles you cut for the head. Line up the bottom of the sheaves with the edge of the cardboard so that they stick out like a crown or a halo. Place the second head circle on top of the first, and lining up the tabs, attach the circles together with the stapler. Do not staple the tabs together.

One at a time, brush both sides of the head, excluding the tabs, with glue, then cover them with a mixture of grains and glitter. Cover the cardboard completely. When the head is dry, fold the tabs outward so that they form a stand for the head. Set the head aside.

Now it's time to dress the Burning Man's body. First, seal up the box with the masking tape, making sure that the window remains open. Lay the newspaper, brown paper, or other covering over your workspace to protect it.

Work on one side of the body at a time. Brush one side of the body box with glue and cover it with grains and glitter. An easy way to do this is to pour a mixture of grains and glitter over the freshly glued surface, then tap off any excess onto your paper-covered workspace. This will also minimize waste. Allow each side to dry and fill in any bare patches before moving onto the next. Leave the top of the box (where the arms are tacked on) for last.

Center the head on top of the box (where you already attached the arm piece), then tack it down with the stapler. Once the head is secured, brush the top of the box with glue and cover with the grain and glitter mixture. Allow it to dry completely before tapping off any excess. Be sure to support the head as you do so! Should the head bend forward or backward, place some palm sized stones (ones you don't mind setting alight—you can always clean them later) in front and in back of his head to support it.

Once he's completely dry, he's ready to burn!

Light up your Burning Man in a safe place (outdoors in a fire pit or bowl) and keep a fire extinguisher close by in case it's needed. At Lammas, have everyone who is participating in your ritual write their intentions and wishes on the small pieces of paper and place them inside. You can also make the Burning Man ahead of time and have him on display in the days (or weeks) leading up to the sabbat. Keep papers and pens near him so that anyone who passes by can add his intentions and wishes. When you light him, have participants concentrate on their intentions; they may even want to say them aloud as he burns. Scatter the cooled ashes over your garden, or on your plants or in your favorite park; the ash is good for the soil, and it will put your good thoughts right to work in the earth.

Any celebration that involves fire is good for a Burning Man build. Think of building one for Yule—a great way to welcome the return of the Sun!

Portable Magic

Mickie Mueller

LAMMAS IS A CELEBRATION of the first harvest; it's the time of the year when grains such as wheat and other bounty were ready for harvest. It is also known as Lughnasadh, a festival to honor the Celtic Sun God Lugh with feasting, drink, and games. In modern times we may feel disconnected from the agricultural cycle since instead of getting our bounty directly from the earth, we harvest a paycheck and even if we supplement our pantry with a home garden, we get most of our nourishment from a grocery store. If like many of us you're out there going to school or earning that paycheck on Lammas, there are still ways that you can tap into the harvest energy of the day and bring it into your life. Put some magic in your pocket and enjoy the sabbat!

Lammas Prosperity Charm Bag

When we think about harvest, we feel the essence of prosperity, make a new prosperity charm to carry today and charge it with Lammas energy. Use a piece of gold/yellow colored fabric about a five inch circle. You can use some or all of these items in your charm: a coin, citrine, quartz, wheat, sun charm, allspice, basil, cinnamon, acorn, or other prosperity symbols of your choice. Place your charm bag ingredients in the center of the fabric and simply bundle it all up and tie it with ribbon or twine. I like to charge my charm bags with my intention and place it by a candle to awaken the energy. Carry it in your pocket for the first time on Lammas and as you think about the first harvest throughout the day, use that to add extra energy to your charm.

Farewell and Closure Spell

Lammas is the time that we say farewell to the summer, the season of growth, and the sun king as the suns energy has noticeably begun to wane. We all have things in our lives that ebb and flow, and sometimes we find ourselves holding on to regretful partings, whether it's people who are out of our lives, things, or situations, and a bit of closure can help us move on. A small ritual to release regrets can be very cleansing and healing for our spirits. This one is so easy but it can really lighten the load you carry on your shoulders. You'll need a slip of paper, a pen, and a pinch of thyme. When you're at home, write down what you wish to release on this Lammas; you can write as few or as many as you wish. Visualize each item as you write it down. When you're done, whisper on to the paper, "I release you with love and I release my regret." Sprinkle it with thyme, an herb of courage, purification, and release. Fold the paper away from you, turn and fold again, always folding away as many times as you feel is needed and put it in your pocket. On your travels throughout the day, drop it in a public trash bin and don't look back.

Jewels of the First Harvest

You might like to wear a special piece of magical jewelry to honor the day; here are some ideas for wearable magic to help you stay mindful of the special day and its energies. I like to wear simple stones on Lammas, citrine or amber is usually my go-to choice mostly based on what I have, but there are other stones that are lovely to wear as Lammas talismans as well. Most of us have some quartz crystal jewelry of one kind or another, which is another good choice for Lammas. Obsidian jewelry is also a great talisman for the day, protection magic is appropriate on Lammas. If you happen to have any jewelry in the shape of an arrow, sword, or spear, those would be nice to wear in honor of Lugh who was a warrior. Whatever you decide, purify it with incense or sage and as you wear it on Lammas let it bring you magic and mindfulness on this harvest sabbat.

Magical Oils and Cooling Lammas Spritz

I love to wear scents to correspond to the sabbats throughout the day. It's usually a scent I don't wear all the time so that when I catch a whiff of it, it keeps me mindful and reverent. For Lammas you can try patchouli oil, frankincense oil, or dragons blood oil either alone or as a blend. If you don't like wearing oil on your skin, you can make a spritz in a little spray bottle—the travel size ones work great so you can take it with you if you wish. Fill the bottle with water, or if you want it to last longer, fill three quarters of the bottle with water and top it off with vodka. Then add a few drops of each oil you've chosen until you're happy with the scent and shake before using. It's very refreshing on a hot day and its magic that goes where you go.

Colors of the Day

When you're getting ready in the morning, consider what clothes you choose to wear on this day of the harvest. Letting the colors set the tone for the day with magical intention is pretty easy and can make you feel magical all day.

Yellow is the color of wheat and the sun making it an appropriate color for your Lammas wardrobe. It's a color of prosperity, but also of creativity and invention, granting the skills to hold on to your harvest and use it wisely.

Orange on Lammas can be a symbol of the harvest, and is also a color of growing opportunities and material wealth. Wearing orange can also relieve depression and promote feelings of safety and warmth.

Brown is the color of the nurturing earth after the harvest. It's a color that speaks of security and strength when you wear it. Also wear brown on Lammas to promote energies of endurance and health.

Sabbat on the Go Tips

Lughnasadh was a festival of competition since the Celtic sun god Lugh was so good at all kinds of games. Today would be a great day to play Frisbee, miniature golf, or horseshoes. Any kinds of games are appropriate to play to honor Lugh, yes, even video games!

Bring some crusty bread with you to enjoy as a snack today, since Lammas translates to "loaf-mass," and bread is one of the traditional foods of the sabbat. I like having bread with lots of seeds and grains for Lammas because it helps me reflect on the harvest.

Lammas is also a day of sacrifice—what a perfect day to donate some non-perishables to your local food pantry. When we recognize that we have enough to share, the universe gives us more, and it helps our community. Make sure you include a couple baking mixes for muffins or quick breads in with your donations.

A Ritual in Motion for Lughnasadh

Melanie Marquis

To reflect the athleticism so often involved in Lughnasadh celebrations of the past, this ritual involves a lot of motion. It's best carried out in the daytime or early evening when there's plenty of light, and it can be performed at any time during or near the Lughnasadh sabbat. It's best to perform the ritual in a wooded area with a thick smattering of twigs and small branches scattered on the ground, or in an open field fraught with weeds. If you can't find either of the above, choose an area that's covered with dead leaves, or anywhere else you feel could be an appropriate place for this rite. The purpose of the ritual is to remind participants of the ancient legends associated with the holiday, and to embrace the rewards of the season that can be gained through our skill and effort. You can enact this ritual with any number of participants, from a solo practitioner to a large group.

Preparations

No tools are needed for this ritual, and the clothes worn should be rugged and dispensable, as you're bound to get a little dirty. You might want to wear a pair of work gloves or gardening gloves to protect your hands. The only personal preparation this ritual requires is to get plenty of rest beforehand, and perform some gentle stretches and warm-ups so your body will be ready to engage in the actions of the rite. The ritual space will be more formally prepared during the course of the ritual itself, but you will need to make a thorough survey of the area prior to getting started. Be sure the area is safe, free from unexpected holes and dips, large debris, or any other obstacles that could cause a person to trip or fall. You'll also need to think about accessibility before your ritual. If you have people in your group with mobility challenges or other disabilities, you'll need to think of ways to adapt the ritual so that it is accessible to everyone. If someone in your group is in a wheelchair, for instance, you might have the ritual on a safer, more predictable surface such as a basketball court. To mimic the leaves, branches, or weeds that might litter a natural area in the outdoors, you could place around the basketball court a number of basketballs. The specifics of rituals can always be adapted in a way that doesn't affect the heart of the magick and that doesn't exclude anyone from taking a full and active role in the rite that's being enacted.

Casting the Circle while Clearing the Field

To begin the ritual, participants gather in the middle of the chosen space. Describe to the participants the boundaries of the ritual space, and imagine together that the area is encompassed in a large circle. When signaled, the ritualists begin their work to "clear the field," just as Tailtiu was said to have prepared the fields of all of Ireland. If you're doing the ritual in a wooded area, have the participants clear the area of any twigs or small branches that might be littering the ground, moving them out from the imagined circle and into the perimeter. If the ground is covered with leaves, carry handfuls and armfuls of them out of the circle and into the outside space. If you're in a weedy field, pull out as many as you can and rush them out of the magickal space. If you're performing the ritual on a basketball court, have participants push, kick, bump, or otherwise force the basketballs to roll off the boundaries of the court. Move as fast as is comfortable. The goal is to utilize all your efforts to clear the area as quickly as possible. As the area is cleared, thoughts of the ritualists might turn to other efforts they have recently put forth in their lives. They might contemplate how each weed, each fallen twig, each armful of leaves, might represent the hardships that have been endured for the sake of success. If you want to add a touch of game and sport, you can make this part of the ritual competitive, with participants or teams each having an individual pile on which to place their collected debris. Continue until the area is deemed to be "clear enough" by everyone involved. If it's agreeable to your group, the individual or team who manages to amass the most in their pile might be chosen to lead the rest of the ritual.

Acknowledging the Harvest

Now that the area is cleared and prepared, the ritual leader or leaders should stand in the middle of the space, with the other participants surrounding them in a circle. The leader or leaders ask each participant in turn, "What have you harvested as a result of your efforts?" The participants can choose to answer out loud, or simply contemplate the question in silence. They might give answers such as, "Through focusing on my career, I've gained a promotion and I'm enjoy my new responsibilities," or something like, "My efforts to watch my diet have paid off in the form of a healthier body." It doesn't have to be a huge accomplishment, just something that you put in effort toward that led to something positive. If you honestly can't think of anything positive, try to identify where you've been directing your energies, and do your best to objectively evaluate what you have gained or lost in exchange.

Next, the participants are asked, "What will you plant now that your field is prepared? What next would you like to harvest?" The participants do this part of the ritual simultaneously to help raise the overall energy. Thinking of their next goals, their next big dreams that they'd like to come true and the efforts they are willing to expend to get there, each participant imagines that they are casting a seed towards the middle of the space to take root in the magickally prepared foundation of earth. The physical actions of planting a seed can be mimicked if desired. Goals and intentions can be spoken out loud, or silently projected through focused thoughts.

Working the Magick

Participants then join in a chant to further magnify the magickal energies now collected in the middle of the ritual space: "We'll make the efforts to make our dreams! The very best harvest the world has seen!" The chant is repeated again and again as the energy rises to a crescendo. When the ritual leader or leaders signal, the energy of the magickal space itself, along with the energies of the intentions and emotions of the ritualists, is directed skyward, up and out of the circle in a funnel of rising power. To finish the ritual, water is given to everyone and a time of rest is enjoyed as stories are shared.

Notes

Mabon

Welcoming the Fall Equinox

Susan Pesznecker

COOLER NIGHTS, DAYS THAT grow ever shorter, leaves shifting to colors of orange and gold, and the urge to bring in one's harvest, whatever that may be....It must be autumn. And the onset of autumn is marked by the fall equinox. Known in various cultures and traditions by a number of names, it remains a time to fill one's larder, both literally and metaphorically, preparing for the quiet darkness of winter.

The fall or autumnal equinox falls on September 22 or 23 (infrequently on September 21) in the northern hemisphere. If you're not sure of the timing where you live, the internet provides a number of sites to help with your calculations. Astronomically, the equinox occurs because of Earth's tilt and its rotation. Our planet tilts about 23 degrees off axis, which means that as it rotates, different parts of the globe are closer to or further from the sun, creating seasons. The fall and spring equinoxes occur at those times of the year when rotation and tilt come together so Earth's axis is equidistant—neither closer to nor further from—the Sun. In technical terms, it's the moment the Sun crosses the celestial equator; to picture the celestial equator, imagine the earthly equator being projected out into space, and you've got it. This alignment creates days and nights that are of approximately equal length, a hallmark of both spring and fall equinoxes. (Although in truth, any almanac will reveal that days and nights are approximately equal for a few days on either side of the actual equinox date). The closer to the equator one lives, the more perfect the equal day-equal night relationship.

In the fall, once we pass the equinox, the days begin to get steadily shorter and the nights longer, building up to the "longest night" of the winter solstice. The Earth's rotation again tips us away from the Sun, bringing colder temperatures and the typical autumn weather. It's a time when we instinctively want to cook up a pot of soup or curl up with a blanket, a cup of tea, and a good book.

We humans know the autumn equinox by many names. In recent years, Mabon has become a craft term many magical folk use to describe it, believing Mabon to be an ancient expression or tradition. Others point to a figure known as Mabon ap Modron or Mabon, which appears in some ancient Celtic folklore and Arthurian legends, attributing the use of "Mabon" to those origins. Still others look to the female Cornish saint named Mabyn—her festival is celebrated on November 18, about half way between the autumnal equinox and the winter solstice—or Maponos, a pre-Christian Celtic/Gaulish god, said by some to be a god of youth.

That said, recent scholarship by historian Ronald Hutton suggests that the modern use of Mabon isn't "ancient" at all and was probably created by author Aidan Kelley in his 1991 book, *Crafting the Art of Magic*. Hutton suggests that Kelly created the term "Mabon" for the fall festival based on syncretism: the bringing together of a variety of ideas for a purpose that now seems more romantic than backed by scholarship. Hutton also mentions the Welsh scholar W. J. Gruffydd, whose publications mention the Welsh figure of Mabon as a Pagan deity and point to that as an origin for the fall equinox's name; however, Hutton points out that this claim remains unproven.

Some modern Druids refer to the fall equinox by the Welsh *Alban Elfed*, said to mean "the light of the water." Such usage seems to be a relatively modern invention, for everything we know about the ancient Druids tells us they celebrated the fire (cross-quarter) festivals but didn't mark the solstices and equinoxes as ceremonial events. That said, I've always believed if something helps a person connect with their own spirituality, it's a good thing. Call the holiday what you want: it's celebrating it that's most important. Although, I also believe that learning more about the real background of our practices only makes them richer.

A number of cultures today celebrate autumn with a harvest festival, although not always on the day of the equinox. China, Korea, Vietnam, and the United Kingdom all have some sort of fall fest as does Japan, which sets their autumn equinox celebration aside as a public holiday. Here in the United States, we don't have a formal autumn festival, but virtually every community marks autumn in some way, whether with hay mazes, fall farmer's markets, cider pressings, or something similar that celebrates the season.

Most magical folk, celebrants of Earth-based traditions, and those who fall under the general neopagan "big tent," mark the fall equinox as one of their important seasonal celebrations, often as part of the Wheel of the Year. The Wheel-as-metaphor imagines that every year rolls by in a series of natural cycles, some or all of which may be marked by a special observance. The solstices and equinoxes as known as quarter days, dividing the year into quarters, with the traditional "fire festivals," or cross-quarter days, taking place on Samhain and the first day or two of February, May, and August. Most Wheel-based festivals honor the nature of the seasonal changes happening around them and cast an eye to what will follow. Different traditions may include offerings, initiations, vigils, and omen-casting in their rituals. Feasting is almost always a common part of these celebrations.

And the typical fall equinox festivity for magical folks? You might expect to see one or more of these ideas represented:

Balance: As the Earth stands poised on the celestial equator and day and night are of equal length, the idea of balance is strong: balance in both our magical and mundane lives, balance between work and play, balance between celebration and preparation, etc.

Bounty: With autumn comes the idea of bringing in one's harvest and preparing for winter. With that readiness comes safety and comfort.

Honoring: We honor the cycles of life and show gratitude for their ever-changing consistency (Changes and consistency? We call that irony, folks!)

Symbolism: Bales of hay, representing the food that is gathered and taken in for winter; colorful leaves; the overflowing cornucopia of plenty; apples, apple trees, and everything about apples; pumpkins, squashes, and gourds; the colors orange, gold, and brown—symbolizing the changes we see in the fields and fauna around us.

Every seasonal celebration brings with it a number of opportunities to engage, enjoy, and experience personal growth. Fall is probably my favorite time of the year. I love the cooling temperatures, the smell of evening woodsmoke, the leaves that swirl around me feet, and the impetus to make rich cups of cocoa and simmer pots of soup on the stove. Everything at this time of year feels magical and full of promise. If you're looking for ways to engage with autumn, here are a few favorites:

Go out for a walk! Sounds simple, but what better way is there to engage with the natural world than to be within it? Dress for the weather, and if you take your smart phone alone for safety, please leave it in your pocket and keep your ears unplugged. Open your senses to the sights, sounds, and smells around you. Be observant for natural signs and omens or for the perfect stone or acorn for your fall altar. As you walk, watch for changes from week to week—even day to day. And don't let the weather stop you: bundle up and walk through rain and wind. It's glorious, and you'll experience Earth's gifts in a primal way.

Make your home an autumn retreat. Put out tablecloths, kitchen towels, bedlinens, doormats, and more with autumn themes. Hang a fall wreath of dried leaves and berries. Light cinnamon-scented candles or simmer cinnamon sticks and whole allspice in a small kettle on your stove to scent the entire house. Redress your home altar in fall colors and decorate with small dried ears of corn, miniature pumpkins, and such.

"Put up" some food. Autumn is inexorably associated with filling one's larder or root cellar so as to be ready for the coming winter. Canning food is simple—to make it even more fun, learn from or work side by side with a friend, and share your results. As you prepare the food, be aware of its gifts to you, and offer thanks to your deities of choice. Stir deasil, echoing the life giving forces of the seasonal wheel. Not ready to try canning? Try drying herbs or apple slices, or freeze apples or plums that you've stewed on the stove top with sugar, a bit of water, and warming spices of cinnamon and nutmeg.

Embrace your inner apple! If there's one food item that symbolizes the wealth of autumn, it might be the apple. Buy local apples from your farmer's market, or if you have a U-pick orchard nearby, harvest a bounty of apples and use them to make an apple crisp, applesauce, or the perfect pie. Sip hot spiced cider. Cut an apple through its equator to discover a perfect pentagram inside.

Visit a local harvest festival. Thanks to the internet, it's easier than ever to find what's going on in one's community. Your local harvest festivals may feature corn mazes, hayrides, cider pressing, bonfires, or other fun events. Participating helps you engage with the season and celebrate your community at the same time. And of course, you can DIY as well. Maybe you can't pull off your own corn maze, but you can have a backyard fire (s'mores, anyone?). No cider press? Puree apples into oblivion in your food processor and drain the results through a fine sieve for your own delicious homemade cider.

Prepare your yard for winter. The best way to do this is to do almost nothing! Pick up sticks and debris, but leave your grass uncut, your fields unmowed, and your shrubs and trees ragged and untrimmed. Leaving your yard on the wild side provides food and shelter for insects, birds, and even small critters through the autumn and winter, helping you support your own piece of the planet. Want to be even more wonderful? Provide a clean water source for birds through the autumn and winter. Do you have planting beds? Plant a cover crop to protect and nurture the soil; you'll till it under in the spring.

Make smudge sticks. I know I just told you to leave your yard alone—but it's okay to harvest some dried-or-done plant matter for this purpose. Bind the material together and roll tightly in newspaper to dry. When dry, wrap in cotton string or embroidery floss to make your sticks. These will be especially wonderful used in winter ritual.

Do something you've never done before! Go on a mushroom hunt—with an expert if you're a novice, please. Harvest acorns and make acorn bread. Make ink from walnuts, wild berries, beets, or other natural ingredients. Make char cloth to use in lighting ritual fires. Peel birch bark and press (an old phone book works beautifully as a plant press) for use as paper in rituals. Harvest wood (live—with the tree's permission—or fallen) for a new staff or wand. You'll find resources on the Web to help with these projects.

Hold rituals for yourself, your family, or your magical friends. In the closing ritual, I'll give you an outline for a fabulous equinoctial ritual. But why stop at one? With a blend of intention, planning, practice, and reflection, just about any autumn activity can be elevated to the level of ritual.

Are you excited? Inspired? I wish for you a joyous autumn, full of color, bounty, balance, and magic!

Cosmic Sway

Charlie Rainbow Wolf

MABON SEES SATURN FINALLY moving forward again, which is great news for those of you who are experiencing one of your Saturn returns. It's now far enough away from Pluto that their energy clash is no longer a concern. However, karma chameleon is still present with the continued opposition to the Moon's north nodes.

The fast moving Moon is coming into play this equinox, too, because it's making a conjunction to the north node in Cancer, and also an opposition to Saturn and then Pluto. The Moon's transits are so fleeting that they only last a matter of hours, but with all this emotion and karma around, extra care should be taken. What seems trivial now might crop up again at a later date, so act with integrity.

The Moon's kiss on the north node as it passes creates a need for emotional security. This usually involves home and family, but it may extend beyond that, particularly if your childhood or your relationship with your mother was a trial. Karmic wounds around dependency, nurturing, or lack of them might reopen if they've not been fully dealt with. While this may be an impassioned few hours, there's also a profound opening to deal with the past by being open to it, and finding the balance between burying it or dwelling in it.

The likelihood for intense feelings and sadness continues with the Moon–Saturn opposition. Sometimes it may seem there's little chance for emotional needs to be met, but this may not be a reality. It could be a fleeting thing, something that's fairly overwhelming during the few hours when the opposition is exact, but fading as the aspect weakens and dissipates. Obviously this isn't a particularly good time for socializing, nor for dealing with authority figures or making important decisions.

As soon as the Moon–Saturn opposition is ended the lunar opposition with Pluto starts. This is yet another brief phase where emotions are high and feelings are intense. Expect mood swings and complex patterns of behavior, no matter how short lived they may be. Any relationship tension that was triggered by the Saturn opposition could well come to a head now. Tempers may flare, and the possibility that this is a make or break time for ties that have been stretched to their limits is very real.

It's not all bad news, though. For one, these lunar transits are intense but quick to pass. Think of them as a sharp shower that clears the air. They bring the rain, but also some much needed freshness. For another, Venus and Mercury are conjunct in Libra one of the two signs (the other being Taurus) that Venus rules.

The Venus–Mercury conjunction is exact for one day but will influence things for approximately seventy-two hours. This is a love connection, where harmony, lively conversation, and getting to know new people are favored. This is a perfect time to travel and socialize. It's a pleasant period, where mingling with others comes easily, and words are kind and lighthearted. Find reasons to giggle; it's good medicine. Not only will it take the sting out of any discomfort the lunar transits might have brought into your life, but laughter is one of the best ways of repelling negative energy and ensuring that future days are brighter.

Mars isn't quite the troublemaker this month either, and is playing nicely with Pluto. This dynamic energy means there's the possibility to get a lot done. Ambition is strong, and it's possible to achieve your goals harmoniously and without disruption. Obstacles seem to remove themselves—this is on a personal as well as a larger scale, and applies to tangible roadblocks as well as ideas or inhibitions that may have been hindering progress. People are generally cooperative, and the chances of new projects and new responsibilities is good. It will certainly bring forth the natural leaders—at least, those who are seeking a position of power. Confidence overall is strong and positive.

Jupiter is once again moving forward this month, and that means the pace picks up when it comes to new ideas and new ways of doing things. It's making a nice transit to Neptune (still retrograde, still in Pisces), which has the potential to be very creative. This aspect feeds hope, and community spirit should be harmonious and optimistic. Spirituality could well seem stronger now, and there's a lot of creativity floating around.

The one caution with this aspect is not to take things for granted. It will be so easy to believe what you want to hear rather than what's being said, particularly when it comes to spiritual epiphanies and enlightenment. By all means, follow the new paths and see where they lead, but don't go blindly. This is a time for reaching out to others, for fighting against social injustices and for championing the underdog, but not one for taking everything on face value. Jupiter wants to help, but when influenced by Neptune, things sometimes aren't all that they seem to be.

Mabon Ceremony: Honoring the Dead

Mabon is the second harvest festival. It's a time of bounty and plenty, of celebrating the abundance and giving thanks for what has been gathered. It's also the time when the day loses its battle with the night, and sunset comes ever faster. Some traditions call Mabon "the festival of the dying Sun," and, as the next festival is Samhain, the festival of the dead, this is actually quite appropriate.

This ceremony is very simple, but so very powerful. You can use it as a group or a solo activity. When used as a group, you might want to make it a field trip of sorts, or to designate a particular place for this activity. You'll need a pen, a small slip of paper or parchment, a spade or a trowel, and a seasonal potted plant for each person present

Cast your usual circle or call the deities as you normally would. When you're ready to begin this activity, ask everyone to write down the name of someone dear to them, someone recently departed, on the slip of paper. These pieces of paper don't have to be large; in fact, this is one instance where the smaller the better.

Once everyone has written the name of the person they wish to honor, using the small trowel, dig down a few inches into the potted plant, and place the slip of paper into the soil. What you do next is largely up to you. At this point you can close your circle and partake in any ritual feast you have planned, or you can wait until later in the day to bring things to an end.

If you have a designated ritual space, place the pots there as a place of honor and remembrance. Another idea is to take them to the local cemetery, and place them on the graves that are unadorned or neglected. The third option is everyone can take the potted plants home with them and keep them in a special place.

There's really no wrong way to do this, the important thing is that the dead are honored with the potted plant. The plant will eventually die too, and the soil will return to the earth. This ceremony isn't just for remembering the dead, but also for paying homage to the turn of the wheel, the equality of life and release, and the cycle of birth, death, and rebirth.

The Old Ways: Mystery Girl

Linda Raedisch

WE THINK OF "LITTLE green men" as the product of the mid-twentieth-century imagination, but one harvest season sometime in the early twelfth century, a little green girl and a little green boy materialized outside the Suffolk village of Woolpit. The children's strange story was not captured by the pen until fifty years after the fact when two chroniclers finally jumped to the task: William of Newburgh (c.1136–1198) and Ralph of Coggeshall (fl. 1200), both of whom claimed to have interviewed people directly involved in the events.

We'll call the girl Agnes, because that's how she was eventually christened. After Agnes had learned to speak the local dialect of Old English, she explained how she and her brother had wandered into a cavern not far from their home and become hopelessly lost among the tunnels. They had been minding their father's flocks when an irresistible tolling music had led them into the caves. The sheep forgotten, the children scrambled onward through the narrow passageways, ears straining to hear the chimes through the rushing darkness.

Moments or perhaps hours later, they emerged within a cavity, perhaps one of the village's clay-pits. Shielding their eyes against the terrifying blaze of light, they knew at once they had not returned to the quiet meadow in which they had left their flock. Looking around, they could make out trees and tall, heavy-headed grasses shimmering in the light of a dazzling sun. By this time, the music had stopped, its place taken by ominous hissing and slashing sounds. The children turned back, hunting for the cave mouth, but the rocks had unaccountably closed up behind them.

Now they were truly lost in this strange, bright world. They had not traveled far into it when they were seized by the reapers, for it was their scything the children had heard. The children were carried in with the harvest and dropped off at the nearest guild hall, a place of wood, bricks, and guttering candle flames, commonplaces with which the children seemed entirely unfamiliar.

In their own country, as Agnes explained later, there was neither day nor night but perpetual twilight. There were churches but apparently no bells, and her people regarded St. Martin "with peculiar veneration." And everyone was startlingly green.

For a long time, neither Agnes nor her brother could speak. And when they could, their speech was unintelligible to the Anglo-Saxon inhabitants of Woolpit. The boy soon succumbed to melancholy, while the girl survived into adulthood, William of Newburgh adding that she married a man of King's Lynn and Ralph relating that she was given a position in the household of one Sir Richard de Calne where her behavior was "rather loose and wanton." The chroniclers disagree over the question of baptism—Did both children receive it or only the girl?—but agree that it must have been the tolling of the church bells at nearby Bury St. Edmonds that had drawn them from their own land.

To be lured inside the earth by enchanting music is typical of the British fairy story, but the subject is more usually drawn out of the mortal realm and into Faerie, not the other way around. Lingering twilight is another hallmark of the Celtic fairy realm. Agnes maintained that she and her green-skinned countrymen were Christians. If they were stray Picts, they may have belonged to the older, more tolerant Celtic Church founded by St. Ninian. Christianized Picts also maintained a special fondness for St. Martin of Tours whose follower St. Ninian had been. But Scotland was a long way from Suffolk, and it is doubtful that any Picts of this time would have been dying themselves either blue or green as their Pagan ancestors had.

It is well known that humans must abstain from eating fairy food or be trapped forever in the fairy banqueting hall. In both William's and Ralph's accounts, the Green Children refuse to tough the local fare until, that is, they are presented with green beans. That's "green" as in freshly picked, not the long thin haricots, which were unknown in England at the time. These beans, given to the children with the haulms still attached, may have been Celtic beans, *Vicia fabor minor*, which have been eaten as an early fall vegetable since Neolithic times, or horse beans, Vicia fabor equine, which are better fed to livestock than to people. Rather than wait for the beans to be cooked, the children tried to eat them raw but had to be shown how to find the beans inside the pods.

Agnes eventually developed a taste for more conventional foods and in doing so lost her green color. If her skin had been dyed green with the herbs woad and weld, the color may simply have been worn or washed away. Or, her greenish pallor could have been a symptom of severe malnourishment. Starvation was an ever-looming specter in those days. Perhaps the children had been abandoned, like Hansel and Gretel. Woolpit was home to a sulfurous well dedicated to the Virgin Mary, renowned for its healing powers, so perhaps the children had been intentionally lost amid the throng of pilgrims.

Ralph claimed that the girl had been "regenerated" by the rite of baptism, illustrating his belief that she was a lapsed or heretical Christian rather than an aboriginal heathen or some species of fairy. As for the boy, William tells us that he "surviv[ed] baptism but a little time" and "died prematurely," which is exactly what one would expect of a vegetal spirit at summer's end.

So was the appearance of the Green Children in Woolpit a historical event or just another fairy story? There are a few more intriguing details to consider. The children did not pop up in the clay-pits naked but in clothing "of a strange colour, and unknown materials," as William describes it. This was the twelfth century, not the Stone Age, so it's hard to imagine what sort of cloth would have perplexed the people of Woolpit. The Anglo-Saxons had been working with wool and flax since time immemorial and would certainly have heard of silk, furs and cloth-of-gold even if they did not own any. The ability to weave cloth so fine that no human can hope to duplicate it is a typical fairy skill, just as shiny fabrics have become a time-honored means of distinguishing the aliens from the Federation-folk on "Star Trek."

Through William, Agnes tells us that her home country of "St. Martin's Land" was divided by a wide river. "The sun does not rise upon our countrymen," she assured her listeners, "but it seems to have shone fully upon this nearby land." Outside the human imagination, there is only one kind of place that fits this description and it is not on Earth.

Could the Green Children have come from a tidally locked planet? Tidal locking occurs when physical events far outside this author's understanding cause one side of a planet to always face the sun much as the same side of our moon always faces the earth. Thus, on one side of the planet it would be forever daylight, on the other, night. The only region where life as we know it would be possible is the narrow "twilight zone" in between, where the inhabitants would enjoy everlasting crepuscularity. This is the state of affairs on the planets Proxima Centauri b, Kepler-1866 b, c, d and e and Star Trek's Daled IV. (Only Daled IV is known to be inhabited.)

But even if the Green Children were aliens, how did they end up in Woolpit? In a ship built to weather the eons, its sails billowing in the solar wind? Or through that fallback plot-saver, the wormhole, this one opening onto a clay-pit in medieval Sussex, just as one would expect to see in an episode of *Doctor Who*. Perhaps the best question to ask is not whether the Green Children were fairies, extraterrestrials, or starving children, but if William of Newburgh should be counted as the world's first science fiction writer.

Feasts and Treats
Blake Octavian Blair

MABON, THE AUTUMN EQUINOX, is now upon us! This second of the three harvest festivals usually arrives to us along with the first visible signs of autumn. Many areas of the country are starting to see sporadic cooler days, signs of summer heat and humidity breaking slowly, and the bright crisp blue autumn sky and the occasional bit of foliage beginning to show sneak previews of small patches of golden oranges and yellows mixed with fiery reds. Along with those changes come tasty treats of the harvest such as squashes, root veggies, and a bounty of apples! Sweet, tart, bright crisp, red, green, yellow, and oh so delicious apples! Here is a menu to take full advantage of the culinary delights presented to us at Mabon! Be sure to bedeck your feast table with the colors of this autumnal harvest with ornamental squashes, beautiful apples, and accent touches of that deep vibrant hue of blue so commonly seen in the sky on crisp sunny autumn days.

Roasted Root Vegetable Medley with Tempeh
Autumn is the perfect season for integrating root vegetables into your menus, and this dish is always an autumnal favorite in our house. It lends a hearty robust flavor sure to bring it to comfort

food status on crisp autumn days making it the perfect entrée for an Autumn Equinox feast. The best part is that it is adaptable to whatever vegetables you can find available seasonally in your local grocery store and neighborhood farmers markets.

Prep time: 15 minutes
Cook time: 50 minutes
Serves: 3–4

1 lb multi colored carrots (or regular if not available), peeled
1 large bunch broccoli
2 medium parsnips, peeled
1 lb cremini mushrooms, quartered
1 lb butternut squash
4 tbsp canola oil, divided
1 tsp kosher salt
1 tbsp all-purpose seasoning
1 cup rice medley
1 lb tempeh, crumbled

Begin by peeling the carrots and parsnips. Then proceed to chop vegetables into roughly uniform pieces.

Placed chopped vegetables into a large mixing bowl. Add 2 tablespoons of canola oil, salt, and all-purpose seasoning to taste. Toss all ingredients until the vegetables are well coated in oil.

Spread vegetables into an even single layer on a large baking sheet.

Cook in a 425 degree F preheated oven for 45–50 minutes until vegetables achieve a golden color.

While the vegetables are roasting, cook the rice medley. I choose a brown rice medley, however, you can substitute the rice of your choice. As the cooking time and instructions for different kinds and mixtures of rice vary, be sure to consult the package instructions of the rice for cooking times and ratios. However, for planning, a general rule of thumb is that most brown rice mixtures will have a cooking time ranging from 35–40 minutes.

While the rice is cooking, add the remaining olive oil and the crumbled tempeh in a medium skillet on medium heat. Sauté for approximately 5 minutes, then stir, then let sit to sauté for an additional five minutes or until golden brown color is achieved. Then remove from heat.

The rice and the vegetables should be finished cooking at approximately the same time. Serve the vegetables over a bed of the rice medley and then top with the sautéed tempeh.

Slow Cooker Chili Mac

One of my favorite things about the start of autumn is the promise of beautiful crisp autumn days. Nothing is better on a crisp autumn day than the alluring smell of dinner in a slow cooker wafting through your home all day as you enjoy the autumn air with your windows open. This recipe is perfect because the cooking of it is mostly inactive, allowing you to do minimal prep and spend the rest of your equinox enjoying the things we are celebrating our gratitude for at Mabon.

Prep time: 25 minutes

Cook time: 3.5 hours (mostly inactive)

Serves: 4–6

2 tbsp canola oil

1 tbsp cumin

1 tbsp chili powder

½ tsp crushed garlic

1 tsp cayenne pepper

½ large sweet onion, chopped

1 15.5-ounce can black beans

1 15.5-ounce can seasoned chili beans

1 15.5-ounce can kidney beans

1 11-ounce can Mexican corn

2 14.5-ounce cans diced tomatoes

2 tbsp brown sugar, packed

¼ cup barbecue sauce

Hot sauce (to taste)
Water (optional as desired for consistency)
1 lb pasta
Salt (to taste)
1 cup shredded cheddar cheese

Add canola oil to a medium skillet and heat on medium high heat. To the heated skillet add the cumin, chili powder, crushed garlic, and cayenne pepper. Allow to toast for one minute and then add in the chopped onion and stir to coat with the spices. Allow the onion to cook, stirring occasionally, for five to seven minutes, or until translucent.

Now, into a five-quart slow cooker, add the onions, black beans, seasoned chili beans, kidney beans, Mexican corn, diced tomatoes, brown sugar, barbecue sauce, and hot sauce. Stir and mix thoroughly until all ingredients seem evenly distributed. You can adjust the consistency of the chili by adding a small amount of water as desired. This is not required nor always needed. Set crockpot to high and cook for a minimum of three hours, stirring occasionally. You can allow this to cook and simmer several more hours if you like, as the longer it simmers the more the flavors will meld together. Once chili is hot all the way through, you can turn to low or warm setting to maintain heat until serving.

Twenty minutes or so prior to serving, you can begin to prepare the pasta. Put a few pinches of salt into a large pot of water and bring to a boil. Add pasta and cook for 9–12 minutes until pasta is al dente. Drain.

To serve, fill bowls with pasta, top with heaping scoops of chili, and add shredded cheese to the top.

Crafty Crafts

Natalie Zaman

I CAN'T BELIEVE THAT it took me as long as it did (years!) to discover the joys of mixing large quantities of cheap cinnamon with applesauce. The recipe was introduced to me as a means of making Christmas ornaments, but the scent—hello, CINNAMON and APPLES!—screams all things autumnal. It's too easy not to try and, oh, the things you can make with it!

Bright Blessings and Fairy Doors

Time Lavished: It takes about 15 minutes to whip up a batch of cinnamon-applesauce dough. After that, it's all about drying it out, which can be done in a couple of hours in an oven, or even a week leaving it out to dry out naturally (depending on humidity). I vote for popping them in the oven and doing something else while you wait—it's quicker, and it makes the house smell nice too.

Coinage Required: You might have all of the makings of the dough in your pantry—if so, awesome. If not, go for bulk cinnamon and the most inexpensive applesauce you can find. All totaled, this craft will set you back about $10–15—and that includes a canister of glitter.

Supplies:

1 cup of applesauce

2 cups of cinnamon

¼ cup of craft glue. Some recipes call for adding craft glue to the applesauce/cinnamon mixture as it makes a more robust dough and durable ornaments. This ingredient is optional.

Bowl

Spoon

Rolling pin

House and door-shaped cookie cutters and/or a knife

Drinking straw

Toothpicks and/or letter rubber stamps

Baking tray

Baking parchment

Ribbon

Glitter—optional, but why ever not?

Small crystals and/or beads

Hot glue gun

2 short, slim nails

Tack hammer

Small flowers for planting

Small tumbled stones and/or crystal points

The flowers and stones are optional, but a fun addition for when you place your Faerie Door.

First, make the dough. Mix the applesauce and cinnamon (and craft glue if you chose to use it) until they are thoroughly combined. Start mixing with a spoon, then work it with your hands. Add a bit more applesauce if the mixture is too dry, or more cinnamon if it's too wet.

Dust a smooth work surface with more of the cinnamon (this is why you use the cheap, bulk stuff), and, if desired a bit of glitter. (Who are we kidding—of course it's desired!) Gold makes a nice contrast while coppers and reds make for a subtle shimmer. Cover

the dough with the cinnamon (and glitter) before rolling it out so that it's about ¼ inch thick.

Mabon House Blessing

Use a cookie cutter to make a house shape, or cut your own. I've found that it's best to stick with simple shapes when working with this dough.

You can leave the house as is, or use the toothpick or rubber stamps to add a simple blessing. Trace the letters with a toothpick, or carefully press the message into the dough with the rubber stamps. Try to "write" out your message in the center of the house. If you make a mistake or if the house doesn't come out the way you want, just return it to the dough pile and roll it out again. Use the drinking straw to make a small hole near the top; this will be for threading a ribbon through for hanging.

Carefully place the houses onto a baking tray and dry them out in a low oven (200 degrees) for about two hours. Check the houses before removing them; they should be completely solid and not floppy or soft in any way. Place them on a wire rack to cool.

Thread a ribbon through the hole you made with the straw. Your house blessing is ready to hang, or given as a gift! The scent should last through the season. When it fades, it can be refreshed with a few drops of essential oil—cinnamon, or perhaps a complimentary scent, like orange or clove. Alternatively, smear both sides of the house with peanut butter, then dip it in raisins, grains and bread crumbs and hang outside as a treat for birds and squirrels and other wildlife friends. You can refill the house when it's empty.

Cinnamon Fairy Door

You can also use this versatile and magical dough (Really! Apples heal and cinnamon invokes passion.) to create a fairy portal. (Note: You may want to make a batch of glue-infused dough. The addition of glue makes for sturdier doors.)

Roll out the dough, then cut it into door shapes with your knife or a door shaped cookie cutter. I like rounded doors—or you can make a totally round hobbit door. Use the toothpicks to draw "wooden" panels, and perhaps cut out a small window. Before they go into the oven, use the straw to make two holes, one at the top and one on the bottom of the door; you will use these to install your door once it's cooled and dried.

Use hot glue to attach a small stone or crystal for a doorknob. Carefully attach the door to a wall or a tree by tacking to the bark with the two slim, short nails. Tap the nails in as gently as possible. If your door feels delicate or starts to crumble, simply lean it against the tree. You can also lay it flat on the ground like a trap door and plant small flowers or outline it with crystals and tumbled stones. Wherever you set it, fairies will love this glittery sweet smelling door, but leaving a tiny cake just outside will also help attract them!

Portable Magic

Mickie Mueller

SOME PEOPLE CALL IT the first day of fall, but us witches and pagans call it Mabon, or the autumn equinox, and we've been feeling a bit of autumn in the air already since this is the second harvest. Now that Mabon has arrived though, it's really starting to feel like fall. Depending on where you live, the leaves may be starting to change, the harvest from local vegetable gardens is well under way, and the transformation from summer to fall is palpable. I love the solstices and the equinoxes because they've always felt like days of significance to me even before I recognized my magical path. How do we celebrate the day of balance any better than finding balance between our magical and mundane lives? If you've joined me on this journey of celebrating sabbats on-the-go in this book, I bet you have some ideas already. I hope you continue to be inspired with little ways to bring magic into your everyday life.

It's Like Apple Pie but Cooler

The apple harvest is well under way at Mabon. I know quite a few Pagans and witches who celebrate this sabbat with the tradition of apple picking at a local orchard. Apples are a symbol of magic of course; if you slice them through the core, you'll find a star inside making a natural pentacle. If you don't have time to visit an orchard in the middle of the week, you can still enjoy the magic of apples on the actual autumn equinox. I always feel like I want the flavor of an apple pie on Mabon, but so often in the Midwest it's still too darned hot to bake. Here's an apple snack that my mother-in-law taught me how to make—it's easy to take along for your lunch break. Slice up one apple into bite sized pieces and toss them in a small plastic bowl with a lid. Sprinkle with about a teaspoon of lemon juice, some sugar or stevia, and cinnamon to taste. Put the lid on and shake it up. It tastes like an apple pie but it's fresh and cool for a special treat on a warm autumn day. If you're missing that pie crust crunch, crumble up a graham cracker in there right before you eat it.

Gratitude Spell

Some refer to Mabon as "The Witches' Thanksgiving," not only a time of feasting and harvest, but a time to express gratitude for what we have. Sometimes life is tough and we tend to focus on only our challenges, but in the season of harvest if we can shift our attention to the blessings in life, we'll manifest more of them. Here's a really easy gratitude ritual you can perform anywhere. All you need is a handful of coins, at least five, but it can be more if you wish. Hold the coins in your left hand and transfer them one at a time into your right as you name each coin for something that you're grateful for in your life. Hold the coin and think about your gratitude, fill your heart with how each one of those things makes you feel with each coin. When you're done, put the coins in your pocket and keep them separate from the rest of your change. Before the day is done, find a donation jar at your local gas station or other shop and donate those coins. Spread that love, sharing the coins is how you thank the universe. Giving to others in need will bring you and the recipients more to be grateful for in the year ahead.

Jewelry of Feather or Stone

Crow and ravens are symbols of Mabon and can be found on costume jewelry for Halloween since they're usually already putting that stuff out this time of the year, you get shopping for two sabbats in one. Both crows and ravens are birds that relate to the harvest, they go along the fields picking at remnants enjoying a feast of their own. They are also deep in the mythos of dark goddesses such as Macha, and The Morrigan whose presence can be felt stronger as we move into the season of death and change. Both of these dark birds are connected to the magic of transformation, fearlessness, adaptability, and intelligence. If you would like to summon up that energy into your life during Mabon, look for a jewelry piece depicting a crow or raven to wear. If you can't find the dark birds of the season or you prefer, there are several stones associated with Mabon. Jewelry made with hematite, amber, lapis lazuli, or tiger eye work nicely with the energies of the season. Pass your jewelry through some incense smoke or sage smoke, then hold it in your hands and speak from your heart to charge your jewelry with Mabon's energy of abundance and transformation.

Wear Colors of the Day

The colors of the changing season represent Mabon in your fall wardrobe. Even though the weather is often still quite hot on Mabon, as we look around and see nature changing we're aware that cooler days are not far ahead. Wearing one or more of the colors of the sabbat can help you embrace the changes happening all around you.

Brown is a harvest color and it's also a color that connects us to nature. Wearing brown on Mabon can remind us to practice generosity, and assure that our resources endure.

Orange, another harvest color always makes me focus on the changing leaves and the pumpkin harvest. To me wearing a bit of orange on the autumn equinox helps me embrace the joy and excitement of fall.

Forest green seems appropriate at Mabon, it's the color of the leaves that are still producing food for the plant, thus getting the last bit out of the waning year. Wear deep green today to focus on planning ahead, success through hard work, and gathering prosperity and abundance.

Black and white is a clever choice to wear on Mabon; it's a day of balance when the day and night are equal. Bringing the contrast of black and white into your look today can help you focus on that balance.

Sabbat on the Go Tips

If you work where you can bring in a vase of flowers, try carnations in fall colors or mums, and mix it with sprigs of sage from your garden or the produce section of the supermarket. Every time you look at it or catch the scent you'll feel Mabon enchantment.

Carry an acorn in your pocket as a charm for luck and prosperity on Mabon. If you find it on Mabon, keep it on your altar to add to your prosperity magic all year.

If you happen to be walking where the wind is blowing leaves from the trees, try to catch one before it hits the ground. Yes, you might look a bit silly, but if you manage to snatch one out of the air, that leaf will bring you good luck for a year. Try it every Mabon.

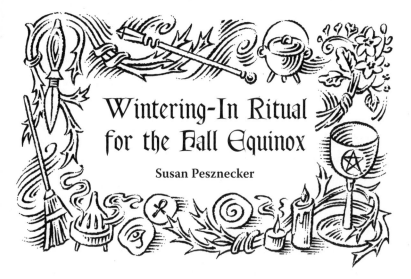

Wintering-In Ritual for the Fall Equinox

Susan Pesznecker

WHEN MAGICAL FOLKS THINK of ritual, they typically imagine an organized (maybe even scripted) activity lasting about an hour. Each tradition has its own ritual design and practices, and there often isn't much variation. Typically a number of people have an active role in the activity, with the rest simply watching and participating as instructed or guided. Rituals are often preceded by preparation and followed with feasting. And then, everyone goes home.

I want you to try something different.

What follows is a day long celebration that wanders from casual to ritualistic moments and which aims, above all, for you to enjoy yourself and participate fully as you connect with the wonderful magic of the autumn equinox. This ritual could be celebrated by you alone—in a wonderful day that would feel like a glorious personal retreat—or could be joined by friends, family, or your magical community. I'm going to proceed as if you're working with a few other people, and you can adjust as needed.

This will be a ritual of wintering-in. While wintering-in (an arcane term describing a process of completing the harvest and getting ready for winter), each person filled their own larder and took stock of their own needs, while also experiencing a tremendous feeling of community—of being a part of something greater and of sharing one's own contribution to that "whole." Working together, the community insured its success and its safety. This ritual will echo these ideals. Set aside a whole day to work through this.

As with all rituals, we begin with intention, move on to preparation, carry out the practice itself, and reflect on the results.

The Days Before (Preparation)

Read through this entire ritual first, then begin planning. Who will attend? What will they bring? Everyone should contribute something to the communal harvest feast and participate in some way. Everyone should also bring a gift—preferably homemade—to share: a canned good, homemade soap, a baked good, or something similar.

Clean and tidy your home and adorn it with autumn colors and decorations. Prepare a fire pit or fireplace, either inside or outdoors, setting the fire so it's ready to light.

Plan your menu. Gather recipes and create a shopping list. If working with other people, you may wish to divide up the shopping and food preparation. Set a time and place for the ritual meal, and let everyone know when to arrive and what to wear.

Morning of the Ritual (Intention and Preparation)

Take a cleansing bath or shower. As you bathe, imagine the water washing away impurities and refreshing your soul—take this with you into the day.

Sit quietly for a moment and consider the nature of the autumn equinox. Is your life in balance? If not, what needs adjustment and how will you accomplish this? What is your harvest for the past year, both literally and metaphorically? What will you tuck away to get you through the winter? Who makes up your community, and how will you come together with them as you move toward winter? Where is your gratitude, and who are its recipients?

Consider your intentions for the ritual: what do you want to accomplish for yourself and/or for the people who will come together?

Set your feast table with linens, candles, centerpiece, and place settings. Your table is an altar space for the purposes of this ritual; add magical items as you see fit.

Consecrate your kitchen—and any other locations where food preparation will occur, e.g., a barbecue)—with the four elements: salt (earth), air and fire (smudge stick or candle), and water. Move deasil through the kitchen, blessing each corner (and the range) and saying, "May this hearth, center of the home, nourish and fulfill us."

Gather the food and drink for your feast. Plan a menu that involves each of these groups, focusing on those that are local and in season. Purchase, if you can, from a local provider or better yet, harvest from your own yard. Shop the day of the ritual or earlier if you prefer. If you're vegetarian, vegan, or have dietary restrictions, please adjust these instructions to meet your needs while retaining the goals of the ritual.

Gather the foods of the land and forest. For this, you'll want some sort of meat: beef, pork, or lamb will work well. Mushrooms would be grand, too.

Gather the foods of the sky. Look to a fowl of some sort: perhaps chicken, turkey, squab, or a Cornish hen.

Gather the foods of the sea. Choose fish or seafood.

Gather the foods of the plain. Select vegetables, fruits, and grains that grow on the ground or on shrubs.

Gather the foods of the tree. Choose fruits and nuts from trees.

Gather the foods of the vine. Choose a local wine or ale, tea prepared from fresh herbs, or a freshly-squeezed cider. Include a separate measure of cider for the fire ritual.

As you gather each of these, murmur a blessing of gratitude and thanks, for instance:

Thank you Earth for gifting me with your bounty. I am grateful.

Put the food away or, if any immediate preparation is needed, take care of it. As you work, remain mindful of your intention and of the richness of autumn's gifts. If you have time, take a walk outside, embracing nature and perhaps collecting a few more items for the harvest table.

At some point as you work, cast an omen, working with tarot cards, runes, or your medium of choice. Reflect on the results.

Midday of the Ritual (Intention and Preparation)

Have a nourishing lunch and wash your hands again, symbolically re-purifying yourself. You're well into the ritual now. Begin preparing your food, keeping focused on your intention and the important work you're doing, preparing nourishment for yourself (and maybe family and others). You'll also want to plan the order in which the food will be presented to your guests.

Heat cider in a large saucepan with stick cinnamon, whole allspice, grated nutmeg, a few lemon slices, and some brown sugar. Save this for the fireplace part of the evening ritual.

At some point in the afternoon, cast another omen, and again reflect on the message.

Evening of the Ritual (Intention and Practice)

As guests arrive, greet them at the door and ask, "What have you brought to share in this community wintering in?" Each should reply accordingly, leaving their gift or gifts in the designated area and taking their food to the kitchen.

Seat your guests at the table as they arrive. When everyone is present, offer a blessing over those present, light candles, and let them know that the celebratory part of the ritual has begun, including the practice of toasts, boasts, and oaths.

Pour everyone a beverage. Say,

The gifts of the vine.

Share a group toast to a successful harvest.

Now, bring the foods to the table in courses. For instance, if presenting the meats first, you might bring them to the table saying,

The gifts of the forest.

Each course should be met with cheers—and possibly more toasts—from those at the table. Pass and taste each course, then bring in the next one—again with cheers and toasts.

Once all the food is on the table, everyone may commence feasting!

When everyone is finished, go around the table and have each person mention something that has gone well for them in the past year: their successful harvest. As each makes their boast, it should be met with more cheers.

Ending the Day (Practice and Reflection)

Have everyone help clear the table, then move to the fire. Light it with ceremony and cheer as the flame builds, saying, "May this gift of fire keep us safe through the coming darkness."

Pour hot cider for everyone, then ask for silence. Have each person, in turn, make their oath: a promise or plan for the coming year. As each oath is made, the group silently raises their mugs of cider and takes a drink.

After all have made an oath, the group briefly moves outside, where an offering of cider is poured onto the soil while one person says,

Mother Earth, we bless these gifts that you have given and share them with you in return. May this gift ensure the richness of next year's bounty. Thank you!

Everyone offers thanks and then heads back indoors, where dessert might be enjoyed, games played, and fellowship shared. When people leave, they select one or more items from the shared gifts. The ritual ends....

After your guests leave, draw a final omen and reflect on what it means to you. If you keep a magical journal, write a note and share your omens. Finish a perfect day with a hot scented bath and soft pajamas.

Blessed be....

Notes

Notes

Notes

Notes

Notes

Notes

GET MORE AT LLEWELLYN.COM

Visit us online to browse hundreds of our books and decks, plus sign up to receive our e-newsletters and exclusive online offers.

- **• Free tarot readings • Spell-a-Day • Moon phases**
- **• Recipes, spells, and tips • Blogs • Encyclopedia**
- **• Author interviews, articles, and upcoming events**

GET SOCIAL WITH LLEWELLYN

Find us on   🐦 @LlewellynBooks

www.Facebook.com/LlewellynBooks

GET BOOKS AT LLEWELLYN

LLEWELLYN ORDERING INFORMATION

Order online: Visit our website at www.llewellyn.com to select your books and place an order on our secure server.

Order by phone:
- • Call toll free within the US at 1-877-NEW-WRLD (1-877-639-9753)
- • We accept VISA, MasterCard, American Express, and Discover.
- • Canadian customers must use credit cards.

Order by mail:
Send the full price of your order (MN residents add 6.875% sales tax) in US funds plus postage and handling to: Llewellyn Worldwide, 2143 Wooddale Drive, Woodbury, MN 55125-2989

POSTAGE AND HANDLING

STANDARD (US):
(Please allow 12 business days)
$30.00 and under, add $6.00.
$30.01 and over, FREE SHIPPING.

INTERNATIONAL ORDERS,
INCLUDING CANADA:
$16.00 for one book, plus $3.00 for each additional book.

Visit us online for more shipping options. Prices subject to change.

FREE CATALOG!

To order, call
1-877-
NEW-WRLD
ext. 8236
or visit our
website

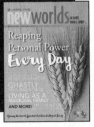

The Witch's Tools Series

With illustrations by Mickie Mueller and contributors from throughout the witchy world, *The Witch's Tools* series delves into the fascinating history, symbolism, and modern uses of various tools, from the athame to the wand. With a variety of spells, rituals, and methods for creating or personalizing each tool, the books in the series present a wealth of knowledge that every age and kind of witch can use.

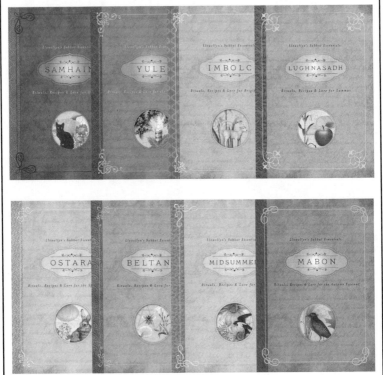